iPhone®

SECRETS

iPhone®
SECRETS

DO WHAT YOU NEVER THOUGHT POSSIBLE WITH YOUR iPHONE

Darren Murph

WILEY
John Wiley & Sons, Inc.

ACQUISITIONS EDITOR: Mary James
PROJECT EDITOR: Katherine Burt
TECHNICAL EDITOR: Todd Davis
PRODUCTION EDITOR: Kathleen Wisor
COPY EDITOR: Kezia Endsley
EDITORIAL MANAGER: Mary Beth Wakefield
FREELANCER EDITORIAL MANAGER: Rosemarie Graham
ASSOCIATE DIRECTOR OF MARKETING: David Mayhew
MARKETING MANAGER: Ashley Zurcher
BUSINESS MANAGER: Amy Knies
PRODUCTION MANAGER: Tim Tate
VICE PRESIDENT AND EXECUTIVE GROUP PUBLISHER: Richard Swadley
VICE PRESIDENT AND EXECUTIVE PUBLISHER: Neil Edde
ASSOCIATE PUBLISHER: Jim Minatel
PROJECT COORDINATOR, COVER: Katie Crocker
COMPOSITOR: Craig Woods, Happenstance Type-O-Rama
PROOFREADER: Word One New York
INDEXER: Johnna VanHoose Dinse
COVER DESIGNER: Ryan Sneed
COVER IMAGE: ©Chad Baker/Lifesize/Getty Images

iPhone® Secrets

Published by
John Wiley & Sons, Inc.
10475 Crosspoint Boulevard
Indianapolis, IN 46256
www.wiley.com

Copyright © 2013 by John Wiley & Sons, Inc., Indianapolis, Indiana

Published simultaneously in Canada

ISBN: 978-1-118-33903-9
ISBN: 978-1-118-38797-9 (ebk)
ISBN: 978-1-118-41684-6 (ebk)
ISBN: 978-1-118-57929-9 (ebk)

Manufactured in the United States of America

10 9 8 7 6 5 4 3 2 1

This book is dedicated to Dana Murph, who keeps me grounded, invigorated, and passionate, my heaven-sent parents, and my late Uncle Jr., who proved to me that life was nothing without love, laughter, dogs, and travel.

—Darren Murph

About the Author

Darren Murph is the managing editor of Engadget, a respected publication in the wide world of consumer electronics. He's written nearly 20,000 posts—enough to earn him a Guinness World Record as the planet's most prolific professional blogger—on everything from speech synthesis to gadget dissection. He's a gadget critic, reviewer, and author, and he splits his time between breaking news, covering new launches at trade shows around the world, and reviewing new consumer gadgets.

He has also been a keynote speaker at NEXT Aarhus (an innovation conference in Denmark) and contributes How-To and hacker guides to Bonnier's *Popular Science* publication. When not immersed in technology, he's a freelancer travel writer for Gadling and Shermans Travel, where he has covered such extremes as Alaska in the winter and conducted an interview with The Travel Channel's own "Bert the Conqueror."

Darren received a B.S. in Supply Chain Management in 2006 from North Carolina State University and an MBA from Campbell University in 2008. In a former life, he troubleshot a Mac lab at NC State University's D.H. Hill Library, shopped for chemicals at DuPont, and watched Nortel sink into oblivion. He's driven a motorized vehicle in all 50 U.S. states, attempted a FaceTime call with the Queen of England, and has an utterly innocent dog named Gangster.

About the Technical Editor

Todd Davis is the Media and Communications
Director and a licensed minister at Hope Chapel in Apex,
North Carolina, near the state's capitol. He grew up on
the Outer Banks and received a B.S. in Communications
& Media Production from East Carolina University.

Todd specializes in video production, web design,
and graphic design. As founder of Shorewire Produc-
tions, he has created web video and graphic arts for
clients ranging from local bands to the regional YMCA.

When he isn't developing iOS apps, creating music,
or crafting custom furniture and cornhole boards, Todd
enjoys spending time with his wife and two sons.

Acknowledgements

To say the writing of this book was a journey would be an understatement of epic proportions. It's my second book, but it was equally enjoyable and harrowing. That said, I couldn't be more thrilled to have taken it, and I have to start by thanking Mary James, my acquisitions editor. Without her taking notice, this project would've never gotten off of the ground. I'm also grateful to Ryan Block and Peter Rojas, the two men that took a chance by starting Engadget, and soon after, hiring me as a freelance editor. It's been an honor to devote my career to covering the world of consumer electronics.

I owe a great deal to editors that have come before me—my teachers and my mentors. Each former and current Engadget colleague is dear to my heart, and without learning from all of you, I would've been in no position to tackle this book. Thanks to my rivals for keeping me sharp, and thanks to the readers for keeping me accurate.

On a more personal note, I'm hugely grateful to my dearest wife, Dana, for not only agreeing to let me sink countless hours into the construction of this book, but for encouraging me all the while. My mother Alice and father Larry have been instrumental in keeping me focused, and I'm forever indebted to them both for their unwavering support and love. To the rest of my family: thank you for believing in me, despite not ever fully understanding what it is that I do.

Special thanks to my technical editor and best friend, Todd Davis, for jumping in headfirst on this endeavor. Writing a guide such as this can be a daunting task, and having a pal and confidante as amazing as Todd enabled me to never truly feel alone. To Sam and Ethan, thanks for letting me borrow your pops.

Finally, I want to thank my late Uncle Jr., who taught me that love, perseverance, laughter, and aimless wandering were vital to fulfillment. He's the freest soul I ever knew, and if there are iPhones in heaven, I'm sure he'll get a kick out of reading this.

Contents at a Glance

Contents

Introduction

Welcome to iPhone Secrets and the universe of iOS. Regardless of whether you're brand new to Apple, iOS, smartphones or computing in general, this book will prove to be the perfect partner in wading through the joys that lie ahead. If you're a seasoned iPhone user, this book peels back the proverbial onion in order to enrich what's undoubtedly already an enriching experience.

The pages ahead will describe how to slip into the nooks and crannies that are scattered about the iPhone world. From little-known tips about tweaking iOS for productivity, to advice on how to make iTunes work *for* you instead of against you, it's all here. This book was dreamed up after Apple's iPhone line had already made an indelible mark on the computing world; in the realm of smartphones, there's the iPhone, and then there's everything else.

In typical Apple fashion, the iPhone is drop-dead simple to use, but perhaps troublingly, there's hardly any information provided in the box as to how to make the most of it. Everything from advanced setup procedures to workflow strategies is covered in detail, with the excruciating technobabble omitted in order to make the most of your time.

I'll even dive into the wide and overwhelming world of apps and accessories, pointing out the best and brightest in order to make your iPhone the tool you'd always dreamed that it would be. Having issues? There's an entire chapter on trouble-shooting, so feel free to get your hands dirty.

I've segmented this book in a way that flows logically for those just picking up an iPhone, but if you're an existing owner, I'll meet you right where you stand. The iPhone is easy to use, but it's a tough device to master. iOS 5 and iOS 6 have introduced a great many new wrinkles to the equation, and even if you feel comfortable navigating prior builds of iOS, this book provides plenty of new morsels to educate you on all that's new in Apple's latest mobile operating system.

More than anything, I hope this book inspires you to see the iPhone as more than just a communication tool or a content consumption device. It's a powerful tool, but only if you possess the knowledge to uncover its deepest secrets. That's why I wrote this book. I should also note that prices provided in the book were accurate at the time of writing, but are subject to change.

What You'll Learn from This Book

iPhone Secrets will teach you more than you ever thought possible about the iPhone—a device you might assume you're already intimately familiar with. Moreover, the book takes a deep dive into all the tentacles that round off a complete iPhone experience, showing you how to master iTunes, the cloud and all of Apple's related cloud services.

You'll learn how to tweak your home panes for maximum efficiency, which apps are deserving of your attention, which accessories are worth splurging on, and how to keep your digital life in order. You'll also gain a greater understanding about iTunes, while also recognizing the incredible streaming power in tools such as AirPrint and AirPlay. You'll understand how the iPhone can become the center of your multimedia-filled life, and how it can potentially take the place of numerous gadgets within the home.

After you've digested this book, you'll be able to fully grok the intricacies of iOS 6, and you'll also learn how to fix any issues that you may run into while pushing the iPhone to its extremes. You'll also learn a great deal about yourself, and how you can take the advice that lies ahead and apply it to your specific usage patterns and needs.

Who Should Read This Book

Anyone who is even remotely interested in Apple's iPhone family, or iOS 6 on the whole, stands to learn something from this book. Even if you've been an avid iPhone user from the start, there's plenty here to educate yourself on. This book focuses on iOS 6, Apple's newest mobile OS. It's without question the company's most substantial overhaul yet of iOS, and I've devoted the majority of the pages ahead to breaking down (and digging into) the subtleties of this new build.

Even if you're familiar with the cloud, you can supplement your existing know-how with the tips and tricks explained here. Your iPhone experience is largely limited by what you've come into contact with. I'll introduce you to new apps, techniques and accessories that you've probably never heard of, all of which are handpicked to advance your overall experience. Whether you think you know it all or have yourself convinced that you know nothing at all, there's plenty here for you. And you. And *you*.

How This Book Is Structured

The fact that this book is many, many times thicker than the actual iPhone says a lot. There's a serious amount of content here and ample avenues to explore. I engineered the layout so that you can read it cover to cover and glean plenty, but it's worth taking a more detailed look at how things are segmented. I recommend sticking *loosely* to how the chapters are laid out sequentially, but those with reduced interest in select portions can skip over and return without any loss in understanding. Plow through the first four chapters, and from there, feel free to choose your own adventure.

The opening chapters revolve around the iPhone selection process, setting things up initially and getting grounded when it comes to iTunes and iOS interactions. Here, you also learn how to arrange your icons and establish an efficient and productive e-mail management system; in my mind, these are cornerstones to enjoying the iPhone.

The middle is where the technophiles will truly find their groove. If there's a nook or cranny within the iPhone universe to be explored, you find it here. These chapters dive deep into advanced functionality and accessories, providing an in-depth look at oft-overlooked settings and scenarios to make the most of your purchase.

The closing chapters are meant mostly for those who aren't afraid of serious tinkering, and also, for those who bundled in a budget to snap up a few accessories. The last chapter offers troubleshooting tips; if you run into issues at any point, feel free to flip to the end and dig in.

Features and Icons Used in This Book

The following features and icons are used in this book to help draw your attention to some of the most important or useful information in the book, some of the most valuable tips, insights, and advice that can help you unlock the secrets of the iPhone.

▶ Watch for margin notes like this one that highlight some key piece of information or that discuss some poorly documented or hard to find technique or approach.

SIDEBARS

Sidebars like this one feature additional information about topics related to the nearby text.

TIP The Tip icon indicates a helpful trick or technique.

NOTE The Note icon points out or expands on items of importance or interest.

CROSSREF The Cross-Reference icon points to chapters where additional information can be found.

WARNING The Warning icon warns you about possible negative side effects or precautions you should take before making a change.

PART I

BECOMING AN IPHONE SETUP PRO

CHAPTER 1

Selecting and Setting Up Your iPhone

IN THIS CHAPTER

▶ Deciding which iPhone is right for you

▶ Going the refurbished route

▶ Selecting a carrier

▶ Dealing with non-expandable storage

▶ Utilizing Find My iPhone

▶ Working with wireless networks

▶ Updating your iTunes build

▶ Organizing your iLife

One of the beautiful things about Apple in general, and about the iPhone in particular, is the complete simplicity of the buying process. Apple's never been one to offer limitless customization options, which just so happens to be a blessing and a curse. This chapter breaks down the options that *do* exist in the blossoming iPhone universe, explains the pros and cons of each, and discusses whether your hard-earned greenbacks should be used for an upscale model. I also dive into the process of managing the storage you're dealt, untangle the mystery of wireless connectivity, and ensure that your PC or Mac is ready to work in concert with your freshly birthed phone. I've also found that iPhone ownership—much like home, car, and pet ownership—is far more gratifying when things are kept tidy. Hence, a deep dive into the organization of your looming iLife awaits.

CHOOSING WHICH IPHONE TO BUY

In the introduction, I made it sound like the process of buying an iPhone was as easy as choosing between chocolate and cheesecake for breakfast. And it is. *Sort of.* But just because there aren't many options, doesn't mean that you have *no* options whatsoever. Apple currently sells three models of the iPhone. There's the iPhone 4, the iPhone 4S, and the iPhone 5. The former two options can connect to 3G mobile data networks, whereas the iPhone 5 can connect to LTE networks. All three models can be found on Verizon Wireless, AT&T, and Sprint in the United States, while a host of pre-paid carriers and global carriers offer them as well. Compared to the original iPhone, which shipped exclusively on AT&T in 2007, the iPhone is tremendously more accessible now than it ever has been.

If you're new to the smartphone world, you might wonder what the real difference is between 3G and LTE. There's a huge difference. LTE, which is available on a growing amount of carriers, is oftentimes five to ten times faster than 3G. It makes browsing the web, checking your e-mail, and taking care of other business on your phone so much faster. Yes, you can *feel* the speed difference. And if you plan on ever using your iPhone as a mobile hotspot to tether your laptop and access the Internet that way, I strongly encourage you to opt for the iPhone 5 if only to have access to those LTE waves.

> **TIP** Don't be confused by marketing lingo; although AT&T's iPhone 4S will show 4G on the home screen, it can connect only to the same 3G HSPA+ towers that an AT&T iPhone 4 can. When I refer to 4G, it's LTE, a true evolution beyond HSPA+ networks.

The iPhone 4 and 4S offer a 3.5-inch retina display, while the iPhone 5 offers a 4-inch, 1136×640 resolution panel. What's that taller screen get you? Room for an extra row of icons or folders on the home screen (and those folders can hold 16 apps each versus 12 on the iPhone 4 and 4S), and as developers build new apps to meet the new specifications, you'll also find programs that enable you to see just a bit more than users can see on the iPhone 4 or 4S. The "take it or leave it" style has always been a polarizing trademark for Apple, but I believe that fewer buying options enables a tighter seal between the hardware and software. Apple's unique in its insistence on handcrafting both the physical device and the operating system (iOS) that runs beneath it, and the only logical way to guarantee a stellar—or at the very least, uniform—experience across the entire iPhone portfolio is to quell deviation with regard to specifications. Supply chain aficionados refer to this as "vertical integration."

Let's dig in to find out which combination is idyllic for those still situated outside of the iPhone Owners Club.

SAVING MONEY THE REFURBISHED WAY

It's a common theme, really. Apple introduces a new product. Apple sees massive demand. Apple sees people lined up for hours in order to get their hands on Apple's new product. But eventually, supply catches up with demand, and if you wait even longer, you'll even find yesterday's hottest commodity in refurbished form.

If you've ever tried to find an Apple product on "sale," you've probably realized that it's a Herculean task. Apple has notoriously tight controls on pricing, and unlike the PC universe, you won't find typical discount stores selling Apple wares for less. Even Walmart is permitted to shave only a few precious cents from their iPhone and iPod touch offerings. So, is there any hope whatsoever to get in on the iPhone cheaply? You bet.

Apple advertises only the MSRP (manufacturer's standard retail price), but I have a tried-and-trusted alternative to paying top dollar. That is Apple's astonishingly well-stocked refurbished store (http://store.apple.com/us/browse/home/specialdeals), which is continually updated as new batches of refurb iPhones flow in. I know, you've done "the refurb thing" elsewhere, only to get a cracked device with miscellaneous crumbs scattered about and a questionable warranty that expired before the postal service could even deliver it. But here's the thing: Apple's refurbished products are better than any other refurbished product I've come across.

You should also look for refurbished iPhones from carrier stores; AT&T will even sell them online.

> **TIP** Refresh Apple's refurbished section early and often; the hottest deals vanish within minutes of appearing, and there's absolutely no way to sign up and be alerted when new stock arrives. Getting a bargain takes plenty of patience and a little luck.

When I say they're "as good as new," I'm thoroughly downplaying reality. In fact, I rarely recommend that people buy an Apple product new. (The iPhone 5 is a notable exception, simply due to the inclusion of an LTE cellular radio.) Refurbished iPhones, just like the company's refurbished Macs and iPods, arrive in fresh plastic wrap with polished accessories, a user guide, and the same one-year warranty that's affixed to new Apple products. The only difference? A drab cardboard exterior compared to the flashily designed boxes you see in the store. Outside of that, you'll be remarkably hard-pressed to tell an Apple refurb apart from a new piece.

▶ Generally speaking, Apple sells refurbished gear only through its online store. Don't bother looking in one of its physical retail outlets; the best you'd find there is a closeout on an old model, or perhaps a used store demo.

Choosing Between Carriers

▶ On average, you'll save anywhere from 8 to 28 percent by buying refurbished, and considering that you get the same warranty, resting easy on that decision should be... well, easy.

Choosing an iPhone carrier used to be easy: it was AT&T or nothing. These days, competition is fierce, and a host of other operators are offering the iPhone. AT&T, Sprint, and Verizon Wireless are the major postpaid operators to carry the iPhone line in the United States (shown in Figure 1-1), whereas Cricket and a smattering of other prepaid carriers are also now offering the iPhone 4, 4S, and 5.

> **WARNING** Unfortunately, Verizon's iPhone handsets cannot support voice and data simultaneously. So, if you're using your Verizon iPhone as a mobile hotspot and you receive a call, your Internet connection will drop until that call is completed. AT&T can easily handle both at the same time.

Globally, the list runs longer than I have the space to list. In general, however, almost every major carrier in the world carries or supports the iPhone. Even T-Mobile USA, the "fourth" major carrier in the United States, supports the iPhone. It doesn't sell them, mind you, but it will happily sell you a T-Mobile SIM card to place in an iPhone that you've purchased elsewhere.

Generally speaking, Verizon Wireless offers the best, most reliable, and widest coverage in the United States. Its LTE umbrella hits far more cities than that of AT&T and Sprint, and if you happen to hit a rural area, you'll stand a better chance of having any connectivity at all on Verizon. Naturally, Verizon also tends to be the most expensive option, but you get what you pay for. Sprint's service is historically the weakest among these three, but it's also the lone remaining postpaid carrier in America to offer the iPhone with an unlimited data plan, so heavy users may be swayed.

As if you needed one more reason to select Verizon as your iPhone 5 carrier, it's also the only iPhone 5 sold in the United States from a carrier that is unlocked from day one. Even if you ink a new two-year agreement with Verizon to get an iPhone 5, the phone they ship you will support Nano SIM cards from AT&T, T-Mobile, and any other GSM carrier in the world. You might not receive LTE on all of those carriers, but basic data and voice services will work. And there's no unlock fee to pay, either.

> **TIP** It's impractical to adequately break down pricing for all possible iPhone carriers with all possible monthly plans. Depending on the size of your family, your data needs, and your voice needs, monthly rates will vary hugely. It's also worth asking your employer if they offer discounts with any one carrier in particular; many corporations will offer employees 5 to 10 percent off of their monthly mobile bills when using a partner operator.

FIGURE 1-1: Choose carefully! Carrier-locked iPhones won't work on other networks (except the Verizon one)

Why does this all matter? Your iPhone's speed and reliability on a network is only as good as the provider it's linked to, and there's absolutely no way to turn an AT&T iPhone into a Verizon iPhone. Even if you currently reside in an area with historically solid AT&T voice and data coverage, I recommend picking up the Verizon iPhone if price isn't a factor. I've traversed all 50 U.S. states, and I can say with authority that AT&T's high-speed reach is markedly less than Verizon's.

NOTE Recently, many carriers (AT&T and Verizon included) have introduced shared data plans. These are typically not great deals for consumers. If you have a grandfathered unlimited data plan, do everything you can to keep it. Although operators tout these shared plans as great for families, they only help to lock you into a carrier, and generally offer a higher price-per-megabyte compared to non-share plans.

UNDERSTANDING THE NON-EXPANDABLE STORAGE SITUATION

What's in a megabyte? Oh, 1024KB, which is comprised of… never mind. I could dig deep into the technobabble surrounding storage and be here for hours, so I'll just cut to the chase: Apple provides three options for storing files locally on the iPhone. You can buy a 16GB model, a 32GB model, or a 64GB model. That's it. Despite the pleading of pundits, there's still no SD (Secure Digital) card slot on the iPhone, which means that the quantity of storage you get can never been expanded via any means whatsoever.

Choosing an iPhone with adequate storage for your needs is of utmost importance. What you probably don't realize now is that you'll need far more storage than you suspect. Much like with our homes, we tend to fill the iPhones in our lives with as much "stuff" as it gives us room for. What, exactly, takes up space on an iPhone?

▶ E-mails

▶ Music

▶ Photos

▶ Videos

▶ Apps

Those are the heavy hitters, seen in Figure 1-2. Things like Contacts, Calendar entries, and miscellaneous To-Do lists also take up space, but they're so insignificant that it's not worth harping on. The long and short of it is this: if you plan on using your iPhone as a serious content consumption machine—loading it down with iTunes TV rentals and every album you've had since the second grade—buy the one with as much storage as you can afford. If you're willing to "clean house" every so often in order to only have the latest and most germane content onboard, the cheaper 16GB edition will do.

The good news is that Apple's taking the focus off of internal storage in many ways with the introduction of iCloud, enabling users to simply stream in content that's hosted *elsewhere*, as opposed to on the device. Granted, this magic seems magical only when you have a solid connection to the Internet, but it's certainly worth considering. Thanks to iCloud—a feature that I devote significant time to in Chapter 16, "iCloud, the Cloud, and iTunes Match"—there's at least a secondary option for storing TV shows, music, and movies, but you'll still need to keep local versions of your most favorite material right on your iPhone. Wireless Internet isn't quite ubiquitous, in a literal sense.

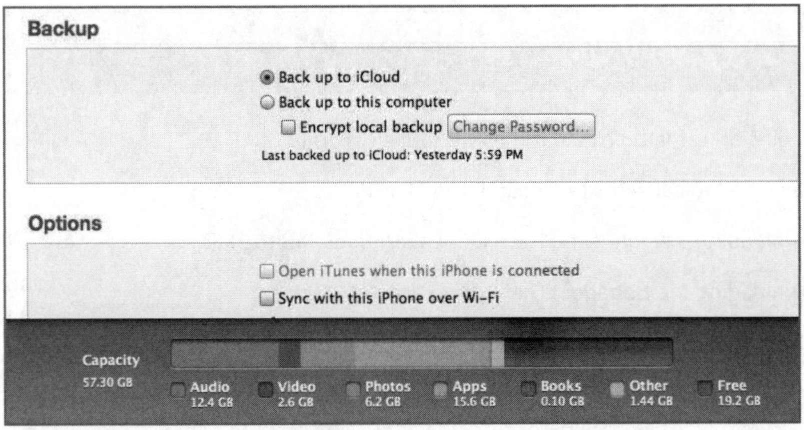

FIGURE 1-2: This capacity gauge within iTunes lets you know what's taking up space on your iPhone.

Thinking About Data Tiers

Defining 3G could take up a book's worth of pages on its own, but I'll try to keep it brief. If you own a smartphone, you're all too familiar with mobile data. It's a constant wireless data connection that enables you to sync up with the Internet, pull down e-mails, send tweets, and remain constantly dialed into your digital life. These days, it's hardly a foreign concept.

You're probably wondering how much data is consumed by doing these various tasks. Just two years ago, this wasn't even an issue at all. All four of the major U.S. carriers offered unlimited data plans with their smartphones, so pondering the strain placed on the network by any given task wasn't something consumers were apt to do. Today, it's different. The networks are being burdened by gaining new users faster than carriers can build new towers, so what we're left with is a world of tiered data plans.

As mentioned earlier, you have a handful of tier choices for iPhone data. But it's nearly impossible to make an informed decision as to which tier suits you best without knowing how much data is consumed by the tasks you do on a regular basis. The sidebar entitled "What's in a Download?" is a rough-and-dirty guide to give you some basic perspective.

WHAT'S IN A DOWNLOAD?

- ▶ Sending an e-mail: around 0.1MB without attachments

- ▶ Loading a typical website: around 0.2MB to 1MB

- ▶ Downloading a single song from iTunes: around 3MB to 6MB

- ▶ Downloading the Engadget Distro app: around 2MB

- ▶ Video chatting over FaceTime: around 3MB per minute

- ▶ Streaming an SD TV show: around 400MB for a 30-minute program

- ▶ Streaming an HD TV show: around 1500MB for a 30-minute program

- ▶ Loading an Adobe Flash-based website (on iPhone): 0MB

Got all that? Good. Most of the major carriers, outside of Sprint in the United States, are pushing a generic 2GB-per-month plan. If you're careful to download apps and app updates at home on a Wi-Fi connection, you probably won't have any issue staying under that barrier. Downloading apps and streaming video are the two easiest ways to destroy a data plan, and although it might be tempting to tether an LTE-equipped iPhone 5 as your home broadband connection, don't. Any carrier will pick up on the heavy usage within a month and will probably disconnect your account.

Keeping Tabs on Data Usage

So, loading a few web pages should take only a few megabytes of your monthly allotment, but wouldn't it be grand if you could see specifically how much data you've used at any given time? It would. And it's possible. Apple doesn't go out of its way to make it clear, but there's a slightly hidden data meter that's always running in the background, calculating how much cellular data you've sent and received right down to the *byte*. It operates in real-time, and it doesn't miss anything.

In fact, it's a fantastic tool for sniffing out "data leaks." If you're using the 3G or 4G connection and you have too many push notifications enabled, you might be consuming data that you never intended to. I strongly recommend disabling push e-mail, Twitter, Facebook, and other social networking apps while using 3G if you're dangerously close to exceeding your monthly allotment. And, of course, you should *really* stop streaming Netflix for 10 hours per day. That's just embarrassing.

▶ Apple's built-in tool only applies to cellular data. There's no built-in way to see how much Wi-Fi data you've used—a real shame given that some home ISPs, like Comcast—are capping monthly usage.

TIP Apple might not support multiple profiles, but if you're brazen enough to jailbreak your device (which voids the warranty, hence I can't publicly recommend it), the iUsers app in the Cydia App Store does just that. My guess is that this kind of functionality will be bundled into the next major iOS release.

To access the meter, visit Settings ➜ General ➜ Usage ➜ Cellular Usage, as shown in Figure 1-3. You should also set up a recurring reminder on your iPhone that encourages you to reset that meter every 30 days. If you don't, it's practically impossible to keep tabs on how much data has been consumed on a new month's worth of data.

FIGURE 1-3: Ah, a fresh cellular data counter. Careful not to run this up too fast!

SQUEEZING THE MOST OUT OF EVERY MEGABYTE

Pinching pennies is never a bad idea. Turns out, pinching bytes isn't a half-bad concept, either. Although the web is largely developed with unlimited home broadband connections in mind, a few companies are mindful of the natural limits applied to wireless broadband. I've compiled a few of my favorite data-saving apps here, all of which available after a quick title search in the App Store.

- ▶ **Opera Mini**—It's a free, fast, and compact web browser for the iPhone. When you request a page, the request is sent to the Opera Mini server, which downloads the page from the Internet. The server then packages your page in a compressed format—dubbed OBML—which requires less data to download.

- ▶ **Skyfire**—If you're a YouTube addict, get the Skyfire browser and accompanying VideoQ app ($3.99), which has a multimedia compression feature that lets users spend less time loading videos and less data accessing them.

- ▶ **Onavo**—This is a free app that acts as a proxy server for your iPhone. Once installed, the app streams data sent to you from Safari, Mail, Facebook, Google Maps, Twitter, and others through Onavo's servers, and then compresses it before sending it to your iPhone. Users also receive access to compression reports and metrics on data savings. The app doesn't shrink or compress information that you send, though, so your image and video uploads will still look as good as possible.

- ▶ **DataMan Pro for iPhone**—If you're constantly fretting your usage, and can't remember to check Apple's built-in usage meter, this $0.99 app provides elaborate notification and monitoring services, enabling you to stay informed and curb usage as your monthly limit approaches. You'll get unmistakable alerts as you're approaching your monthly limit, helping you to dodge those pesky overage fees.

SETTING UP (AND UNDERSTANDING) FIND MY IPHONE

Find My iPhone is a brilliant service that ships with every iOS 5- and iOS 6-equipped iPhone (see Figure 1-4). If you update your existing iPhone to Apple's latest mobile OS, you will have it. Swell, eh? Put simply, it's a software/hardware solution that allows your

Apple ID to keep tabs on the movement of your iPhone, and if it's ever lost or stolen, you can rather easily track it down. Think of it as OnStar tracking, but for your iPhone.

FIGURE 1-4: Make sure you tick the top option here during your initial setup. Failing to do so will result in endless tears from yours truly.

Setting up this service didn't used to be so simple. In a prior life, this service required a MobileMe account, a paid service that only the hardest of hardcore Apple loyalists were apt to spring for. Sensibly, Apple figured it prudent to bring this highly valuable service to *all* iPhone owners, completely free of charge.

MobileMe was (mercilessly, albeit understandably) killed when iCloud was introduced.

Enabling the service is as simple as accepting the opt-in notification for location-based services upon iOS install, choosing to turn Find My iPhone on, and creating an iCloud account. If you skipped this process while rushing through the startup screens in iOS, simply visit Settings → iCloud → Find My iPhone, and flip the toggle to On. I can't emphasize this enough: please, take five seconds and enable this feature. It's never been easier to proactively protect your investment in anything.

Once active, it's downright staggering what you can do should your iPhone become lost or stolen. For starters, you can sign into www.icloud.com on any web browser in order to see precisely where it's at based on its GPS coordinates. If you're near a pal with an iOS device of their own, there's a Find My iPhone app that allows you to use *their* device to locate and interact with *your* lost device.

And when I say, "interact," I mean *interact*. You can force a pop-up message onto the screen of your misplaced device, encouraging anyone who finds it to drop it off at a given location or phone you at whatever number you please. The message you write is completely customizable. Moreover, you can force the alert to make an audible sound—even if you had the Mute function on when you lost it!

If you're concerned about ill-willed thieves prying into your personal information, you can remotely set a lock-screen password requirement, and if you know that it has somehow fallen into the wrong hands, you can remotely delete *all* of its contents (see Figure 1-5), but you won't be able to track it if you do. Clearly, this is a last resort recommendation. If (and when) you do retrieve it, a simple restore from iCloud will bring it back to the state you left it in. Did I mention all of this was free?

FIGURE 1-5: Wipe away. You can restore it in a few clicks with iCloud.

WORKING WITH NETWORKS

Despite being a highly useful offline product, the iPhone is truly at its best when connected to a live wire. And by that, I mean no wire at all. Ensuring that your iPhone is connected to the Internet—be it over Wi-Fi or 3G—ensures the best possible experience, and allows you to take full advantage of iCloud, Game Center, e-mail, and a litany of other incredible features that simply aren't available offline.

Right from the get-go, iOS's startup process asks you to connect to a Wi-Fi network in order to fully set up your device. *That's* how integral the Internet is to the overall experience. So, it goes without saying that you should be near the web before you venture too far into iPhone setup. I recommend venturing to Settings ➔ Wi-Fi each time you situate yourself in a new place. As soon as you're in, the iPhone begins an automatic perusal of the surroundings in search of nearby Wi-Fi networks. Connecting to one is as simple as tapping the one you're after and entering the security password (if applicable).

I encourage you to use Wi-Fi whenever you can, particularly when you're home. If you're on a tiered data plan, there's no need in relying on a cellular network when Wi-Fi is around.

BENEFITS OF THE MOBILE HOTSPOT

You may be buying an iPhone for the sake of having the Internet in your pocket. And that's fine. But wouldn't it be nice if you could share the Internet connection on your phone with your laptop, desktop, or any other Wi-Fi device? You can! The iPhone 4, 4S, and 5 all offer a Mobile Hotspot option in the Settings ➔ General ➔ Cellular ➔ Set Up Personal Hotspot. Effectively, this takes the 3G or 4G LTE connection coming into the phone, and sends it back out over Wi-Fi for nearby devices to leech off of. Technically, this process is known as "tethering."

Carriers all approach this differently, with some charging more for it, some letting you do it for free, and some enabling it gratis if you sign up for a mobile sharing plan. Even if you don't think you'll tether, you'll probably find a situation where it'd be handy. If you're a business traveler, don't even debate it; you'll need tethering. Due to this, the iPhone 5 becomes a strong candidate over the 4 and 4S. Being able to tether using LTE waves is a huge boon; given that it's five to ten times faster, your laptop will be able to browse the web using your iPhone's cellular radio much, much faster.

If your home router is located a great distance away from where you typically use your iPhone, and you're pulling your hair out from dropped connections, it's probably worth investing in a Wi-Fi repeater or extender. My personal favorite is the AirPort Express. For one, it's an Apple product, which practically guarantees smooth sailing within the ecosystem. Two, it's widely available for less than $100—far less if you buy it from Apple's refurbished store. Three, it's wildly compact, and a new AirPort Utility app (free in the App Store) enables you to have complete control of the AirPort Express' settings and security right from your iPhone—no Mac or PC required.

> **TIP** Although somewhat unrelated, the AirPort Express is also an exceptional travel partner, just like your iPhone. With the built-in Ethernet jack, it allows hotel Ethernet connections to instantly be shared with all of your devices on your own, homegrown Wi-Fi network. It quite literally converts a wired Internet connection into a wireless one, and you have absolute control over the SSID and password. Particularly in those hotels that charge you *per connection*, paying for just one while sharing the love among your iPhone, tablet, and laptop will make any frugal traveler smile.

UPDATING AND READYING ITUNES

Make no mistake: iTunes is still a very real, and very necessary part of the iPhone experience. Apple has gone to great lengths in order to convince the world otherwise, but unless you've grown up entirely enveloped in Apple's ecosystem, you'll still find the occasional talk with iTunes a necessity. To Apple's credit, iOS, iTunes Match, and iCloud have made iTunes interactions far less necessary than in years past, but keeping the primary middleman between your stored files and your iPhone in tip-top shape should be considered a mandate.

> **CROSSREF** iTunes is discussed in more depth in Chapter 4, "Wrangling iTunes"; Chapter 16 is dedicated to the subjects of iTunes Match and iCloud.

The truth of the matter is that iTunes is updated on a far more regular basis than iOS. Apple tends to make only major, deliberate changes to the latter, whereas the former seems to be in a perpetual state of improvement. Or perhaps "repair" is a better term, depending on your perspective. At any rate, it's extremely wise to ensure you have the very latest copy of iTunes installed on your PC or Mac before attempting to set up your iPhone for the first time, or upgrade your existing iPhone for its initial encounter with iOS 6.

> CROSSREF Newer isn't always better, though oftentimes it's required.
> I offer instructions on where to find older builds of iTunes online in Chapter 18,
> "Jailbreaking and Troubleshooting."

You have two options when it comes time to update. Either use Check For Updates within iTunes itself, or cruise over to www.itunes.com and download the new installer from Apple. Once the latest iTunes is fired up, and your iPhone is plugged into your computer via USB, a quick tap of the Check For Update button should get things underway on your device. Have a look at Figure 1-6 for a clearer understanding.

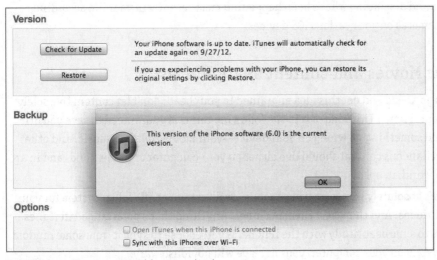

FIGURE 1-6: Fingers crossed for an update!

ORGANIZING YOUR ILIFE FIRST

"Sheesh, *another* step in the process before I even dive into my iPhone?" A fair question. But yes, that's exactly the case. I've set up a number of iPhones in my time, and I've consistently found that those who put in the proper efforts ahead of time are more greatly rewarded afterward. The entire iPhone experience is enriched by being organized, and a few key portions of Apple's iLife suite tie directly into the fabric of iPhone.

How iPhoto Ties into iPhone, and Vice Versa

The first program worth mentioning is iPhoto. Granted, this won't apply to those who aren't using a Mac (or, OS X, given that Apple's desktop OS can technically be hacked onto machines designed for Windows), but it's a surprisingly robust piece of software that's worth dabbling in if you're a self-proclaimed shutterbug. One of the real joys of using iPhone comes in the form of sharing photos. The built-in slideshow feature enables owners to quickly and beautifully share vacation and family pictures without having to lug a full laptop and external hard drive worth of photos to a relative's abode. Unless you organize your images ahead of time, they'll show up as a scattered mess on your iPhone. "Garbage in, garbage out" has never been so accurate.

I dive deeper into Photo Stream in Chapter 16—one focusing solely on the merits of iCloud—but suffice it to say, this is yet another method for pulling down captured shots and displaying what's been happening most recently in your life according to the cameras on your various iOS devices.

How Movies and Content Share Homes

Let's go ahead and get this idea engrained in your head: don't let content live solely on your iPhone. Thinking of it in the following terms is guaranteed to save you grief should something go wrong on your device—your movies, photos, music, and other miscellaneous content should live either on your computer or in the cloud, and in an ideal world, in both.

It's absolutely worth creating a robust, well-cataloged file folder system for your local videos. And then, sort them in iTunes. Anything that's prearranged in iTunes tends to sync beautifully with the iPhone. If you choose to sync it from some random filesystem on your computer, your mileage will obviously vary.

As you'll learn in the chapters to come, syncing is a *huge* part of iPhone life. I've an inkling that Apple's doing all that it can to change that, but we aren't there yet. Apple would love nothing more if everything you could ever want were available on demand from the cloud. As it stands, you'll be reaching back to your computer for a great many files, and things aren't going to become magically organized on your iPhone if they're strewn about on your home computer.

Realizing that content will be living in two places is a bit tough for some to wrap their head around. But as an ardent supporter of backing up everything on your computer, it's something that's worth managing. If you acquire something fresh on your computer, make sure it's placed in the same filesystem or program that you initially sync your iPhone to. That way, updates are shared with no fuss to speak of. If you happen to download a new app or iTunes record on your iPhone, I discuss how to transfer those to your PC in the pages to come. The key is making sure the data continues to flow both ways, even after the initial setup. Computing families that talk together, stay together.

SUMMARY

It's important to carefully consider which iPhone is right for you. Perhaps saving a bit on the iPhone 4 or 4S is worth giving up the LTE that's only included on the iPhone 5. If saving money is a priority, opting for less storage capacity or even a refurbished iPhone might be the way to go. The same careful consideration should be applied to choosing your carrier.

You can set up your iPhone in the blink of an eye. But that's not the path you should take. Putting a proper amount of effort into cataloging and organizing your content before setting your iPhone up will ensure that subsequent syncs are smooth and predictable, and that no data is haphazardly left out or lost.

The proactive iPhone owner is the happiest, and I've provided a number of methods for keeping an eye on your cellular data usage, as well as managing your network situation. Utilizing the Mobile Hotspot function on the iPhone 5 enables lightning fast tethering access for nearby laptops—a huge deal for business travelers. AirPort Express is not only a highly recommended iPhone accessory, it's a travel companion that I never leave home without. Just like my iPhone.

Icon Placement and Organization

Thinking about the setup involved in tailoring your iPhone specifically for you is worth the effort. Once you have things just so from an initialization standpoint, it's time to ponder the overall look and feel of iOS. Remember: this is your phone, a highly personal extension of you. After whisking through the first handful of setup panes, you'll be abruptly dropped onto the home screen. Where do you go from there? Here. This chapter explains how to best tweak the iOS home screen for productivity, how to best arrange your Dock, and how to position icons that I'm sure you'll end up using the most. The fact is, it doesn't take a great deal of time to get your icons and apps situated in a manner that's ideal, and it'll save you precious time and frustration in the future. When you first get an iPhone, there's not a whole lot on there. But soon, if you lack a proper attack plan, you'll be overwhelmed with the sheer quantity of apps and information on board. Thankfully, there's a method to controlling the madness, and I discuss shortcuts and suggestions for creating a sorting system that works best for you.

OPTIMIZING PLACEMENT FOR PRODUCTIVITY

Ever wondered why people tend to place things in easy-to-reach spots whenever possible? Because it makes perfect sense. If you let it, the iPhone's home screen will eventually become an out-of-control slew of panes that simply arrange icons in the order in which they were downloaded.

The iPhone has been around since 2007, and by and large, the visual styling of iOS (formerly known as iPhone OS) has not drastically changed. Users who are choosing now to jump on the iPhone bandwagon for the first time certainly have a lot to grow familiar with. But even for iOS veterans, the explosive growth of the App Store has made organization a continual challenge. When your app collection grows on a weekly or even daily basis, you won't want to completely rewrite rules for placement. Rather, it's wiser to construct a scheme for organizing that scales and applies even when new apps join the fray. (And with the amount of innovation happening in the App Store, join the fray they will!)

> **NOTE**   With iOS 5, Newsstand was introduced, and Apple has made it impossible to file it away inside a custom e-reader folder. I guess Apple's not too comfortable with Newsstand and Amazon's Kindle app being buddy-buddy in a folder, but it's worth mentioning that most Apple-installed apps simply cannot be deleted from the device.

▶ If you're coming from the world of OS X, the term "Dock" is a familiar one. For those not so familiar with the Mac universe, it's the semi-translucent row of icons that remains glued to the bottom of the iPhone's display, regardless of what pane you swipe to. You'll find something similar on Android phones, but it's a foreign concept in the Windows Phone, which relies on a unique tile system.

Placing Highly Used Icons in Easy-to-Reach Spots

It might sound obvious, but it's worth clarifying. The iPhone, due to its shape, tends to place your thumbs in the lower right and left hand corners. Predictably, those are the two hottest spots on the entire screen, and they're absolutely the easiest and most convenient to access. The iPhone Dock has room for a grand total of four icons (it's filled up in Figure 2-1, showing two fewer than the maximum of six possible on the iPad), but don't be fooled. You can actually stuff many dozens of apps into that lower bar without ever reaching for a jailbreak.

iOS 5 and 6 contain a feature called Folders, which is Apple's simplistic, albeit entirely satisfactory solution to now having well over 650,000 apps in the App Store. I dive deeper into folders in a bit, but suffice it to say, I'm a big fan of using 'em for the sake of organization. Unfortunately, you can't choose a folder color, lock a given folder, or change the font of a folder title without jailbreaking your device. These customization options are hugely requested, though, so I'm holding out hope that we'll see them in future iOS builds.

FIGURE 2-1: Choosing which four get the Dock spot is tough.

WARNING It's vital to think about where an app should be slotted as it's downloading. Moving it to a sensible folder right away prevents your mind from expecting it to be somewhere that it's not, and it also prevents you from relaxing your efforts to maintain a clean and well-sorted grid of applications. There's no digital rug to sweep things under on iOS; it's either categorized nicely, or it sticks out on its own like a sore thumb.

The Dock as a whole is without question the most important locale for apps. It's the only row of apps that retains its position regardless of what pane you're on, and taking it one step further, the apps on the far left and far right of the Dock should be the ones you use the most. Remember that whole "close to your thumbs" thing? Yeah. If you're looking for a little advice on which apps you're *likely* to use the most, here goes.

- ▶ Phone
- ▶ Contacts
- ▶ Mail
- ▶ Safari
- ▶ Messages
- ▶ App Store
- ▶ Music
- ▶ Photos
- ▶ Settings
- ▶ Maps
- ▶ Facebook
- ▶ Game Center
- ▶ Passbook
- ▶ Twitter

My personal recommendation is to make Mail and Safari the bookends, unless you have a stellar reason to do otherwise. From there, I'd create a folder (as seen in Figure 2-2) to house relatively similar apps that would normally be overflow—apps that would've been numbers 7, 8, 9, and 10 if the Dock were longer.

> CROSSREF If you're looking for the Siri app, you can stop. Siri isn't an app; she's a part of the entire operating system. She can be summoned from anywhere by holding the Home button for a couple of seconds. I dive deeper into mastering Siri in Chapter 14, "Utilizing Your Personal Assistant: Siri."

An ideal Dock, in my mind, consists of two of your most commonly used applications (Mail and Safari for me) and two folders of overflow. You can cram up to 16 apps in each folder with the iPhone 5 (though prior iPhones are limited to 12 per folder), but nine per folder is optimal. Why? Because you'll see miniaturized icons of the first nine apps in any folder, which—surprisingly enough—are large enough to make out what they are should you encounter a brain fart while trying to remember which apps are in which folder.

FIGURE 2-2: Folders... they do an iPhone good.

TIP Neither iOS 5 nor iOS 6 allows for multiple user profiles. This means that owners who need a certain grid of apps at their fingertips for work and another set handy for play simply don't have the option of switching on the fly. If that's you, here's my solution—use one or more of your home screen panes to house your favorite additional "at home" apps, while other home screen panes house the apps most frequently used for work. It's not quite a two-profile compromise, but it's still better than fragmenting across two devices for work and home.

Pegging the Edges

The corners are undoubtedly the place to nail your favorite apps. The bottom corners are the easiest to reach, while the top two aren't lacking on the tantalization scale, either. But sadly, some estranged law in some scientific field I'm not qualified to opine on has asserted that only four corners be applied to each rectangle, and I know good and well you'll need hasty access to more than four apps or folders.

Just as surrounding yourself with good company is a wise move in life, it's also wise to surround your moderately used applications with your favorites. That's right, it's time to head to the edges. The outskirts of the app grid are naturally easiest to access (see Figure 2-3) without having to relocate your hands or fingers, and conversely, the central region of each home screen is where I leave my most infrequently used programs.

FIGURE 2-3: Sorry, Newsstand—it's tough to get a seat on the edge!

TIP Unfortunately, Apple doesn't include any sort of launch counter to clock how many times you open any given app, so it's a bit tedious to actually keep track of which programs are being used the most. It's delightfully easy to relocate an app, however, but more painful to relocate nine. Thus, I strongly recommend using folders whenever possible. If you realize you need to move your Travel or Foreign Language folders to a hotter spot on the grid due to an upcoming trip, you're now moving two icons instead of dozens.

Picking a uniform *modus operandi* and sticking with it is crucial in allowing the iPhone to become just an extension of your brain. If you know precisely where the apps that you need most given your current situation will be, it is far easier to locate them. Even if the apps or folders themselves change with the season, the placement is of the utmost importance.

Thinking Through Folders

Folders are perhaps the most wonderful introduction to iOS from an organizational standpoint, although they're often overlooked in the frenzy of slapping as many mouth-watering applications as possible onto the iPhone upon the initial unwrapping. I'm not blaming the masses—grabbing hold of an iPhone for the first time is indeed a thrilling experience—but if you're calm, cool, and collected enough to be perusing these pages, you're probably thoughtful enough to add a bit of order to your iPhone.

As mentioned previously, you can shove up to 16 apps into a single folder with the iPhone 5 (or 12 in prior iPhones), and you can name each one anything you desire. I recommend stopping at nine per folder in order to see each and every app thumbnail within each folder, but those with highly trained memories can feel free to go overboard.

NOTE Creating a folder is as simple as long-pressing on one app and hovering it above another. A moment later, a folder is born, and the iPhone does its darndest to suggest a satisfactory folder label based on the categories of the apps you're bringing together. In my opinion, these suggestions are generally too vague. Productivity doesn't mean much; you're better off with separate folders of Photography apps, Word Processing apps, and Financial apps.

OPTIONS FOR MASTERFULLY ORGANIZING YOUR APPS INTO FOLDERS

Outside of a few choice apps that you simply use over and over, the only true way to keep your iPhone organized over the long term is to rely on an elaborate system of folders. It's daunting at first, but far less harrowing than seeing 80+ apps untidily strewn across countless home panes. What's difficult, however, is a wholesale change of how you arrange apps within a folder system. This sidebar shares with you three proven—if not a touch unorthodox—methods of attacking the issue of folders.

How to Organize by Genre

This is absolutely my preferred way of organizing folders. But I'm a person who thinks in terms of subjects and topics, so it jibes with my natural mental flow. Before I get too physiological up in here, I'll reiterate that Apple's suggested folder names are simply too vague for me. They work fine if you're only inter-ested in lumping things broadly together, but you have many home screens to work with. If you end up with 40 or so folders, so be it. I'll take highly specific folders—ones that I can recall their contents at a mere glance—over folders that could contain just about anything.

Looking for suggestions on app folder names?

- ▶ Apple Apps
- ▶ Cloud Storage
- ▶ Navigation
- ▶ Foreign Languages
- ▶ Travel
- ▶ Streaming Video
- ▶ Streaming Music
- ▶ Online Radio
- ▶ Web Browsers
- ▶ Word Processors
- ▶ Social Networking
- ▶ Camera Apps

- ▸ Video Apps
- ▸ Video Calling
- ▸ VoIP
- ▸ Magazines
- ▸ Analytics
- ▸ To-Do

How to Organize by Color

Color, you ask? Why, yes! Not everyone's inclined to think about apps in terms of natural categorization, and in fact, some respond better to visual stimulants than descriptive phrases. I can't take complete credit for this one—a dear friend of mine at The Verge, Ross Miller, first brought this to my attention—but it is actually far more useful in practice than it sounds in theory. The majority of applications I've seen in the App Store are launched with a logo that rarely, if ever, changes. And even if the design is mildly overhauled, few apps ever change their logos entirely.

Here's an example of how this can work: create a folder called "Red." Now, pop i.TV, Netflix, Photo Booth, and iTunes Movie Trailers. Black & Red? The AP's mobile news app and Opera Mini come to mind. Blue? There's Engadget, Skype, Twitter, Facebook, Dropbox, Distro, Echofon, FlightTrack Pro, PS Express, and Safari.

Because some apps simply don't use an icon that relies heavily on one single hue, this method works best if you reserved color-themed folders for your most frequently used apps, and then categorize the rest using the genre method. It's a hybrid system, but it might be just what your cranium ordered.

How to Organize Alphabetically

I'm surmising that you'll be able to guess what I'm going to say next. This here is the most elementary method of all, but setting it up isn't quite as straightforward as you might imagine. A simpleton may create a different folder for every letter of the alphabet, and while that's a fine approach, I'd bet that you'll see quite the imbalance shortly after.

Folders N and S are apt to be overflowing, whereas less commonly used letters remain barren. Thankfully, it's fairly easy to create S2 if S1 fills up, but you may be better served by Sa-Sm and Sn-Sz. Depends on how heavy an app user you are, really.

(continues)

(Continued)

> If you go this route, I'd still look to place the letter folders you frequent most around the edges of your first home screen; just because your apps are in alphabetical folders, doesn't mean your folders have to be arranged in alphabetical order too.

Giving Each Home Screen a Purpose

The first home screen—the one that loads up after the Slide To Unlock screen is slid aside—is clearly the most significant. Communication, productivity, and your favorite content/game applications should reside here, but what about the other 10 panes? The iPhone and iOS 5/6 provide 11 total panes to work with, and if you're genuinely able to fill them all up, you've most certainly accomplished something.

The wild thing is that some of you might come close. If you're the type who tends to leave no stone unturned—and thus, no pane left blank—the aforementioned categorization methods may need a bit of tweaking. Start off by keeping your first home screen reserved for your most commonly used apps and folders. The first screen should always be home to the popular crowd. The good news is that science has yet to prove that apps have feelings, so those relegated to subsequent panes aren't apt to delete themselves in an act of rebellion.

> **NOTE** One of Apple's unofficial official trademarks is the art of letting people discover its products on their own terms. Apple smartly realized that placing artificial boundaries around the possibilities here would have been a poor decision. Instead, it created an accessible App Store that has—in effect—allowed *users*, not Apple itself, to dictate what the iPhone is truly capable of. Chomp, a free app, is great for searching through hundreds of thousands of apps to find ones you'll use. So great, in fact, that Apple acquired the company's talent in early 2012.

▶ You can't create a folder as a placeholder. In fact, you need two apps before you can create a folder. In other words, download a fair amount of desired programs before diving headfirst into folder creation.

If you're wondering about customization on the home screen, it's as simple to change as visiting Settings → Wallpaper. You can assign different images for your Lock Screen as well as your home panes, but you can't assign a different image for *each* individual home pane. For best results, ensure that you select an image with a resolution higher than the display of your iPhone, or better yet, crop it ahead of time in a photo editing program like Preview, Lightroom, or Photoshop. From there, you can just e-mail it to yourself, long-press to Open in Safari, and then save it to your Camera Roll. Once it's there, you can easily select it for wallpaper or home pane use.

Apple doesn't allow each page to be labeled. You can call your folders anything you want, but there's no naming panes. What I suggest, however, is giving each overflow pane a theme. It's certainly not as obvious as a label, but until Apple adds that function, this is about as close as you can get.

Looking for an example? Let's say you're a huge news junkie, and you've downloaded just about every possible news application hosted on the App Store. Creating News 1, News 2, and News 3 is clearly not specific enough, so you can theme an entire pane for news apps instead. I'd create folders for Sports, Politics, Technology, Science, Travel, and whatever other niche you're into, and for apps that encompass all aspects of news, you can pop those into a General folder. Just like that, you've assigned an entire pane to host news apps—no confusion about what lives where.

As for deleting apps? If you'd prefer, you can delete from within iTunes and then sync with your iPhone. If you're on the go, you can just long-press an app, wait for it to start jiggling, and mash that X in the top-left that appears. If you'd like to protect your precious apps from being deleted, simply visit Settings → General → Restrictions, and flip that Deleting Apps toggle. While you're in there, you can also restrict the ability to install new apps, use FaceTime, open your Mail, and a host of other things. It's a great way to put some boundaries on what can and can't be done with your phone—particularly if it's routinely in the hands of a child.

> **TIP** When organizing panes by theme, I generally leave my absolute favorite, most-used app from each theme as a standalone icon in the top-left corner. Not only does it prevent me from having to dig into a folder to access a favorite app, but it provides a glanceable way to see what theme is represented. For instance, the ESPN ScoreCenter app is in the top-left of my Sports pane, left out of a folder for better visibility and "marking" purposes.

Examples of themes that tend to flesh out well:

- ► News
- ► Sports
- ► Audio Streaming
- ► Video Streaming
- ► Communications
- ► Productivity
- ► Business

▶ For the Kids

▶ Games

▶ Sharing/Storage

It'd be swell if Apple included a way to lock all panes except for that one dedicated to kids, but at least you can go ahead and arrange one specifically for their eyes. In iOS 6, a new Guided Access feature allows you to disable the Home button and disable touch in specific areas of the screen, but it's largely only useful to keep kids in a single app that you've already loaded.

GENERATING A WORKFLOW

At long last, it's the culminating of all the work you've put into the art or organizing. Once you've populated your Dock just so, arranged your most commonly used apps along the edges of the first home screen, and organized your home panes by easy-to-recognize themes, it's time to focus on a workflow.

The most challenging thing about using an iPhone once you pick it up is finding what you're after, particularly if you're keen on keeping dozens upon dozens of applications on your device. I take a closer look at Push Notifications in future chapters, but I'll mention for the sake of organization that they are completely valuable tools when properly set up and minded.

A great number of applications have been updated to support the more useful, less invasive push system first unveiled with iOS 5, and honed in iOS 6. In prior versions of the operating system, push notifications simply popped up in the center of the iPhone's display, regardless of what app you were currently engrossed in. Taking a note from Google's Android, Apple decided it prudent to shift notifications to their own pull-down bar at the top of the display (shown in Figure 2-4), where they'll collect and sit until you manually go and sift through.

I suggest enabling push notifications for any app that you use daily. Things like Facebook, breaking news apps, e-mail, and perhaps your favorite podcast can send you push notifications whenever a new message, alert, or issue awaits. With a reliable push system, you're presented with only the important changes upon reentering the iPhone universe, giving you a head start on which apps to check in on first. Those that haven't sent you a notification are probably less urgent to reload.

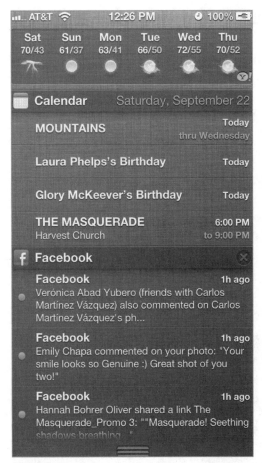

FIGURE 2-4: Have a look at iOS 6's drop-down notification window.

TIP It's easy to get overwhelmed by push notifications. Being alerted of every MLB score update is probably overboard. Being alerted of a new iMessage from your significant other is probably useful. Well, provided your relationship is in good standing. At any rate, be careful to not enable push alerts willy-nilly, and to take advantage of iOS 6's VIP list. You can select specific people from your contact list to receive push notifications from in practically every scenario.

For times when sifting through pages or folders just seems too burdensome, there's always a way out. At the initial home screen—the one that automatically presents itself just after the lock screen—just swipe toward the right one time, and up pops a simple search bar. That's called Universal Search (shown in Figure 2-5).

FIGURE 2-5: Universal Search—just type, and it'll start finding.

▶ No need to type out a full term. Universal Search updates and rearranges results with each additional letter you press.

That search bar is remarkably powerful. And it fields results incredibly quick. What's most useful about the Universal Search function is that it actually digs *into* applications when it searches. In other words, searching for "Facebook" not only pulls up a shortcut to the Facebook app, but also any e-mail messages within the Mail app that relate to Facebook (see Figure 2-6). It's also capable of searching within Contacts, Music, third-party apps, and Calendar. New to iOS 6, Spotlight now tells you which folder a certain app is in, which is most useful when you have two identically named apps that serve different functions in varying folders.

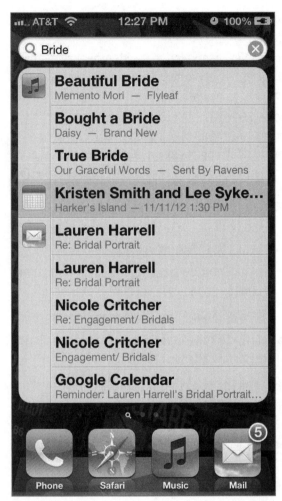

FIGURE 2-6: It's not just for finding apps...

Best of all, there are two shortcuts that appear for every search: Search Web and Search Wikipedia. Even if you can't find what you're looking for, one of those can probably help. I actually recommend using the Universal Search bar as a shortcut to Google search something. No need to actually launch Safari and search; just whisk over to the Universal Search bar, peck your query in, and select the Search Web option.

While we're on the topic, let's dive into a few settings that'll increase your efficiency. Apple provides a way to add your own keyboard shortcuts by visiting Settings ➜ General ➜ Keyboard ➜ Shortcuts. Add as many of these as you like for frequently used phrases, and since they're automatically synced over iCloud, anything you input on your iPhone will also transfer to your iPad (assuming you own one). Just be sure to visit Settings ➜ iCloud ➜ Documents & Data and flip that to On.

Just above the Shortcuts feature is a Keyboards icon that adds other keyboards. You can add various languages—only useful if you're multi-lingual, of course—but the real kicker is Emoji. iOS 6 has added a ton of new icons here, enabling frequent iMessage users to have a bit of fun with graphical characters.

When you're typing, you can also hold down (almost) any letter to get a pop-up menu of alternative characters—pretty useful for properly typing words with foreign origins. If you're in the mood to ruin someone's day, you can activate Caps Lock by simply double-tapping the Shift key. Thankfully for those trying to expand their vocabulary, iOS enables users to long-press on any word in an e-mail or document and witness a Define pop-up; tap that, and you'll instantly be educated on the word's definition. Here are a few more of my favorite timesaving tips when generating a workflow:

▶ If you're tired of targeted advertising, head to Settings ➜ General ➜ About ➜ Advertising and flip Limit Ad Tracking to On.

▶ For heavy Safari users, head to Settings ➜ Safari and flip Private Browsing to On.

▶ While browsing an article in Safari, click the Reader icon in the Address Bar to view a stripped-down version that's far easier on the eyes.

▶ In just about every app—Safari and Twitter included—a gentle tap at the top of the app or page will automatically scroll to the very top.

▶ Near universally, iOS 6 supports pull to refresh, which allows you to press and slide downward (in a Twitter stream, for example) in order to have that stream refreshed.

▶ To save an image from the web or an e-mail to your Camera Roll, just long-press on it and select Save Image.

▶ To activate an LED flash for any incoming alerts, head to Settings ➜ General ➜ Accessibility and flip LED Flash For Alerts to On.

▶ If you're having trouble viewing icons or text, visit the Accessibility menu in Settings and flip Zoom and/or Large Text to On.

▶ Taking another step, the VoiceOver feature in the Accessibility menu will read aloud screen icons and actions, and you'll find plenty of tweakable options within.

- Try out AssistiveTouch in the Accessibility menu to add hot corners to your screen for easier navigation.

- To quickly turn VoiceOver, AssistiveTouch, Invert Colors or Zoom on and off, visit Accessibility and activate Triple-click Home; tapping your Home button three times will trigger it.

- In the pull-down Notification Center, swiping across the Weather icon will bring up a multi-day forecast, while tapping on it opens up the Weather app.

- If you're annoyed by those constant keyboard clicks, visit Settings → Sounds and flip Keyboard Clicks to Off.

- With iOS 6, you can now simply pick a song from your Music library to be associated with any alarm in the Clock app (edit any alarm, then look in Sounds).

- Newer iPhones and iPads with iOS 6 will now find a Late Night option in Music EQ settings—sweet dreams!

- If you're being bombarded with random messages, visit Settings → Notifications → Messages and choose My Contacts Only under Show iMessage Alerts From.

- In iOS 6, visit Settings → Notifications → Do Not Disturb to establish the hours when you want your alerts silenced; if you still want all calls to come through, just select Allow Calls From → Everyone.

- To add or remove items from your pull-down Notification Center, visit Settings → Notifications. To prevent clutter, only add the ones you'll actually use.

- New in iOS 6, there's an entire Privacy portal in Settings → Privacy. Turn as much of that stuff off as needed until you're comfortable.

- Passbook is still a blossoming app; open it to visit the App Store and see what apps currently support it. For now, airline boarding passes and digital gift cards are the highlights.

- In iOS 6, you can send a message back to someone if they're trying to ring you while you're on another call. To edit the messages, visit Settings → Phone → Reply With Message.

SUMMARY

Just as important as setting your iPhone up right is the art of organizing the applications that make it what it is. It's vital to think about the kind of layout you'd prefer, choosing a methodology for arranging folders and giving themes to each home screen. I suggest keeping your most highly used apps in the Dock, even if that means tossing a folder or two down there. Yeah, folders can fit into the Dock, too!

The iPhone's edges are the easiest to reach, so keeping your most commonly used programs around those is advisable. You'll also be more apt to maintain your sanity if you take full advantage of folders, but placing only nine apps in each ensures that you can view all of the app thumbnails. In general, Apple's folder name suggestions are just too vague for serious cataloging; they are, however, useful for thinking of themes for home panes.

The easiest way to dig through information that builds up on the iPhone is the Universal Search function, which not only pulls up app names, but information tucked within Mail, Contacts, and more.

Finally, I reviewed some of my favorite timesaving settings that help to generate a smooth workflow. I recommend diving into Settings and making the tweaks that make sense for you.

CHAPTER 3

Managing Your E-Mail Accounts with iPhone

IN THIS CHAPTER

▶ Mastering the Gmail app
▶ Perfecting the Mail app
▶ Managing multiple accounts
▶ Tweaking the settings

Have you looked at how most folks use their iPhone? More often than not, it's being used with a finger. As voice calls fade to history and text-based communications grow, more and more individuals are using their iPhones predominantly as e-mail machines. The iPhone is actually quite great at doing just that, but understanding the intricacies of how the iPhone handles e-mail is vital to avoiding inefficiencies and frustrations. In this chapter, I do a bit of composing of my own, digging through the App Store's vibrant third-party library in order to overcome some of the limitations and stumbling blocks related to e-mail. I also show you a few alternatives to the factory Mail app, including Gmail's own app. Finally, I touch on e-mail syncing and the smattering of options available to keep your iPhone, iPad, and desktop web browser on the same page.

MASTERING GMAIL'S IOS APPLICATION

If you aren't an avid Gmailer, perhaps this section won't be near and dear to your heart. But if you are, it's probably worth a look-see. Most iPhone owners dig right into the conventional Mail app settings—the e-mail app that Apple loads into each and every iPhone Dock it sells—and proceeds with the built-in Gmail registration and setup tool. And that works. It's quick and painless, and for most, that's that.

But there's actually an alternative—an alternative that I'm convinced is far better in almost every way. After months of radio silence, Google was finally able to launch a Gmail iOS app into the App Store (see Figure 3-1). The upside is that this replaces the old method of using Safari to browse the Gmail web app; the downside is that it's mostly an HTML5 web app wrapped into a standalone program. That said, it still manages to support the lion's share of Gmail features that most users simply can't live without (Archive, Labels, and so on).

FIGURE 3-1: It may look like a web app, but it's the Gmail iOS app.

Why Gmail's iOS App Trumps Mail

The Gmail iOS app works mostly like the company's web app, but in a far friendlier form. There are also a few new tricks up the program's sleeve that make it even easier to use the native app over the watered-down version through Apple's own Mail app. For starters, the Gmail iOS app supports notifications within iOS 5 and iOS 6. That's a huge improvement over using the web app, because users can now get notified of new e-mails immediately (using a built-in "push" service). You can then hop into Settings ➜ Notifications to change which kinds of notifications you see, and how you want to be alerted to new messages. You can even have those notifications show up in your lock screen and the drop-down menu; or, for those who receive far too much e-mail, turn any of the notification options off.

> **WARNING** Apple claims that iOS 5 allows for "multi-tasking," but the reality is quite different than the multi-tasking you're accustomed to within Windows or OS X. Think of it more like "background support." You can let Safari or Mail load messages in the background while composing a graph in Apple's Numbers app, but you cannot load a split-app view that shows two or more applications on-screen simultaneously.

Another perk of using the Gmail iOS app is the ability to "Send-As." Basically, those using their single Gmail account as a repository for multiple other accounts (from work, school, etc.) will be able to reply to business-or education-related messages using their business-or education-related e-mail address. No more switching e-mail addresses or accounts in order to reply from a specific address; you can select which identity to send from right in the composition window.

Perhaps most importantly, Google's Gmail iOS app knows how to handle e-mail threads and archives. iOS 5/6 has improved its handling of threads, but I've still seen many occasions where the built-in Mail app rendered a 20+ message thread incorrectly, whereas this app always displays things just as I've come to expect from within Gmail. Archives are also a major part of daily life for Gmailers, and if assigning a label to a message before archiving it is vital to keeping your inbox organized, you'll be happy to know that this portal nails it every single time. Colored stars, too, can only be fully executed within Gmail's iOS app.

> **WARNING** Unfortunately, Apple still refuses to let you choose a third-party app as your default e-mail client. This is supremely frustrating when you select E-Mail a Link from any number of applications that support sharing; if you don't have Apple's own Mail app configured, you cannot use Gmail, Sparrow, or any other third-party e-mail app to accomplish the task. You're simply out of luck.

Inputting Text via Keyboard and Voice Dictation

Unlike the iPad, there's no pull-apart split keyboard when using the iPhone in a horizontal orientation. Like the iPad, however, Apple still won't allow you to load a custom keyboard into iOS. Even with iOS 6, there's still a single factory keyboard option; there's no Swype or SwiftKey here. It's a crying shame, too.

Apple's stock keyboard was easily the best onscreen option when the iPhone launched in 2007, but these days, many superior alternatives exist for the Android. Instead of giving those same opportunities to iPhone users, Apple has implemented something else—voice dictation.

When composing a message in the Gmail iOS app, simply move your cursor (via touch, of course) to the body of the e-mail. Once there, you'll notice the virtual keyboard change ever-so-subtly. To the left of the spacebar, there's now a microphone icon (assuming you're using an iPhone 4S or iPhone 5). Tap that, and you'll soon be composing your e-mail with your vocal cords (shown in Figure 3-2).

FIGURE 3-2: Speaking your emails can be much faster than typing them.

NOTE Voice dictation is a magical thing, but unfortunately, it's the kind of magic that requires access to the Internet. Essentially, spoken words are ingested by the phone, shot out to a transcription robot via the Internet, and then returned to your screen. Without a Wi-Fi or cellular data signal, voice dictation simply won't work. It's a shame, too, as Google's own voice dictation works offline over on Android. Perhaps Apple will take its own service offline in the future, but it's online or bust for now.

Dictating e-mails (or any document, really) can be a huge time saver, but it's also a point of frustration for many. To get the best results from the voice dictation feature, I first recommend being on Wi-Fi or a 3G/4G data connection. If you're in a remote locale where only GPRS or EDGE (2G or older) data services are available, the service will struggle to return results. Secondly, try to speak clearly and boldly in a room with minimal background noise, and aim your mouth directly at the microphones on the bottom of your iPhone. Pausing and stuttering will almost certainly introduce errors in the text that are eventually returned to your display.

Finally, try to only speak three to four sentences at a time. If you speak for much longer, the voice dictation app will simply cut you off mid-sentence, forcing you to remember where you left your train of thought. It's also worth mentioning that dictating generally means "talking like a robot." You have to think ahead for the best results—you literally need to say the word "comma" if you want a comma to be inserted. Same goes for "new paragraph" and "question mark." If you speak like you're writing—instead of like you're talking to a best bud face-to-face—you'll face far fewer frustrations.

NOTE I've harped on Gmail a lot here, mostly because it's widely viewed as the best web-based e-mail service out there. Currently, the major rivals—Hotmail and Yahoo! Mail—do not have native iOS apps, but both can be set up within Apple's Mail app. Still, having a dedicated app ensures that Gmailers get access to the bells and whistles that make this service so great.

PERFECTING THE MAIL APP

Even if you're dead-set on using the Gmail app to check your e-mail, there's plenty of reason to *also* establish your addresses within Apple's Mail app. I generally discourage duplicity with things like this, but as I alluded to earlier, there *are* certain benefits to having an e-mail account registered with an app that's so finely woven into the core of iOS. Universal Searches won't pull up findings within your e-mail accounts unless they're established in Apple's own Mail app (shown in Figure 3-3), and push notifications cannot be sent down through Safari if you're trying to use an e-mail system's web app.

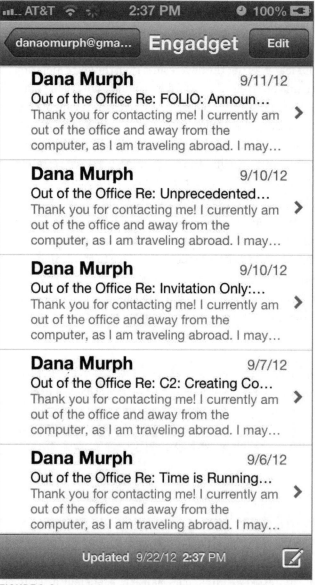

FIGURE 3-3: Simple and clean is Apple's iPhone Mail app.

Beyond all that, though, Mail is a fantastic app on its own, but there are an abundance of settings and options to tweak—things that most folks don't ever take the time to investigate. Good thing you aren't lumped into *that* crowd. Apple makes it stunningly easy to get an e-mail account registered in Mail... provided you're using a Gmail, Yahoo!, Microsoft Exchange, iCloud, Aol, or Hotmail account. Those are shown in Figure 3-4.

▶ Any POP or IMAP e-mail account can be set up in Mail, but these are pre-programmed to fetch all the required backend data with a simple username and password.

FIGURE 3-4: Take your pick. Plenty of automated e-mail setup awaits.

Here's a stunner: Mail setup leads you to all sorts of other non-mail related things. I'll give you a moment to let that sink in. Apple has intelligently realized that you may not want to suck down associated contacts, notes, and calendars for every single e-mail account you load into Mail. To that end, each new account you create gives you the option to toggle the aforementioned extras off or on. If you're looking to add your work e-mail address to Mail just for the sake of having it there in case of an emergency, but you've no desire whatsoever to see any weekly conference calls on your personal calendar, just venture to Settings → Mail, Contacts, Calendars → and select each account individually. See for yourself in Figure 3-5.

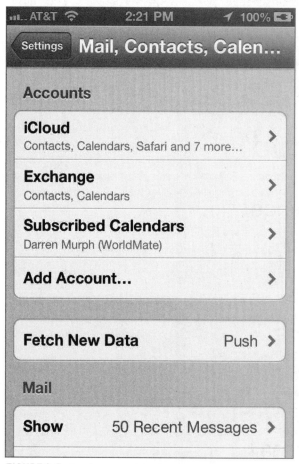

FIGURE 3-5: Syncing everything? Nothing? You've got options.

You've probably heard a thing or two about "push" and "pull" systems related to e-mail. The iPhone handles both. Push accounts—such as a Gmail account—automatically alert your iPhone that a new message has arrived, even if it's asleep or idling. It requires no action whatsoever on your end. Naturally, this "always alert" state has a slightly negative impact on battery life (think of it as your iPhone sleeping with one eye cracked open), but more detrimental is the data required. If you're using cellular data, or you're counting kilobytes with more intensity than calories, you may want to disable push altogether.

> **NOTE** As an example, I added my Engadget work e-mail into the Mail app for one reason, and one reason alone: sharing. Any time I see a tweet, a YouTube video, or any other piece of media that can be shared via e-mail, Apple forces me to use its Mail app to do the sharing. Until iOS enables you to change the default mail application to a third-party one, you'll have to use an account programmed in Mail to share over e-mail.

To do this, surf over to Settings ➔ Mail, Contacts, Calendars ➔ Fetch New Data. Right up top (shown in Figure 3-6) is a toggle to disable or enable push wholesale. "Fetch" is another term for "pull," where you give the iPhone a time interval in which to reach out to your connected accounts and pull in anything new since the last polling time. My suggestion is 15 minutes for those addicted to their digital lives, and hourly for everyone else. Manually is fine, but why force yourself to remember what to refresh when the iPhone will do it for you? Push forces updates to your phone as soon as they happen; pull (or fetch) retrieves information on a schedule that you dictate. iCloud information is set to Push, but other third-party accounts give you additional control.

Another tip is to dig one level deeper. If, while in that same window, you tap Advanced, you'll be able to tell each and every mail/calendar account how you want it to push or pull. Perhaps pushing your personal account while only pulling your work account hourly is an ideal situation, as it saves precious battery life and data where you can most afford to. *Just don't tell your boss.*

▶ Push is a godsend for keeping you informed, but it can quickly become overwhelming. I've known people to disable push at 6PM each day in order to remove distractions and focus on family. It's worth considering.

▶ By default, Mail allows you to swipe to archive. If you'd rather swipe to delete, visit Settings ➔ Mail, Contacts, Calendars and toggle Archive Messages to Off in the account(s) you have loaded.

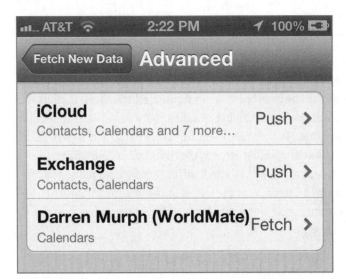

FIGURE 3-6: Pushing or fetching options can be applied separately to various accounts.

RECOMMENDED MAIL SETTINGS

In the effort of saving you time, I recommend the following settings under the Mail options in Mail, Contacts, Calendars.

▶ Show ➔ 500 recent messages: It doesn't demand that much extra space, and it's awesome to have a huge history when sifting for something offline.

▶ Preview ➔ 5 lines: The more glanceable information you can get your hands on, the less time you waste diving deeper into something that's not important.

▶ Minimum Font Size ➔ Medium: Unless your eyes are troubling you. The Giant setting is highly useful for some, and highly hilarious for everyone else.

▶ Show To/Cc Label ➔ On: In most cases, the more information you have to glance at when communicating, the better off you are.

▶ Ask Before Deleting ➔ Off: You can always resurrect things from the Trash if you need to.

▶ Load Remote Images ➔ Off: Selecting On is a great way to accidentally buy into a phishing scam.

▶ Organize By Thread ➔ On: Attempting to read e-mails sans threads could cause your iPhone to burst into tears.

There's another hidden gem here that more advanced users may very well appreciate. While in Settings ➔ Mail, Contacts, Calendar ➔ Add Account..., there's a nondescript Other option beneath all the branded, pre-configured solutions. *Mysterious!* I'll dig into the specifics of popping an unorthodox e-mail account in here in the section "Password and Multiple Account Management," but for now, I'd like to draw attention to a foursome of obscure (to the simpleton, anyway) options below Contacts and Calendars. If you were hoping to connect an LDAP or CardDAV account for pulling in the former, or a CalDAV/Subscribed Calendar for the latter, here's your opportunity (as shown in Figure 3-7). Make sure you bring your server address, username, password, and a crafty description, though.

If you're one of those folks (like me—no shame in confessing it) who have a multi-tude of shared Google Calendars, getting them to populate in the iPhone's Calendar app is far more difficult than it should be. Although you may assume that simply flipping the Calendar toggle to On in your added Gmail account would be enough, that *only* adds the sole Google Calendar that directly links to said account. If you've access to shared Gcals from your significant other, colleagues, bosses, sports teams, and so on, they won't just "show up." Defies logic, but it's true.

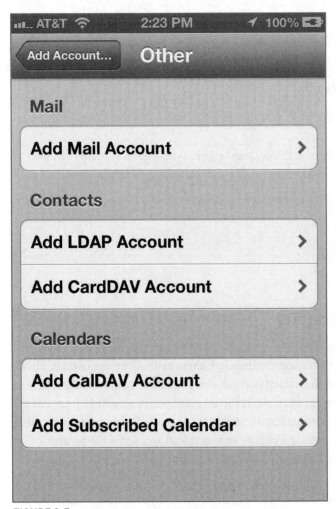

FIGURE 3-7: Got your own mail settings? Punch 'em in here!

WORKING GOOGLE INTO APPLE'S APPS

Thankfully, there is a way to link the iPhone's Calendar app to all your shared Gcals, but it certainly takes a little elbow grease. Here's how it's done.

1. Head to Settings ➔ Mail, Contacts, Calendars ➔ Add Account.

2. Select Microsoft Exchange, and then input your full Gmail address into the Email and Username fields.

3. Leave Domain blank and insert your Gmail password in the Password field.

4. Tap the Next button in the top-right, and when the Server field emerges, punch in **m.google.com**.

5. On the following screen, ensure that all options are toggled off except Calendar.

6. Now, open Safari and head to `m.google.com/sync`; find your iPhone in the list after logging in and select it.

7. From there, tap to add any or all of your shared calendars, and once saved, your Calendar will update in a matter of minutes if you're on a solid Wi-Fi connection.

Tweaks for Productivity

Although the iPhone's Mail app is fully capable of handling as many e-mail accounts as you can throw at it (within reason, naturally), there can only be one default. This is actually more important in relation to third-party apps that allow shortcuts to "mail" things from within. For example, if you select to e-mail an article from a news magazine, it'll send from your default account. If your work is fairly strict about what passes through its mail servers, make sure your personal account is the default at Settings ➔ Mail, Contacts, Calendars ➔ Default Account.

NOTE With the introduction of iOS 6, Apple is finally letting people add documents, videos, and photos right from the Compose screen of a new message within the Mail app. It's a major improvement from iOS 5, where you couldn't attach a wide variety of media once you started composing a new e-mail.

Also, leaving "Sent from my iPhone" as your signature may seem a bit pretentious and played out—and let's be honest, it sort of is—but it definitely gives recipients a heads-up to expect curt replies, stranger than usual formatting, and a glut of typos. Better safe than sorry, right?

If you're planning on traveling with your iPhone (you should!), pay close attention to how your calendars are displayed. Over in the familiar Settings → Mail, Contacts, Calendars → Calendars section, make sure you deliberately choose to turn Time Zone Support on or off. Off will please those who want to see what times their events are with respect to whatever time zone they're currently in. On will please those who may change position in the world, but never mentally leave the time zone where their work takes place. In my world, Engadget revolves around Eastern Time, so my iPhone is flipped to On. Even if it's 3AM on a Thursday in Sydney, I want to be reminded that it's noon on Wednesday so far as my work is concerned (see Figure 3-8). There's hardly a productivity (and reputation) killer more ruthless than a confused time zone.

> For what it's worth, I changed mine to something less colorful: "Sent from my mobile device; apologies for brevity and typos."

FIGURE 3-8: In a New York state of mind, regardless of location.

Avid archivists should also know about another swipe trick: sweeping left or right across a message *in the list of messages* will bring up a red Archive button, which does exactly what you think it does upon pressing.

Mark As Unread is another beast entirely. It feels like Apple changes the location of this feature on every iOS release, and it's located in a somewhat hidden spot in iOS 5/6. I use this function all the time for e-mails I want to peek momentarily, but to which I don't have time to fully reply at the moment.

Within an opened message, you'll need to take the following steps:

1. Click Details in the upper-right corner.

2. Click Mark.

3. Click Mark as Unread.

I mentioned earlier that multi-tasking is more like backgrounding on the iPhone. That doesn't mean that you should avoid keeping mental tabs on what's lurking behind your Mail pane. When composing an e-mail that requires you to reference something stored on Dropbox, in Numbers, on a web page, an address in Maps, or practically any other application, a simple double-tap of the Home button will pull up apps that are currently running in the background (as shown in Figure 3-9). It'll only show the four most recently used at first, but a swipe from right to left will reveal more (and more... and more).

Just tap whatever app you need to reference in order to hop into it, and then do the same bottom-bar emergence trick as before in order to find Mail sitting there in the lower-left corner. Your message will remain just as you left it, ready to accept a new thought or even a paste of text that you copied from a different app.

Choosing Your VIPs

It's distasteful to talk about in public, but let's be honest: there are e-mails that can wait, and there are e-mails that can't. What determines the split? The sender, of course. With the introduction of iOS 6, Apple has added a new VIP system that enables you to select and label certain people in your Contacts list to be more important than the rest. People like significant others, bosses, children, and so on. From a mail perspective, this is hugely important when it comes to seeing important messages first.

Much like the arrival of a text message, you can allow any VIP that sends an e-mail to an account established in your Mail app to have their message show up on your lock screen. Think of it as a "high priority" alert. While in the Mail app, you'll also get a new VIP inbox, where you can sift through messages sent only from folks who you've deemed highly important (see Figure 3-10).

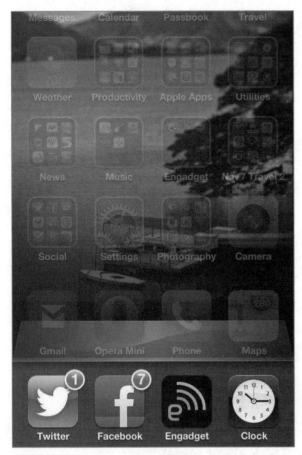

FIGURE 3-9: Background apps are shown in the bottom bar.

Password and Multiple Account Management

Look, you're a popular person. There's no need to feel ashamed about having eight e-mail accounts. (At least, you can keep telling yourself that.) All jesting aside, there are a few snippets you should know about having a cadre of accounts within Mail. For one, the notification bubble on the Mail icon—which represents a view of how many unread messages you have—shows the *sum* of all unread e-mails across accounts. There's unfortunately no way to force the icon to only show unread message counts for a specific list of accounts, which might not bother those who go to great lengths to maintain a "zero inbox" in their most used account.

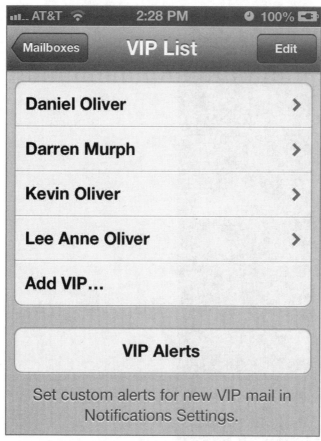

FIGURE 3-10: The worst part about VIP labeling? Choosing who to omit.

▶ One idea is to switch less-important accounts to manual fetch, so you aren't distracted by push notifications (and a surging unread count) from accounts that aren't urgent.

I've already touched on the importance of carefully selecting which account is your default, but changing from one to the next is fairly simple. While in the Mail app, just tap Inbox ➔ Mailboxes in order to pull up a list of your accounts. I recommend naming them with care. If you have more than a couple, using just your name, "personal," or "work" may not be descriptive enough.

For now, Apple has no feature that allows you to lock specific apps or e-mail accounts. Once you're through the optional lock screen password—which you established in Settings ➔ General ➔ Passcode Lock—you've access to everything. This is particularly troubling when you need to hand your iPhone off for a work presentation, but would rather your nosey colleagues not "accidentally" read your e-mail or spot any personal push notifications.

To date, there's no app in the App Store to remedy this, but jailbreakers have an option. A few, actually. FolderLock, Lockdown Pro, and Locktopus can be found in Cydia or BigBoss repositories, and all are priced at under $5. These apps allow you to enable very specific locks for apps and content, and again, my suspicion is that Apple sees the light here and integrates similar functionality into a future iOS build.

S/MIME (Secure/Multipurpose Internet Mail Extensions) is one of the more advanced security features that most common folk will just gloss right over, but for those obsessed with keeping track of signed messages (or those that have this requirement due to the sensitive nature of their work), it's a great feature to tap into. Apple has enabled support of this by default within iOS, and you'll need to dig into Settings → Account → Advanced for each e-mail account in order to enable it on each account. From here, you can opt to receive signed messages and sign them yourself, but you'll need to procure a certificate elsewhere, first. Once in possession of that (VeriSign's a good place to head for that), just e-mail it to yourself and have iOS install it.

▶ Jailbreaking isn't for the weak spirited, or the cowards, but plenty of information is out there on Google for those who want to dive in. It voids your warranty, though, so you're operating at your own risk!

SUMMARY

Although the iPhone has "phone" in its name, it's clearly more than that. It's an e-mailing machine, and iOS 6 has added plenty of new features (VIP lists, for example) to highlight this aspect. Simply managing the influx of information and notifications is a job in and of itself, but Apple's notification options allow you to surface e-mails from the people most important to you.

Google finally succeeded in bringing a native Gmail app to iOS, and while it's far from perfect, it does give avid Gmailers access to the subtle extras that make it so compelling. A native Gmail app has kept many on Android; the addition of this app into the iOS ecosystem could be a great reason to switch. Managing multiple accounts—and perhaps even multiple tools for sending messages—is tricky but worth the effort.

CHAPTER 4

Wrangling iTunes (While Maintaining Your Sanity)

Apple has gone to great lengths in order to remove the PC (or Mac, for that matter) from the list of necessary items when first setting up an iPhone. With the introduction of iOS 5 (and continued in iOS 6), the idea of "PC-free" was not only introduced, but also forced to the forefront. Think of it less as an option, and more like the new regime. Not that I'm complaining—making the iPhone more of a standalone device can mean only good things for mobile professionals, not to mention those who just aren't interested in learning the intricacies of a computer operating system in order to properly set up their iOS-based device. Despite the remarkable efforts, though, an iPhone's potential is still only fully realized with the help of a partner, and as with most right-hand men, iTunes is both a blessing and a curse at times. This chapter will help you tame a necessary evil, and show you how to make iTunes work with you (as opposed to the obvious alternative).

MASTERING THE INITIAL ITUNES SETUP

When Apple initially launched iTunes on Windows, it aptly proclaimed that "Hell Had Frozen Over." By bringing the liaison used with every modern iPod and iPhone to the archrival operating system, the company took a huge step in opening itself up and finally playing toward the demands of the masses. Not surprisingly, it has been consumer electronics—not Macintosh computers—that have forced the company's shares northward and placed them on a nearly unbelievable path of record-breaking quarters. But the irony in Apple's clearly tongue-in-cheek statement is that there's more "hell" in iTunes than any other piece of software designed in Cupertino.

Year after year, and release after release, iTunes remains the most griped about piece of Apple software. Granted, it's about the only piece that works on 95+ percent of personal computers, but there is much to learn about an application that's both a requisite to maximum iPhone enjoyment and an absolute thorn in the side of computer users the world over. As with most frustrating things, iTunes doesn't have to be the boss of you, but you'll need a bit of underground knowledge in order to gain the upper hand.

> **NOTE** Long before the iPhone was on the public radar, Apple decided it was prudent to make iTunes a multi-platform affair. If you're worried because you don't own a Mac (and have no interest in joining that club), don't let it stop you from considering an iPhone. Perhaps miraculously, Apple has designed the iPhone to be functional with or without a Mac nearby, with the common link being the iTunes software. iTunes is free to download for both Windows as well as OS X at **www.itunes.com**, and updates to both platforms have historically been pushed out simultaneously. Phew!

Creating Your Initial iPhone Profile

One point that Apple doesn't make nearly clear enough is just how important the initial iTunes/iPhone marriage is. As with any bona fide matrimony, getting these two off on the wrong foot will unquestionably lead to heartache, if not outright disaster. Being that prenuptial agreements are null and void in the computing space, it's better if you don't have to resort to a night of reformatting every other week. The trick? Thinking about how you want your media arranged *before* pressing every "Okay, Move Along!" confirmation button you see.

Intro to iTunes

It's helpful to know what iTunes is going to ask of you before actually approaching the point of no return. Although owners of the original iPhone can sync most of their applications, music, and preferences to a newer iPhone sans a PC, iPhone owners who are new to the entire ecosystem will inevitably end up touching iTunes sooner rather than later. I suggest plugging your iPhone into your Mac or PC and ensuring that the latest release of iTunes is installed, and the latest version of iOS is running on your phone.

One of the more vexing quirks of Apple is its insistence that you keep your software and hardware up-to-date. I generally recommend holding off on updates for at least a week or two after their release in order to see whether issues crop up (surprise incompatibilities with automotive iOS systems, for instance), but it's smart to have everything up to date at the point of first contact. Like I said, getting off on the right foot gives you more control over where to take the relationship from there.

Updating both is as simple as navigating to iTunes in the top menu bar and activating the Check For Updates option. If you're connected to the Internet, your iTunes should search for any available iOS updates when you initially plug it in.

Post-updates, I strongly recommend registering the device when iTunes prompts you. Chapter 1, "Selecting and Setting Up Your iPhone" covered the Find My iPhone feature, but suffice it to say here—this is the first step in ensuring that you can track down your lost or stolen iPhone. Trust me, although it's easy to just click Never Register, it's absolutely worthwhile to go ahead and hand over some information.

The next step is undoubtedly important: you're aiming to either restore your iPhone from a backup (applicable to perfectly happy owners of older iPhones) or create a new profile. For the sake of iOS newcomers (and those who just need a fresh start), the following sections assume that you're checking the latter.

DOWNGRADING TO OLDER IOS BUILDS

Owners of older iPhones using an outdated version of iOS, take note! It's vitally important to make sure you can find a copy of your existing iOS build *before* updating, as well as the outdated iTunes version that you originally used to install it with. Why? Because not all updates are better. The latest iTunes builds won't let you "downgrade" to older iOS builds, even if you have the restore file handy. Don't be anxious to update if you don't have to; if what you have works, well, stick with it until some new feature pulls you ahead. (*You know, like iMessage and iCloud.*) Be sure to visit **www.oldapps.com** for archived iTunes releases and **www.iclarified.com** for archived iOS releases.

The Whys, Whats, and Wheres of iTunes

Before going any further, you'll be best served by having a few other ducks in a row in advance:

▶ Are you using Google Calendar, an Exchange calendar, iCal, or something else for your date-tracking needs?

▶ Have you migrated all of your contacts into Gmail or into the Mac Address Book?

▶ Are all of the photos you want on your iPhone sitting in organized folders within iPhoto?

▶ Have you compiled an assortment of music for your iPhone, and thrown it all into a dedicated playlist within iTunes?

▶ Have you converted your favorite video clips into formats optimized for iPhone?

▶ Are your downloaded apps all up-to-date, and are they arranged in folders and on the home panes that you want them to be?

CHOOSING TO SYNC YOUR CALENDAR

▶ On a PC? Don't bother trying to find Apple's Calendar—that's a Mac-only affair.

Believe it or not, Apple's iPhone actually syncs amazingly well with Google services. Rivals they may be, but they both understand that they need one another. I'm an avid Gmail and Google Suite user, and if you're like me, your entire world would crumble around you if Google Calendar failed to send reminders for a 24-hour period. The trick when setting up your calendar is to know ahead of time whether or not you'll be using Apple's built-in Calendar.

If you use Google's Calendar, make absolutely sure that you tell iTunes *not* to sync your calendar. It's a complete nightmare to have two conflicting (or worse, overlapping) calendars running on your iPhone. It goes without saying that the same is true for any other calendar service other than Apple's Calendar; if you use Exchange or any other Cloud-based calendar service, don't let the initial calendar sync happen. (If you happen to dabble in both Calendar and something else, feel free to have two calendars installed—just make sure you don't end up with duplicate entries.)

CHOOSING TO SYNC YOUR CONTACTS

Overseas travelers stuck in a hotel room with no native cell service will certainly appreciate having a few pals from back home on speed dial, even if that means dialing a username instead of nine consecutive numbers. The rules you read with calendars apply here; iTunes will give you the option to sync Contacts from the OS X Address Book application should you choose. Pick wisely, because having duplicate (or triplicate!) contacts is confusing to wade through and frustrating to eradicate.

ORGANIZING YOUR PHOTOS

The iPhone is an ideal tool for displaying photo slideshows to colleagues or coeds, and the built-in Photos application nicely sorts images into folders. But if you want to save yourself tons of time, you need it all nicely sorted on your computer before you sync. On the Mac, the easiest way to do this is to toss the images you want on your iPhone into iPhote.

There's no iPhoto on the Windows side of things, but Windows users can make similar arrangements using Adobe's Photoshop Album or Photoshop Elements.

iTunes is smart enough to automatically resize gargantuan JPEGs into more sensibly sized files for use on the iPhone, but it's not smart enough to guess which image should go in which gallery. For those who've never sorted their heaps of vacation photos (*raise your hands—I won't judge*), this task is downright daunting, but organizing things in iPhoto prior to that initial iTunes sync is time well spent.

If, for some reason, you'd rather avoid those programs altogether, you can choose the Sync Photos From option in the Photos pane of iTunes (shown in Figure 4-1) and then select a file folder with your desired photos in it. It's a bit messier, but doesn't require as much legwork on the organization front.

> **TIP** iPhoto is also capable of displaying photos on a map based on location (geotagging), which helps you easily visualize where you and your iPhone have been based on photos captured. I discuss this in detail in Chapter 13, "Utilizing the iPhone's Camera."

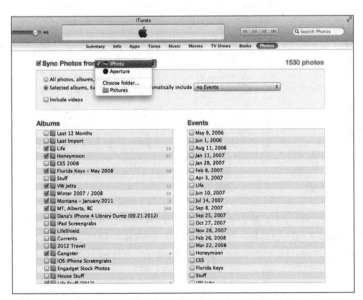

FIGURE 4-1: The Choose Folder option is for those who'd rather avoid using a dedicated photo-management program.

READYING YOUR MUSIC FOR THE IPHONE

When it comes to music, I'm happy to report that no third-party program is needed. iTunes, the same program used for syncing purposes, is also the program I recommend using to manage your music. It's not the most streamlined tool for playback, and older machines tend to have a tough time dealing with how many resources it ties up, but it's far and away the most sensible for use with iOS products. Syncing music to the iPhone using any program other than iTunes is a hassle that's simply not worth dealing with, and if you happen to get an iTunes gift card, you'll find that it's even more logical to keep grandfathered and digitally purchased music in one central location.

You need to think about storage before syncing music over; I have amassed well over 80GB of music, and if you're in a similar boat, you'll be in the unfortunate position of not being able to sync 100 percent of your tunes to your new phone. Time to pick and choose! The easiest way to do this is to create a new playlist within iTunes, as shown in Figure 4-2.

FIGURE 4-2: Creating a new playlist is as simple as a single click... or pressing Cmd+N (Control+N for PC users).

Go ahead and decide how much room you're willing to sacrifice for music. Roughly 50 percent of your storage is a safe bet, leaving the rest for e-mails, Dropbox attachments, apps, and photos, but feel free to adjust based on your particular needs.

NOTE Thinking about storage? Boring. But trust me—it's vitally important! Running out of room when you least expect it is a real bummer, and nothing seems to swell uncontrollably like music. Leaving 50 percent of your available storage open for productivity tasks, unsuspected photo dump sessions, and all-night app download-a-thons is a wise move. Just force yourself to be smart about what's in your music playlist; if iTunes tells you that you haven't "Starred" or listened to a particular song in more than six months, you'll probably be okay without it on your iPhone.

From there, create a playlist that's easy to recognize ("iPhone Music" works magically), and then sift through your gigantic library, dragging and dropping your absolute favorites into the list. Those willing to put in the extra time and effort could actually create a number of playlists and simply add up how much storage they each require. Have a look at Figure 4-3 to see where the fun begins. iTunes handily tells you exactly how much space a given playlist takes up on a small line at the bottom of the software—keep an eye on that to make sure you aren't overloading things.

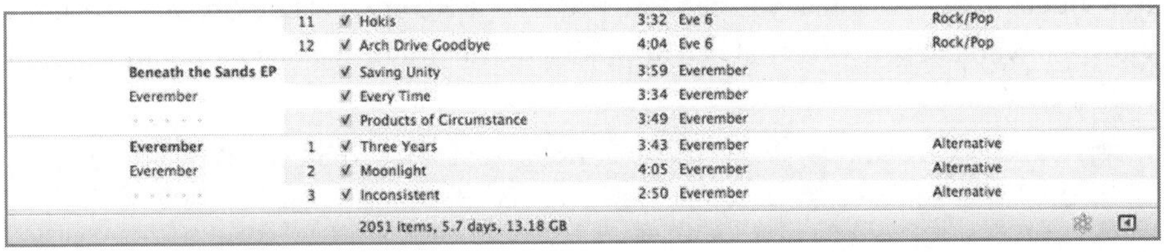

	11	✓	Hokis	3:32	Eve 6	Rock/Pop
	12	✓	Arch Drive Goodbye	4:04	Eve 6	Rock/Pop
Beneath the Sands EP		✓	Saving Unity	3:59	Everember	
Everember		✓	Every Time	3:34	Everember	
. . . . .		✓	Products of Circumstance	3:49	Everember	
Everember	1	✓	Three Years	3:43	Everember	Alternative
Everember	2	✓	Moonlight	4:05	Everember	Alternative
. . . . .	3	✓	Inconsistent	2:50	Everember	Alternative
			2051 items, 5.7 days, 13.18 GB			

FIGURE 4-3: Total songs, total playtime, and total storage requirements. Pay close attention to that last one.

Once you're satisfied with your selections, it's important to tell iTunes very specifically what music you want synced. By default, it'll attempt to sync your entire library until it runs out of room, but that'll leave no extra space for apps, photos, and whatever else. You need to simply click the Selected Playlists, Artists, Albums, and Genres selection and then check off the individual playlist choice(s). iTunes will bring over only the tunes in those lists, not your entire library.

TIP It's important to remember, however, that you need to manually add any new music to your iPhone-specific playlist; otherwise, those new tunes won't migrate over in future syncs.

PREPARING YOUR VIDEO CONTENT FOR THE IPHONE

When it comes to putting films, TV shows, or home movies on your iPhone, you have two main options. The first is the one that Apple hopes you choose frequently. There's a movie and TV rental store right within iTunes, and as you'd expect, anything purchased or rented from there will land pre-formatted to fit on your phone. That's notable for two reasons: First, it's optimized for size, so it won't take up unnecessary space. Second, it's optimized to fit the screen resolution of the iPhone, so it's guaranteed to look crisp and not distorted. In other words, renting or buying content from the iTunes Store removes gobs of hassle, and anything downloaded from there immediately files itself nicely into an iTunes subsection on the left rail.

But what if you're dealing with footage you've already captured? Home videos or Digital Copy films acquired as part of a DVD or Blu-ray combo pack might not always be optimized for viewing on the iPhone, and unlike with photos, iTunes isn't built to convert them without your intervention. The good news is that iTunes is *capable* of doing it, but you need to put in a little elbow grease. Just visit the Advanced menu to create versions for iPod, iPhone, iPad, or Apple TV. If you want more control over how videos are re-encoded, you can also use iMovie HD or Final Cut Pro, or any other video-conversion software that can downsize to the resolution of your phone.

> **TIP** For easily compressing your own videos, Elgato's Turbo.264 HD dongle is the best in the business. Too bad it only works with Macs!

UPDATING YOUR APPS

If you're new to the iOS/iTunes ecosystem, you won't have any apps to worry about updating, but if you already have a few kicking around, it's worth updating them all before throwing them on the iPhone. Within the Apps section of iTunes, you can simply click Check For Updates below your cadre of apps to get the process started, but as with most everything else related to iTunes, you'll need a live Internet connection to accomplish anything.

If you're an organization junkie, which you likely are if you're poring over these words, you'll want to put extra effort into arranging your apps in a sensible fashion *within iTunes*. I discuss specific patterns and recommendations in the pages to come, but it's worth knowing up-front that you don't want to sync your apps haphazardly, only to then manually arrange them on the device. If you do the arranging within iTunes, that layout "sticks" to your profile.

> **TIP** If there's one thread that repeats itself here, it's this: take the time to organize iTunes prior to your initial sync. It's worth it.

UNDERSTANDING ACCOUNT LIMITS

You might assume that content purchased in the iTunes Store can be played back only on the machine that you originally used to complete the transaction. Or, if you're in the other school of thought, you might assume that a single purchase in one place should be readily available anywhere else. With the introduction of iTunes Match and iTunes in the Cloud, Apple has vastly extended the usability of iTunes purchases, but when it comes to actually playing things back and syncing via hardwire, there are still a few limitations that you need to know about.

Authorized Computers

In the iTunes world, your system is either authorized or deauthorized—there's no in between. In order to access purchased content, play it back, and—perhaps most importantly—sync it to your iPhone, you need to have access to a live Internet connection as well as your iTunes credentials. In essence, iTunes requires you to log in before doing any of these tasks as a means to double-checking your purchase history before allowing you to copy that content onto other devices (such as your iPhone).

The good news is that five computers can be simultaneously authorized. For the vast majority of consumers, that's plenty. A home desktop, a laptop, perhaps a work machine, and a Netbook shared by the family. But if you're one of *those people* (much like myself, I might shamelessly add) and have more than five machines within reach, you'll need to figure out which of the five you want to authorize.

If you attempt to play a song purchased on iTunes from the DRM days, you'll need a username and password. If you punch that in, you've just authorized a machine.

How to Deauthorize and Authorize

This proves particularly tricky when visiting a friend, and wanting to play back content that you purchased on a foreign machine. If you're already at your five-machine limit, their copy of iTunes will inform you when you attempt to authorize a sixth. Stuck? Not quite. There's a fairly simple workaround, but Apple curiously buries the option in a place most folks don't think to look.

▶ Regardless of anything else, Apple's hard limit is five authorized machines.

You need to first log in to your iTunes account on the guest machine, and then click your username in the top-right corner. Once you reenter your password, a full profile page is shown. The typical fields are there (name, address, and billing information), but if you scroll all the way to the bottom, you can see how many computers you currently have authorized. From there, you click Deauthorize All (shown in Figure 4-4) in order to remotely deauthorize all five machines and start back at one on the guest computer you're in front of. Yes, this means you'll need to reauthorize the systems that you just canned at a later date, but that's as simple as signing in again.

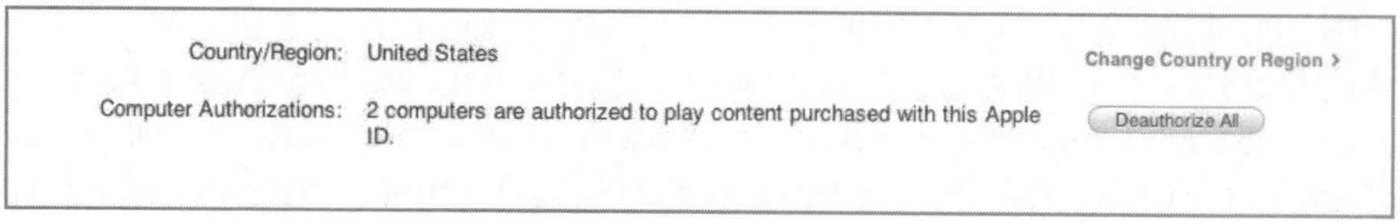

Country/Region:	United States	Change Country or Region >
Computer Authorizations:	2 computers are authorized to play content purchased with this Apple ID.	Deauthorize All

FIGURE 4-4: Click the Deauthorize All button to start fresh.

WHAT CAN BE SYNCED, AND WHERE?

▶ Always remember to sign out and deauthorize any guest computers once you're done using them.

Syncing files between a computer and an iPhone can be a magical, if not a mysterious, experience for the uninitiated. With a few choice clicks, content housed on a PC becomes content housed on a phone, all neatly organized and ready for mobile consumption. Apple purposefully leaves many of the particulars vague for the sake of simplicity—a company value that oftentimes annoys power users who would rather have access to the minutiae going on behind the scenes.

Where Files Go in a Sync

Unlike Android 2.*x*, which allows users to simply mount their devices and drag content over as they would on an external hard drive, iOS takes a vastly different approach. For instance, the MP3 files stored on your computer are renamed and reorganized when synced onto an iPhone, and then shuffled into an esoteric file pattern that only iOS can accurately digest. Why mention this? Because getting files off of your iPhone isn't nearly as easy as getting them on it.

Let's say your hard drive fails, and the only place your music remains is on your iPhone. You might assume that a simple "reverse sync" to the new PC would be all that's required to shift those files back from the iPhone and onto a new system. Sadly, it's not that easy. The reason likely has nothing to do with Apple, but with the RIAA and MPAA—America's two largest content overlords. They look out for the rights of content creators, which means that they usually end up frustrating end users in one fell swoop.

If iOS were allowed to reverse sync content unchecked, you could theoretically purchase thousands of songs and movies, and then place that purchased content onto an unlimited amount of guest computers, thereby distributing "stolen" content at will. In reality, this makes it impossible to use your iPhone to restore any lost files. *Bummer*.

▶ These bodies, among other things, largely control what content gets released, how it's released, and what you can/ can't do with it once purchased.

NOTE   For honest restoration situations, there is a way to reach into your iPhone and pull your stored music back into your computer. For Mac users, there's a free program called Phone to Mac, and it's useful for rescuing songs from your iOS device and placing them back on a new or different computer in an organized fashion. For Windows users, SharePod accomplishes the same thing. I obviously recommend against piracy of any sort, but it's great to have these programs in your back pocket just in case disaster strikes.

If you plug your iPhone in to a new machine, you *can* right-click on the mounted device and choose to Transfer Purchases back to the connected machine (as shown in Figure 4-5). It works like a charm for content that you've procured via the iTunes Store, but that's the extent of the functionality. Any content you purchased elsewhere—be it a physical record store or Amazon's rivaling MP3 service—is not eligible for a reverse sync.

FIGURE 4-5: While in the Apps or Music section in iTunes, right-clicking your device's name brings up a Transfer Purchases option.

> **NOTE** Apple's nice, but it's not *that* nice. Although re-downloading apps and music you've purchased within the iTunes Store is kosher, it's not Apple's responsibility to do so for content procured elsewhere. Because this function only checks your prior receipts within the iTunes Store, any content not matched up there will not be available for download. In other words, make *sure* you have a great backup solution for your other content, be it an in-home NAS (Network Attached Storage) or Time Machine, or an off-site solution like Mozy (**www.mozy.com**).

How to Revert Your iPhone to a Prior State

If you manage to create problems for yourself while using your iPhone—perhaps while downloading a problematic app or otherwise—Apple makes it fairly painless to restore your device to a prior state. If you allow it, Apple backs up every single morsel of your iPhone before every new sync, so if something goes wonky, you can plug it back in and select the Restore button (shown in Figure 4-6) to revert the entire system to a place of peace—before trouble struck.

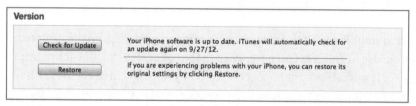

FIGURE 4-6: Don't worry if you tap Restore by accident—Apple gives you one final chance to confirm.

OPTING OUT OF A BACKUP

As mentioned, there's tremendous value in allowing iTunes to back up your device while it's still in a recent, useful state. Should anything go wrong, it's extraordinarily comforting to know that a backup is available to get your iPhone back on its feet. But the harsh reality is that we're all busy, and sometimes, too busy to sit around and wait for a system backup to complete.

It's a situation that occurs quite often in my world. You purchase a new album from iTunes, you drag those new tunes into your iPhone Music playlist, and you plug in your iPhone to add those songs. It sounds like it ought to be a simple two- to three-minute process, but if it's been a month or so since your last sync, the initial backup process could take in excess of 20 minutes. In other words, you have 20+ minutes of waiting ahead of you before the new tracks even think about migrating over.

When you're rushing out of the door, this scenario is a buzz kill of epic proportions. Thankfully, Apple makes it possible to opt out of backups, but unsurprisingly, it doesn't go out of its way to advertise that.

OPTING OUT OF A BACKUP

Here's how to opt out of the backup process: Once you've initiated a sync to add new files to your device, you'll spot a tiny X to the right of the Backing Up message. Just click that X a single time (shown in Figure 4-7), and iTunes will immediately jump to the transfer process, leaving you ready to eject your iPhone and be on your merry way in mere minutes. Realize, however, that any restoration you do in the future won't contain any files that were added on sessions that you opted out of the backup. Opt at your own risk, so to speak.

FIGURE 4-7: No time for backups? It's as easy as clicking that tiny little X on the right.

HOW TO MANAGE MULTIPLE COMPUTERS

It won't take you long to realize that Apple intends for you to use one computer to manage your iPhone. Have a couple of machines at home, plus one at work? Brace for frustration. The good news is that most of the multi-machine mayhem can be calmed with a few sly workarounds, discussed in this section.

Secrets on Partial Syncs

Believe it or not, you don't have to sync everything from one machine to your iPhone. But it's not as easy as being able to pick and choose what comes from where. Users can sync music and contacts from one host machine, while another is used only to sync photos and apps.

The trick is to be exceedingly careful about what you check to sync. If you carelessly leave the Sync Music box checked on a machine with no music on it, your iPhone will soon be devoid of Devo (and whatever else you had on there). From there, the only way to get the tunes back is to resync with the machine from which the tunes originally came—there's no "Undo button" for syncs.

> **TIP** A partial sync makes sense when your music library is on a home desktop, but everything else is stored on your laptop.

Cautions on Using Secondary Machines to Add Content

One common misconception is that you can use Machine A to sync your music, and then use Machine B to simply add a newly downloaded album, while keeping your existing playlist in-place. Unfortunately, this is absolutely not the case. The reasoning, as best I can tell, relates back to the same piracy concerns as explained earlier. In an ideal, honest world, Machine B would be able to suck down your existing music structure, back it all up, and then add the newly downloaded tunes atop that. The concern here is that you end up giving Machine B a wealth of content that perhaps the owner didn't actually purchase. So, Apple makes it impossible, *except* for music purchased in the iTunes Store. In theory, if every single song on your iPhone were acquired via the iTunes Store, this scenario would be possible. Food for thought, anyway.

But the secret here is that the same is true for apps. The difference, notably, is that most consumers will have acquired every single app on the iPhone via the App Store. Only developers who have side-loaded test programs would run into issues with an app not being eligible for transfer in a reverse sync. So, this situation would work with apps, but there's a catch. A new iTunes master wouldn't recall the exact app structure that you painstakingly organized on Machine A, so if you pull over your apps, add a few newcomers, and then resync with Machine B, all of your created folders are eliminated, and you're left to manually reorganize the location of every single app.

SUMMARY

iTunes is a powerful tool, and it's one that will almost certainly become a necessity in your continued iPhone use. It's of paramount importance to organize your photos, music, movies, and apps before making the initial iPhone sync, and it's vital that you deselect contact and calendar syncing if you're planning to pull those tidbits from the Cloud on another service (Google, Microsoft Exchange, and so on).

Planning ahead and staying organized within iTunes is the best way to guarantee a seamless and satisfactory experience when syncing with iPhone, and it's important to always let the program back up your phone whenever you have ample time. If you're in a pinch, opting out of a backup is as simple as clicking a single X, but remember to plug your device back in when time is more plentiful in order to keep your restore file current in case of disaster.

Finally, I recommend against having multiple iTunes masters on a single device. Although it's possible to pick and choose which machine syncs which sections, this method makes it impossible to have a whole restoration file, leaving your iPhone susceptible to vast downtime if problems ever arise.

PART II

ACING THE ADVANCED FEATURES

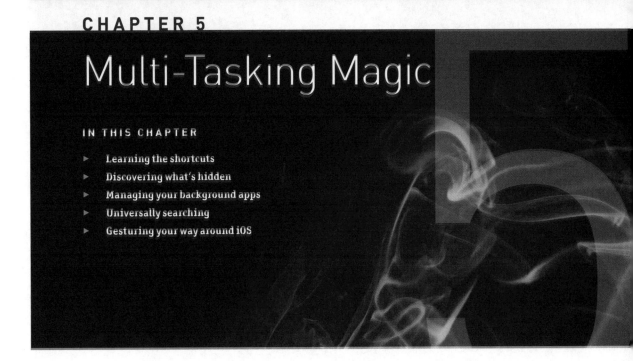

Multi-Tasking Magic

I've alluded to this before, but Apple's definition of multi-tasking on the iPhone doesn't jibe with the definition that was (and still is) used within the desktop operating system realm. iOS 5 and iOS 6 can most certainly have multiple applications running at once, but you'll be forced to look at 'em one at a time. In my estimation, that's more like "backgrounding," but this chapter doesn't spend any more time arguing semantics. Instead, I explain how to make the very most out of what Apple has to offer in terms of multi-tasking (or whatever you prefer to call it), and how to think about your workflow in a way that follows logic in the iOS world. You learn about shortcuts, dig deep to figure out what's hidden, and learn to manage the apps that are running in the background. You even learn about reducing resource load by killing apps that you aren't actively using, and I show you why Apple's Spotlight is the unsung hero of iPhone productivity. Finally, I touch (ahem) on the expanding world of multitouch gestures, which Apple has placed at the forefront of iOS discovery. Your iPhone is nothing without your touch, and having the full gamut of gestures in the forefront of your mind will undoubtedly improve your overall experience.

SHORTCUTS GALORE

Half of the fun in owning an iPhone is "discovering" new ways to use it. At first, it's little more than a mystery. Pop a couple of productivity apps on it, and soon it's an essential part of your workday artillery. But there's another part of the equation, and that part is usability.

The iPhone, without even understanding the concept of multitouch, is immediately and infinitely usable. There's just something intrinsically natural about control via touch, and few companies have implemented it as well as Apple has on the iPhone. But smooth scrolling on web pages and seamless shuffling of photos is just the tip of the proverbial iceberg.

Mashing Buttons

Go on, admit it: you always were one of those kids who couldn't resist pressing the big, red button, despite obvious warnings to avoid doing so. Apple's minimalistic approach means that there aren't too many buttons and switches on the iPhone, but that *also* means that each and every one of them is highly important to understand.

I'll start at the top. Up there, you'll find what rocket scientists affectionately call the power button. I'll give you a moment to ponder its possibilities. In all seriousness, the power button itself does have a few undercover features, some of which are only revealed when used in conjunction with other buttons. Aside from turning an iPhone on from a powered-off state, a single press will also turn on and off the display. More-over, holding it down for a few short seconds will bring up an otherwise impossible-to-find option to turn the unit off entirely. It's also not a bad idea to do this every week or so. Even the iPhone can get caught up in its own mire sometimes, and giving it a fresh start every six or seven days helps to ensure that it doesn't become too bogged down. If your iPhone ever becomes completely unresponsive and unusable—yes, this can and has happened—holding down the power button as well as the Home button for approximately 10 seconds will initiate a "hard reboot."

NOTE A hard reboot on the iPhone is the equivalent to holding down the power button on a Mac or PC computer in order to force a shut down. It ain't pretty, but sometimes it's the only way out.

While I'm on the topic of using your power and Home buttons in conjunction, I'll speak about one other function this tandem can pull off. Mashing the Home and power buttons simultaneously will cause a white flash and a camera shutter sound. That song and dance is to let you know a capture of your iPhone display was just taken and stored for safe keeping in your Photos app. It's the same place that photos taken from the iPhone camera are housed, and they can be easily pulled over to your Mac by firing up iPhoto and initiating an import. Each captured image is saved natively as a .PNG file, with a resolution matching that of the device you're on.

Screenshots and Hidden Bars

The two-button screen capture feature is a real godsend for those working in the media industry, but it's also equally beneficial for consumers. Troubleshooting remotely becomes a lot easier when you can capture onscreen errors in order to show others, and those who need to permanently capture something onscreen for offline viewing later will also be thrilled to have this in their back pocket. Curiously, screenshots aren't saved in their own folder. They're just saved in the Camera Roll as images taken with your onboard camera. You can, however, easily e-mail, iMessage, or tweet screenshots by searching in the Photos app.

NOTE With every new iteration of OS X and iOS, Apple has grown ever more attached to multitouch gestures. In a way, the company pioneered this para-digm as the primary control mechanism on slate-style smartphones, and while it's obviously widespread at this point, the touch response on iOS prod-ucts remains world-class. What started out as a fascination with two-finger gestures (like pinch-to-zoom) has blossomed into four-finger gestures that can accomplish any variety of tasks. Apple even ushered the Magic Trackpad into existence in order to bring the gestures that people were learning on iOS products onto its laptops and desktops. If you've yet to explore what using all of your digits can do on the iPhone, you're only feeling a part of the experience.

Pressing the Home button twice in quick succession will bring up—for lack of better terminology—the multi-tasking menu. It's a Secondary Dock bar that contains each and every app that you have currently running in the background, even if they're idle. They are arranged from most recently used (left) to least recently used (right). Have a gander yourself in Figure 5-1.

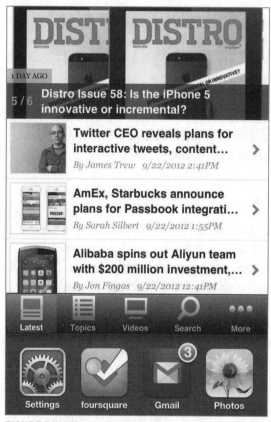

FIGURE 5-1: The Secondary Dock, sitting pretty beneath Engadget's iOS app.

▶ That Music icon in the hidden panel will morph into the Movie panel if you have a clip playing, and the middle controls will then dictate said clip instead of your background music.

Swipe from left to right on that multi-tasking menu, and you'll spot a new layout with a few vital buttons and sliders. While you're in this Secondary Dock bar, I'll explain the other shortcuts here. The left most icon controls the orientation lock (preventing the screen from shifting when the phone tilts), whereas the trio of buttons in the middle control music playback (skip backwards, play/pause, skip forward). The right most icon (Music) will pop you directly into your music application. If you've most recently used Videos, you'll see that shortcut in place of Music. I've found that double-tapping the Home button and using that Secondary Dock bar to get into my Music app is far more convenient than exiting to the home screen and then hunting for the icon. Furthermore, knowing that this shortcut is always available may encourage you to stash your Music app on a less important home pane, saving more room for other apps on that all-important first pane.

Although the iPhone's native lock screen still isn't as useful as some lock screens that are available to jailbroken devices, there is one highly appreciated extra tossed into iOS 5 and iOS 6. If you double-tap the Home button while the screen's locked, you'll get a top bar that allows you to play/pause a track, move forward or back within the last accessed playlist or album, and even adjust the volume—all without ever sliding to unlock the device. Have a peek in Figure 5-2.

FIGURE 5-2: Trigger your Music controls, right from the lock screen.

Furthermore, just bringing up the lock screen will present a small "slider" icon in the lower-right corner. Slide that upwards, and you'll be taken immediately into your Camera app. This was implemented in order to give users quicker access to their cameras in order to not miss so many crucial moments. Once the Camera app loads, you can flip the phone horizontally and use the Volume Up button as the shutter button. You can, of course, use the virtual onscreen shutter button if you prefer, but the physical button along the top just feels more like a conventional camera motion.

MASTERING YOUR INNER KEYBOARDER

Not surprisingly, the iPhone relies on touch for just about every interaction. But there's one antediluvian aspect that's oft overlooked, though just as important: the keyboard. Although you can admittedly get quite a bit accomplished on the iPhone sans any input on a QWERTY layout, its uses become significantly limited. In fact, Apple itself has shown extra care of late when it comes to the device's onscreen virtual keyboard.

From day one, critics extolled Apple's slate for having a remarkable keyboard and input system, and despite having to type on a flat, hard screen, composing e-mails and the like on it is actually quite enjoyable. And quick, to boot. But as I've witnessed on the Android platform, one keyboard really doesn't fit all. I've known many people to jailbreak their iPhone *solely* for the opportunity to install a modified keyboard. Unfortunately, even iOS 6 doesn't allow for custom keyboard installations, but I touch on using voice dictation in place of keystrokes in Chapter 14, "Utilizing Your Personal Assistant: Siri."

Kbrd Shrcts

▶ TextExpander (www.smilesoftware.com/TextExpander) is a remarkable $35 program for Windows and Mac that lets you assign short abbreviations to frequently used snippets of text.

Kids these days. Who has time to actually type out full sentences? All jesting aside, there's more to keyboard shortcuts within iOS 5 and iOS 6 than LOL and JK, and Apple has intelligently pulled in functionality from things like TextExpander in order to make the overall typing experience faster, without reverting to commonly known acronyms to do so.

There's no third-party app required here. Just surf over to Settings → General → Keyboard → Shortcuts in order to get started. The idea is pretty simple, as evidenced by Apple's one inclusion from the factory: omw. When typing omw on the iPhone, it'll automatically expand to "On my way!" By pressing Add New Shortcut, you'll be able to add any number of similar shortcuts. Perhaps g2g for "good to go," or iirc for "if I recall correctly". Figure 5-3 provides another idea. These shortcuts make it easier for legitimate typers to quickly type out *actual* words and phrases, but on the other hand, quick messagers may actually *prefer* the shortened version out of respect for space. At least Apple's giving you the option.

FIGURE 5-3: Finally, a customizable option. Go crazy!

▶ Apostrophes are important. But not when using a virtual iPhone keyboard. If you simply type a normal contraction (such as doesnt, cant, wont, dont, and so on) sans the apostrophe, iOS 5 and iOS 6 will add it automatically. Don't waste time doing it yourself.

While you're in this Settings pane, I'll discuss the five shortcut sliders that Apple flips on by default. Auto-capitalization, auto-correction, check spelling, enable Caps Lock and "." shortcuts are all useful to keep on in my estimation, but it's worth making special mention of two of 'em. Auto-correction can be a serious pain for those who use iMessage frequently. Yo is almost universally corrected to something other than yo, and you'll need to get used to tapping the X in the bubble that pops up a suggested word if you prefer to skip it. The "." shortcut is actually one of the more useful ones in the keyboard; just press the spacebar twice after a standard sentence is complete, and it'll automatically add a period, space out once and prime your next letter to be capitalized as you begin a new sentence. Handy!

Long-pressing and Hidden Commands

Speaking specifically for the U.S. English keyboard—which is the only one this feeble brain can understand—there's a bit of extra value in trying out the oh-so-popular long-press. Long-pressing select keys will bring up menus containing extra characters, and if you press the .?123 key in order to switch over to the numeric pad, the trick works on a few keys there, too. Finally, a double-tap of the Caps Lock key (it's the up arrow just below the A and Return keys) activates caps lock, and another single-tap deactivates it. (A single tap capitalizes just the next letter.)

► While in Safari, you'll notice a convenient .com key there at the bottom after tapping the address bar. Long-press that for a multitude of other domain name endings, such as .net, .org, and .edu.

> **TIP** In the same vein as TextExpander, Safari lets you create an app shortcut to just about anything. Many great websites already have iPhone apps in the App Store, but not all of them. Although you can certainly create a bookmark within Safari for any site, some of your most highly loved sites can end up on a home screen pane or in an app folder. Simply tap the Share icon in the center of the bottom menu bar within Safari, and then select Add to Home Screen. Customize the title, click Add, and then adjust it to the position you want on the home screen. Just like that, an app-sized web shortcut.

► Speaking specifically for Pages, Apple's acclaimed iPhone document processor, there's a laundry list of shortcuts to learn. Head to www.apple.com/support/pages/shortcuts to learn more. Use the time you'll save for something fun and daring.

Although the onscreen keyboard is certainly capable of handling its fair share of e-mails, those who are drop-dead serious about input into the iPhone may opt for a docking or Bluetooth keyboard. When using an external keyboard, the world of shortcuts opens up even further. If you're familiar with shortcuts within OS X, many of those work on iPhone as well. Here's a list of surefire keyboard shortcuts that external typists should do their best to commit to memory.

- ► **CMD+C** (copy)
- ► **CMD+X** (cut)
- ► **CMD+V** (paste)
- ► **CMD+Z** (undo)
- ► **CMD+Shift+Z** (redo)
- ► **CMD+Delete** (deletes current line to the left of cursor)
- ► **CMD+Up** (top of document)
- ► **CMD+Down** (bottom of document)
- ► **CMD+Left** (start of line)
- ► **CMD+Right** (end of line)
- ► **Option+Delete** (nixes the word to the left of the cursor and its preceding space)
- ► **F1** (dims the display)

- **F2** (brightens the display)

- **F7** (prior track)

- **F8** (plays or pauses music)

- **F9** (forward track)

- **F10** (mutes volume)

- **F11** (volume decrease)

- **F12** (volume increase)

- **Eject key** (displays or conceals onscreen keyboard)

On the off chance that you're typing a word without actually knowing the definition (or, perhaps more likely, you spot a curious word that your mate typed), you can simply long-press the befuddling word in order to bring up a Define option. As a bonus, the pop-up definition box is just gorgeous (see just how gorgeous in Figure 5-4), proving once again that few details were overlooked.

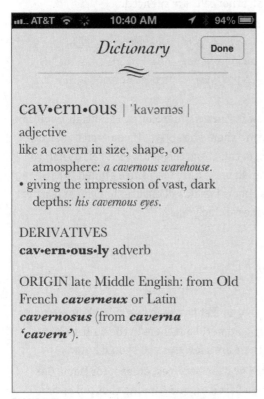

FIGURE 5-4: Definitions never looked so beautiful.

SCREENING YOUR PHONE CALLS

It may not be smiled upon, but keeping an overly close eye on who exactly is calling may be useful at times. Apple has really stepped things up in this department with iOS 6. At long last, iPhone users are given options other than Accept or Reject when it comes to dealing with an incoming call. By default, iOS 6 users can select Reply With Message or Remind Me Later by swiping up on the icon to the right of the Slide To Answer window. The former is remarkably useful. If you see a call come in, but you just can't take it at the moment, a couple of quick taps will shoot a text or iMessage to the caller with a pre-configured message ("I'll call you later," for example), or you can input a custom message.

If you're going into an important meeting, just toggle on Do Not Disturb mode within the phone's Settings menu. From there, calls will be silenced and sent to voicemail if you so choose. Within Settings ➜ Notifications, you can further customize how your phone reacts to Do Not Disturb. For example, you can allow Favorites and VIP callers to still ring through, while all other calls are silenced.

> **NOTE** I recommend switching Repeated Calls to On. This will allow a call through on the *second* attempt. If it's an emergency, and someone calls you back immediately after missing you once, it's probably worth the interruption.

Another beautiful aspect of this new feature is Quiet Hours. Essentially, you can schedule a daily time when Do Not Disturb should be active. If you aren't keen on receiving notifications, text messages, or calls from the hours of 10PM to 7AM, you can set that up while in this same menu. Experts have long since argued that we're growing dangerously connected—this simple tweak will ensure that you at least get a decent night's rest without your iPhone waking you.

MAKING THE MOST OF MAPS

As an avid traveler, having the world in my pocket has been one of the biggest boons to smartphone ownership. There's a big, bold world out there in the built-in Maps application, but to best experience it, there are a few tips you should know.

For starters, you'll need to activate Location Services, at least for Maps. Get going by heading to Settings ➜ Location Services, and flipping that top option to On. You *should* already have this active if you have Find My iPhone active, and while you can switch some apps off if you're uncomfortable with everything having access to your current coordinates, keep it on for Maps. Without it, well... you won't do much navigating.

> **TIP** Every so often, a new wave of fuss will be made over location-based services on mobile devices. But if you're using it only for Maps, there's nothing to get worked up about. If you're tremendously paranoid about your location being shared, you can disable it altogether and not use one of the iPhone's greatest features. By the same token, you should probably put away every credit card you own as well, given that the powers that be can certainly trace your movements in other ways. Moral of the story? Location services aren't the devil—just use them judiciously.

While you're on this pane, hop on down to System Services. The top six options, all of which should be on by default, are just fine to leave that way. But I strongly recommend switching the Status Bar Icon to On. Why? With that active, you'll get a location services icon in the top menu bar (beside the battery life indicator) whenever an application is using your location. Think of it as a heads-up to when your coordinates are being shared, and if you object to some unknown app doing so, you'll be able to quickly shut things down and uninstall it, or adjust the preferences to disable location sharing on that particular piece of software.

Now that your sharing preferences are squared away, let's focus on a few hidden features of Maps. You won't go far without getting your bearings, so you'll need to dial up a Wi-Fi or 3G/4G connection and tap that northeasterly arrow in the lower left. That's the shortcut for pinpointing your current location—a useful thing to tap before starting any guidance.

Once you've searched for a locale you'd like to head to, tapping the pin that drops enables you to seek directions (shown in Figure 5-5), and once that pop-up emerges, you can *typically* get walking, driving, and public transportation directions—provided that you're in a proper city for the third option, of course.

That's all pretty straightforward, but it may be easy to overlook that turned page corner in the lower right. Pull that page toward the center, and you'll uncover a few options—mostly visual tweaks—that may prove pleasing. Underneath, you'll find four Map options (Standard, Satellite, Hybrid, and List), and if you're in a dense population center, that Traffic overlay will give you a real-time view to congestion on the roads surrounding you. Perhaps the most useful nugget is the Drop Pin function (shown in Figure 5-6), which allows you to place a visual marker on an area that you'd like to remember—perhaps your hotel in a foreign city—to act as a central point of reference. I dive into the Print function in Chapter 8, "Cutting the Cord: Utilizing Wireless Functionality," but suffice it to say, those zany enough to actually think about printing a virtual map can do so (wirelessly, to boot) from this options pane.

FIGURE 5-5: Tap that title for directions and bring your appetite!

FIGURE 5-6: Peeling back the options pane in Maps

MANAGING YOUR BACKGROUND APPS

Apple's iPhone is chock full of surprises, including one that involves apps running in the background. The art of multi-tasking is truthfully still being mastered by iOS, but we're a lot closer to true multi-tasking today than we were even a few generations prior. iOS won't allow you to have two separate apps open and onscreen at the same time—the closest you'll come to that is the use of multiple tabs within Safari—but thanks to an expertly constructed backgrounding scenario, flipping back and forth among programs is just about effortless.

But, as with all computers, the iPhone has its limits. There's but a specific amount of memory in the device, and while it'd take a hardcore poweruser to truly see a performance dip from using too many programs at once, those who fail to do a bit of housekeeping may unintentionally end up seeing the same.

> **NOTE** Apple designed the iPhone so that end users wouldn't have to actively think about what is or isn't running. By and large, you can just use the iPhone at will without ever stopping to think how many programs you have open, and you'll never see a performance hit or a decrease in battery life. But why leave it to chance? Managing your background apps is categorically simple, and it's well worth the time investment.

The first step to managing is figuring out what wheels are in motion. By initiating a double tap of the Home button, you'll spot the Secondary Dock at the bottom. It's a sight you should be familiar with by now, but here's something you may not have known. Each app in that tray is active, albeit idle, in the background. Each app is also claiming its own share of resources—however small—which may eventually impact performance and battery life if the build-up becomes too great over time.

Since the app you used longest ago will be all the way at the end of line, I suggest swiping towards the right until you reach the last app there. Then, long-press on any infrequently used app that you aren't planning to use soon. A small minus sign will appear in the corner of the app icon (shown in Figure 5-7); give that a tap to close the app, freeing up whatever resources were assigned to it.

▶ An alternative way to get a fresh start is to simply hold down the power button and reboot the iPhone, but unlike Android, there's no built-in app manager to kill all programs. You'll have to do it manually if you don't reboot.

FIGURE 5-7: Minus means gone!

SPOTLIGHT: UNIVERSALLY SEARCHING

Without qualification, one of the most useful aspects of OS X is Spotlight. It's simple, well integrated, and eerily accurate. In short, Spotlight is a baked-in search apparatus that peeks into whatever folders and filesystems you deem fit in order to find programs, documents, and even snippets of code hidden *within* documents. And while this functionality has been on the iPhone in the past, it's even better in iOS 6.

As described earlier, accessing Spotlight is as easy as swiping toward the right from the home screen. From there, you can simply start typing, and the iPhone will begin to shoot out tailored results with each additional letter or character.

But here's a tip: Apple lets you customize (to some extent) what Spotlight will index and search. In order to see what's being included (or, perhaps more importantly, excluded), you'll need to head to Settings ➜ General ➜ Spotlight Search and have a gander at the options (shown in Figure 5-8). Unfortunately, you can't include web apps here, so avid users of the Gmail HTML5 app won't be able to use Spotlight to dig through archived messages.

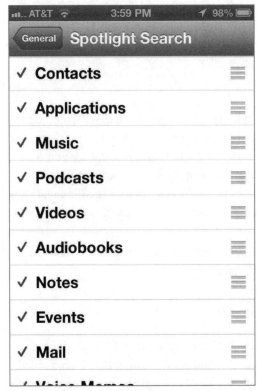

FIGURE 5-8: Don't want your contacts cluttering Spotlight results? Uncheck 'em!

> **TIP** Using Spotlight to look for a reminder or a calendar event is highly recommended. No more sifting through days on end looking for that one birthday of that one colleague that you can't quite remember the name of. Even if you know the first two letters (or just "birthday"), Spotlight should come through in the clutch.

While I'm on the topic of searching, I should also point out that Apple is now giving Safari users the ability to change which engine it uses for searches initiated in the top-right Search bar within the browser. A look at Settings ➜ Safari ➜ Search Engine provides a trifecta of choices: Google (default), Yahoo!, and Bing. My personal preference remains Google, but those who tend to prefer either of the alternatives can change it here.

GESTURES TO LIVE BY

Gestures have always been a crucial part of the iOS experience, and Apple is keeping that trend alive with the touch input experience in iOS 5 and iOS 6. Everything from gesturing back to the home panel to pinching in order to zoom within the Camera app is included, both of which I highlight in detail in this section.

Shutterbug Swipes

Within the Camera app itself, you may not expect too many extras with regard to touch. Turns out, that's absolutely not the case. For starters, you can pinch-to-zoom in order to get tighter or farther away from a shot, but remember—you're dealing with *digital* zoom here, which introduces a plethora of noise in order to get closer to your subject. Optical zoom, which isn't available on the iPhone, is the type of zoom that's preferred, as it doesn't inject pixilation into your resulting images after zooming.

Remember, it's also possible to hop directly into the Camera app by swiping up on the icon in the lower right from the lock screen.

Pinching and Zooming

It's as universal as it gets on the iPhone: pinching and zooming. One technique provides a smorgasbord of effects throughout iOS, and it's something that I recommend you learn, STAT. In the Photos app, this simple act of taking two fingers onscreen and pulling them closer together allows one to zoom in on a shot; reversing the movement zooms out. While in Safari, pinching in brings a full page in view, while pinching out allows you to focus in on a specific area of images or text.

In Maps, as mentioned, pinching and zooming helps you to get a broader or tighter view on the area that immediately concerns you. This technique is popularized in a litany of third-party apps, making it nigh impossible to list out what it'll accomplish in every scenario. One thing's for sure, though: it'll almost certainly do something in every app, so be sure to give it a go before fussing with a less intuitive way to navigate.

SUMMARY

I'll never discourage you from discovering the iPhone in a way that suits you. Part of the magic is the ability for the iPhone to become whatever it is you want it to be. But we're all in a hurry, and this chapter was designed to give you a look at shortcuts and navigation tips that'll make your time with iPhone both productive and efficient.

Half the battle is knowing where to start, and shortcuts are as important as ever with iOS 5 and iOS 6. From keyboard shortcuts to gesture-based navigational tricks, there's an easier way to get around. Long-pressing buttons and apps enables you to get where you're going with fewer steps, and searching for content, apps, and text clippings via Spotlight is bound to keep your wild-goose-chasing to a minimum.

Finally, it's important to fully realize the power of gestures. Don't stop with just single-finger swipes to the side. Multi-finger gestures are more powerful and prevalent than ever within iOS 5 and iOS 6, and more often than not, their uses aren't entirely obvious. Simply initiating these swipes (along with the pinch-to-zoom technique) could help you fall in love with any given program all over again.

CHAPTER 6

Taking FaceTime (and Those Other Video Calling Solutions) to the Next Level

IN THIS CHAPTER

▶ Getting comfortable with FaceTime

▶ Friending and finding

▶ Understanding connection requirements

▶ Integrating Skype

▶ Tying Google Voice into the equation

▶ Avoiding traditional communication charges

The cameras on the iPhone have long since been world-class, and while many people use them primarily for Instagram, far-flung family members can use them for something more special. The concept of video calling itself isn't hard to understand, but the primary issue that has kept it from hitting critical mass is the difficulty in finding and organizing contacts. The conventional phone number, for all of its faults, still excels at being easy to distribute, catalog, and reference. A username, however, is vastly more flexible. Internet-based chatting applications such as Face-Time, Skype, and Google Voice are infinitely more approachable, and anything with access to the World Wide Web can join in. In this chapter, I discuss the ins and outs of using the iPhone as a video communication tool, and I point out the intricacies of getting (and staying) connected inexpensively via video while traversing the globe.

MAKING FACETIME YOUR GO-TO VIDEO CALLING APP

▶ Desktop owners can dive in as well, thanks to Apple's 27-inch Thunderbolt Display with FaceTime HD camera ($999), but you'll need a Mac with DisplayPort in order to use it.

In a way, Apple took video calling to a mainstream audience in a way that no prior company had. Skype was well on its way, and the recent acquisition by Microsoft will no doubt hasten that, but it was FaceTime that truly got people talking.

To start, it's helpful to know which products can use FaceTime. Sadly, owners of older iPhones (anything prior to the iPhone 4) are left out. Right now, you'll need an iPhone 4 or newer, the iPod touch (again, with a front-facing camera), or any modern-day Mac to enjoy the spoils of FaceTime. Smartly, Apple has made FaceTime a platform in which a phone number isn't required to use. Although you can still request a Face-Time call with an iPhone user by pinging their number (as shown in Figure 6-1), the majority of devices are pinged by e-mail address. This is particularly handy if you own multiple FaceTime-equipped products; regardless of whether you're on your iPhone or Mac, people can initiate FaceTime calls with you using your same e-mail address.

FIGURE 6-1:   Let's FaceTime, shall we?

How to Find Friends with FaceTime

One of the biggest strengths of FaceTime is that no accounts, in the most literal sense of the word, are required. You simply provide the e-mail address that's associated with your iCloud or iTunes account (called an "AppleID"), and boom—it's connected. Now, people can search for you on FaceTime with just your e-mail address, so I highly recommend using an e-mail address that the bulk of your friends, peers, and colleagues are already familiar with.

> **TIP** FaceTime defaults to using the e-mail address tied to your iTunes and iCloud account, but you can easily add another e-mail in Settings → FaceTime → Add Another Email. Be aware, however, that you can only add addresses that have never been used with Apple's ecosystem before. Also, you'll need access to the addresses you add, as you have to verify each one before FaceTime will enable that address to be linked to your profile. Once that's done, however, folks can connect with you via FaceTime with more than just one e-mail address. It's a great trick for those who have several active e-mail accounts.

You may be wondering, "How on Earth do I know if any of my friends have Face-Time, and if they're connected over Wi-Fi?". The unfortunate truth is that making and receiving a FaceTime call is far more difficult than simply ringing a phone number, mostly because FaceTime calls require users to be on a Wi-Fi connection when using iOS 5 or earlier. With iOS 6, Apple has enabled support for FaceTime over cellular data, but not all carriers are going to join in. Moreover, some carriers—like AT&T in the United States—force users to pay extra for the privilege. In addition to that, video calls eat up around 3MB per minute, and if you're using a fairly limited, tiered data plan, a handful of FaceTime calls could easily put you over your monthly limit.

Thus, I strongly recommend using Wi-Fi for FaceTime calls unless you absolutely can't wait. To add some perspective, a FaceTime call over 3G will blow through AT&T's entry-level 250MB plan in 83 minutes. That's right—video chatting with your mum on Mother's Day for under 1.5 hours will obliterate your data pool *for a month*. Yikes.

> **NOTE** Interestingly, FaceTime is a protocol that could be adopted elsewhere. To date, no other companies have created applications based on the platform that Apple has built, leading to a serious amount of fragmentation. For example, you can't FaceTime someone simply by finding them in your Skype contact list. Too bad there's no easy way to merge all of the most popular video calling apps into one!

▶ Outside of data usage (and if your carrier charges for the luxury of completing calls over its cellular data network), FaceTime is completely free. No matter which FaceTime member you call, in what country, across what ocean, it's always free.

How to Make FaceTime Calls Over 3G/4G

With the introduction of iOS 6, Apple also enabled FaceTime over 3G/4G on the iPhone. It's a feature that was already enabled on apps such as Skype and Fring, but until the newest build of iOS, FaceTime *required* Wi-Fi on both ends of the conversation. But here's the trouble—it's up to individual carriers to support it. Some don't support it because their networks simply can't handle the excess load of so many high-bandwidth FaceTime calls. However, some carriers—such as Rogers in Canada and the major players in the United States—have enabled it. It's up to your provider to charge extra for it or not, so I recommend checking around with whichever carriers have service nearby to understand their policies.

> **TIP** If you're familiar with Cydia—a repository for apps in the world of jailbroken devices—you'll need to search for My3G. That's your ticket to enabling FaceTime over a 3G/4G connection without ponying up for your carrier's permission.

The other workaround for those looking to avoid carrier fees for FaceTime initiation doesn't require any tomfoolery. Well, not any of the warranty-voiding kind, that is. If you fire up a mobile hotspot—which should get you online via a 3G or 4G network, depending on what model, carrier, and plan you select—you'll be able to connect your iPhone to it.

Essentially, the phone will be connected via Wi-Fi, so it won't check to see if you've paid the carrier entry fee for FaceTime calls using cellular data. Of course, you'll need to be mindful of the data plan attached to your mobile hotspot, but otherwise you'll be in the clear.

> **NOTE** If you're planning to use the mobile hotspot trick to FaceTime over a cellular data network with any level of frequency, I strongly recommend selecting one of Verizon Wireless' LTE hotspots. Its 4G LTE network is the fastest and most widespread 4G network in the States, and it's expanding at a breakneck pace. There's plenty of bandwidth to handle clear FaceTime calls, but remember—the faster your Internet works, the easier it is to blow through your monthly allotment.

Video Calling from 35,000 Feet

There's this crazy invention from the future, and it just so happens to be available today. It's called Gogo, and for all intents and purposes, it's Wi-Fi in the sky. Gogo has been around for a few years now, but they're still expanding to various new markets and airlines. In a nutshell, a Gogo-equipped plane enables you to connect to the Internet while sitting 10,000 feet in the sky, in an airplane. In the United States, Delta, Virgin America, and JetBlue are your best bets for finding a Wi-Fi flight, and if you want to pass your time while cruising from point A to point B, there's really no better way.

Frequent fliers are well advised to spring for a monthly pass, but even those who find themselves on an aircraft only every so often can buy a single-flight pass for under $13. You'll be able to spot Gogo on your flight by connecting to the Gogo network once you're above 10,000 feet. If you pass the point of "It's okay to use electronics" and you don't see this network, you're on a disconnected flight.

Why spend so much time poring over in-flight Wi-Fi? Because it relates directly to FaceTime. If you manage to get onboard an aircraft with Gogo, you can connect your iPhone to the network, and from there, make and receive FaceTime calls. It's important to realize that Gogo is little more than a highly extended 3G cellular network, so you shouldn't expect stellar performance. That said, I've seen it work in a number of instances, and it's certainly a fantastic way to pass the time and touch base with your loved ones. Just remember to use headphones with an inline microphone—your fellow passengers probably aren't interested in overhearing your conversation.

WARNING Gogo has already blocked select VoIP ports on their service, locking Skype users out. I suspect it's only a matter of time before they do the same for Fring, FaceTime, AirTime, and a slew of other Internet calling applications. It's probably less of a bandwidth thing, and more of a passenger distraction thing.

Showing Off Your Surroundings

Although the front-facing camera is obviously there to enable video chatting, the iPhone also touts a rear-facing camera. Might as well take advantage of it! During a FaceTime chat, simply tap the Camera Rotate icon (it's positioned beside the End key) in order to flip your camera to the rear-facing one. On the other end, your recipient will see whatever is facing the rear camera. This is an excellent trick for showing off the kids without having to physically turn the iPhone around, and in the same vein, the person you're chatting with can tap that button on his end to give you a different perspective. In case you're wondering, the audio will remain the same regardless of which camera angle you're using.

▶ The mini window that shows off your own face (what the person on the other end sees) can be relocated by tapping it, holding it, and dragging it to another corner.

I also recommend that you be cautious of the lighting behind you. If you're in a sunny park, for instance, and the sun is unleashing its wrath on your neck, there's a better-than-average chance that the person you're chatting with will see nothing but a silhouette of your mug. It's a good idea to minimize the light flooding in behind you, particularly for those who sit next to large windows. You're not only the envy of the working world, but you're now tasked with repositioning yourself before initiating a FaceTime call. Congratulations!

> **NOTE** iOS 6 is tailor-made for multi-tasking, and this applies to FaceTime, too. If you need to hop into another app while on a FaceTime call, simply press the Home button to reach the home screen. On the other end, your recipient will see a frozen image of you, but your audio will still work. You can continue yapping while fiddling in another app, and once you return to the FaceTime call, the video feed will pick back up again.

TROUBLESHOOTING FACETIME

FaceTime was engineered to be simple, but it's worth covering a few trouble-shooting angles in the event that you hit any snags during use.

▶ FaceTime doesn't like firewalls. Hotels are full of them. If you're trying to video chat with your family back home, you'll need port-forwarding enabled on ports 53, 80, 443, 4080, 5223, and 16393-16472 (UDP). Rather than using the hotel Wi-Fi, try using a mobile hotspot or heading to a nearby café.

▶ If you need to tweak the ports on your own router, open a browser page and cruise to 192.168.1.1 (or consult your router's tech support line).

▶ If you can't make any FaceTime calls, be sure it's enabled in Settings ➜ FaceTime.

▶ Remember to position your face just north of where you probably think it should be; otherwise, the person on the other end gets an eyeful of your nostrils.

▶ If you're having a conversation within iMessage and the person hops on Wi-Fi, you can tap the FaceTime icon in the top-right to initiate a video chat from there.

NOTE Although video chatting is a bit of a futuristic experience for most, the most magical aspect is the cost savings. By replacing conventional landline and cellular networks with the Internet, consumers can significantly cut the costs that are oftentimes associated with non-local or global calling. Part of the Internet's magic is being able to send bytes across fibers that end up looking like someone's face on the other end; the other tidbit is just how cheap it is to access this compared to the options of just a few decades ago. That notion alone is causing a generation of landline droppers to also drop phone numbers that are directly linked to legacy carriers, a point which I explain in detail a bit later.

INTEGRATING SKYPE INTO THE WORKFLOW

Skype's main advantage is the traction behind it. By landing at the right time, offering the right features, and enabling people across the world to call and chat with each other for free, Skype has amassed millions upon millions of users. Chances are, if you know someone with a smartphone, they also have a Skype account.

The other *major* advantage to using Skype on the iPhone is cross-compatibility. Skype is available on every major platform—both desktop and mobile—giving you a far larger pool of potential chatters. Because Skype supports Windows, Mac, Android, BlackBerry, iOS, Windows Phone, and myriad other operating systems, you stand a far greater chance of finding all of your friends on Skype than on FaceTime. As it stands, you need an OS X or iOS-enabled device to use FaceTime, so unless you hang with an Apple-only crowd, there's a good chance that some of your buds will feel alienated.

The good news is that you can have FaceTime and Skype running concurrently on the iPhone, ready and able to accept calls from either platform at a moment's notice. Furthering the good news, Skype for iPhone supports video chatting, and although it doesn't use the FaceTime protocol, it still works just fine with the built-in cameras.

NOTE Skype for iPhone is a free download in the App Store, and it accepts the same login credentials that you've probably already been using with a different form of Skype. If you're new to Skype, installing it on the iPhone will allow you to register with a new account and find friends via username or e-mail address.

Replacing Your Landline with Skype

Unlike FaceTime, which is a highly specialized application, Skype is a multifaceted communications tool. Just tap that dialpad icon along the bottom of the app, and a conventional dialpad appears (see for yourself in Figure 6-2). You'll need to purchase Skype Credits (which can be done in your Skype account) in order to dial out to phone numbers across the globe, but if you're looking for a great reason to drop your land-line, this just might be it.

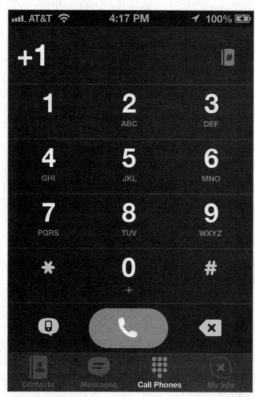

FIGURE 6-2: A telephone... on your iPhone? It's true!

▶ International travelers can't always initiate free Skype-to-Skype calls, but using Skype to dial back to wherever home may be is always cheaper than roaming on a foreign cellular network.

Calling actual phone numbers from within Skype ranges from a few cents per minute on a pay-as-you-go plan, to $4.49 per month in an all-you-can-call plan that services the United States and Canada. Skype's full list of calling plans can be found at www.skype.com/intl/en-us/prices, and no matter how you slice it, it's a far saner deal than a traditional landline. Pair up a Bluetooth headset with an iPhone and a Skype subscription, and you'll wonder why you didn't cut that cord long ago.

Skype for iPhone beautifully melds the conventional calling side and the VoIP/ video side, so you can always hop from a familiar dialpad to a list of Skype usernames with no fuss to speak of. I always recommend dialing a Skype username (for voice or video) first. Skype-to-Skype calls are always free within the app itself, but if you dial a phone number, that'll cost you. You can check your Skype Credit balance from within the app, as seen in Figure 6-3.

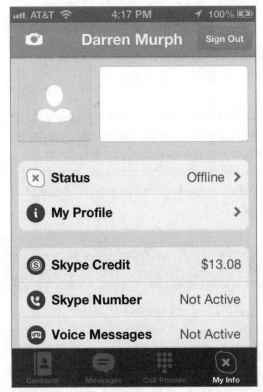

FIGURE 6-3: Skype Credit allows you to dial conventional phone numbers from within the app.

Doubling Down on VoIP

Of course, dialing out is only half of the equation. If you still want people to be able to ring you via Skype, you'll need a Skype Online Number. Basically, this is a brand new phone number—one that looks like any other number on the outside— but instead of ringing a landline, it rings whatever device you have Skype enabled on. By visiting Skype's website, you can apply for an Online Number, and perhaps even more amazing is that U.S. users can procure a number from a country *outside* of America. That's right—you can claim ownership of a Hong Kong phone number without actually having property there. Welcome to the future.

If you're a business owner who deals with foreign nations, stocking up on various "local" phone numbers in these countries could save you a bundle on roaming rates, and it'll certainly make it easier for your clients (and perhaps more importantly, potential clients) to phone you.

> **WARNING** Although a Skype Online Number makes total sense for a lot of things, it cannot be used for emergency calling.

Finally, Skype calling logs and conversation histories can be viewed from any Skype device, which cannot be said for a traditional landline. It's also easier to manage digital call records for business owners, and because your iPhone can go with you, so too can your phone number. I'm a firm believer that the phone number as we know it is a thing of the past, and it's only a matter of time before people begin porting those numbers to Internet-based hosting services such as Skype.

SKYPE EXTRAS

Skype for iPhone is full of subtle additions that enrich the overall experience. I've included a list of my favorites here.

▶ You can send an instant message while a video call is ongoing, which is particularly useful for pinging just one person while you're on a group call.

▶ Skype can automatically forward your calls to a number that you dictate; just click into your profile and flip the Call Forwarding switch to On.

▶ Skype is capable of sending conventional text messages (SMS) via the dialpad.

▶ If you set up a secondary Skype account on your iPhone and set it to auto-answer, you can mount it on a wall with the camera facing into your living room; dial that account from your mobile, and you now have a homegrown security camera.

▶ QuickVoice (free) and Audio Memos 2 ($0.99) can record calls and notes for future playback.

VIDEO CALLING APPS YOU'VE NEVER HEARD OF (BUT SHOULD)

FaceTime and Skype for iPhone are probably enough for most folks, but for hardcore iPhone communicators, there are plenty more options out there. In fact, some of those options fill tiny holes that are glossed over by the two power players.

- Google Voice, though buggy at times, is a must-download. Much like Skype Online Number, getting a Google Voice Number is infinitely powerful. It not only allows you to dial out and receive calls to/from a conventional looking number (although it eats up voice minutes in the process), but it also enables you to receive e-mailed transcripts of voicemails.

- While we're talking Google, the Google+ iOS app also supports "Hangouts," which enable free group video chats for your pals that are also using the service.

- Fring (free) supports group video chatting with up to four participants, and unlike FaceTime, this app allows video calling over 3G or 4G, regardless of carrier. It's also cross-platform, so you can use your iPhone to video chat with pals using Android or Nokia devices.

- ooVoo (free) is a sassily-designed messaging app that supports six-way group video chats, and also allows you to converse via audio and IM. It also lets you record your sessions.

- WhatsApp Messenger ($0.99) doesn't support video calling, but it does support group chatting, multimedia messaging, and a whole heap of platforms (Android, BlackBerry, Nokia, and so on).

- Tango (free) supports video calls over 3G and Wi-Fi regardless of carrier, and it's one of the only cross-platform alternatives that has a future with Windows Phone 7.

- Nimbuzz (free) supports video calling, but additionally, allows users to have a host of other communication protocols open. It also supports push notifications.

SUMMARY

Although "phone" is in the title, your iPhone is a potent all-around communicator. It's just as adept at handling video calls as it is voice calls, provided you have a broadband-quality data or a Wi-Fi connection. FaceTime, Apple's built-in video calling program, is not a standalone app. Instead, you're able to start a FaceTime call from within the Contact card of each person stored on your device.

If that single program isn't enough, there are plenty of other paid and free options in the App Store. Skype is the most well-known, and adds a ton of value by virtue of being a cross-platform program. In other words, you can Skype someone on a Windows PC from an iPhone, without worrying about compatibility issues.

The phone number attached to your carrier is old news. Grab yourself a Google Voice Number and download a number of VoIP and video calling apps in order to make more calls for less money. The more you rely on data rather than voice minutes, the closer you are to getting rid of your reliance on a particular carrier.

CHAPTER 7

Streaming Your Multimedia Without Wires: AirPlay

With the introduction of iCloud, Apple took a stand—a stand against wires. Cords have always been a necessary evil that plagued consumer electronics, and while people have managed to consolidate somewhat over the years (the multifaceted Dock Connector is proof of that), one cable is still one too many in my mind. I'm still waiting on wireless power to be a reality across the board, but until then, I'll have to be content with technologies like iCloud and AirPlay.

The latter of the two is the focal point of this chapter, where you dive into the underpinnings of one of Apple's slickest tether-free implementations yet. AirPlay is an overarching term that describes a wireless protocol that's capable of distributing audiovisual content with no cables to speak of, and the real magic of it is the simplicity in setup. Still, a hassle-free setup doesn't mean that there aren't nooks and crannies to explore. If you're buying an iPhone and aren't taking the time to explore its wireless streaming possibilities, you're selling your purchase short. Let's dive in and make sure you nip that in the bud.

THE IN(PUTS) AND OUT(PUTS) OF AUDIO STREAMING

For years, most average consumers assumed that setting up a wireless home audio system would require a professional installation, gobs of money, and tons of research. And in a lot of cases, those assumptions are both warranted and accurate. Whole home audio systems have traditionally required a high-end receiver, plenty of in-wall cabling, mounting brackets galore, and a networked remote to dictate the orchestra. (Those remotes alone could easily cost $500+.) These days, things are a bit simpler—particularly for iPhone owners.

> **NOTE** AirPlay is a relatively new term, even for Apple loyalists. The term was introduced at a September 2010 iPod launch event, but rather than being entirely new, it actually took the place of a term that has existed since 2004: AirTunes. Over the years, Apple realized that people were interested in streaming more than just audio. With video in the mix, converting AirTunes to AirPlay made more sense than using two separate protocols. Even today, AirPlay is in its infancy. The true potential lies in the hands of Apple's blossoming developer army—an army that has already developed over 100,000 iPhone-specific apps. Optimists might say that Apple's headfirst approach into wireless video streaming is only being tested on the iPhone, iPod touch, and iPad, with the real killer app to be the forthcoming Apple-branded HDTV. At this point, those are still rumors, but the smoke that leads to fire is certainly becoming tougher to ignore.

▶ *AirPlay Mirroring is currently only available for the iPhone 4S, iPhone 5, iPad 2, and the new iPad. Owners of older iPhone handsets, the iPod touch, and the original iPad aren't able to enjoy the spoils without a jailbreak.*

Beginning with iOS 4.2, Apple enabled the movement of video from the iPhone onto other devices without the use of a cable. But there's a lot more to talk about now that iOS 6 is out and about. At first, only select applications could stream video, and a heap of limitations kept the functionality in check. But with iOS 5 and iOS 6, AirPlay Mirroring has been unveiled. I describe it more in the "Tapping the Power of Apple TV" section, but in short, this feature allows iOS devices to wirelessly beam their displays to any screen that has an Apple TV connected to it. Think of it as wirelessly projecting your iPhone's display onto your HDTV.

All that said, audio is still at the core of AirPlay, and while the "Tunes" doppelganger has since been dropped, it's still very much a part of the overall experience. To better understand the intricacies of AirPlay, it's important to understand how AirPlay-compatible products are divided. AirPlay sender devices include the iPhone, other iOS products and computers running iTunes. All of these are capable of broadcasting audio or video wirelessly, for something else entirely to catch and comprehend. Those "catching" devices are called AirPlay receivers. As of now, there aren't too many receivers to keep track of. The AirPort Express—which I recommended earlier as a fantastic iPhone companion from a networking standpoint—is the primary AirPlay receiver from an aural perspective. Outside of that guy, there's the Apple TV and a small but growing stable of AirPlay-compatible A/V receivers and speakers.

Configuring AirPlay on Your iPhone

Considering that at least some external equipment is necessary to receive any wireless streams emitting from the iPhone, Apple has hidden AirPlay's settings from view until your device *detects* one of those outside products. If you have an AirPort Express, an AirPlay-certified A/V receiver or speaker, or an Apple TV, you'll see a new icon in a semi-concealed place that you wouldn't otherwise see. First off, you need to ensure that your iPhone and your AirPlay accessory are connected on the same Wi-Fi network. If they are, the "discovery" process happens automatically on the iPhone, although you may have to reboot it if it doesn't recognize the device(s) right away. To find out, simply double-tap the Home button to bring up the Secondary Dock bar at the bottom. Swipe from left to right twice to bring up the control bar, and look for a rectangular icon with an arrow on the bottom. That's AirPlay, and it's shown in Figure 7-1.

> **TIP** Here's one little-known fact about AirPlay: Any previously paired Bluetooth speakers (such as the fantastic Jambox from Jawbone) will *also* show up in the list of AirPlay-enabled devices, allowing you to start streaming music even to Bluetooth devices from the same menu, using the same controls. Handy!

FIGURE 7-1: "Hi. I'm AirPlay. Let's stream something."

Press that icon, and your discovered devices should be shown. You select the one to which you want to stream give it a moment to pair, and you're configured. If only washing dishes, mowing the lawn, and filing taxes were this easy....

> **TIP** While you're in the setup mood, it's worth your while to download Apple's Remote app from the App Store. It's a free program that allows your iPhone to control your Mac's iTunes library wirelessly. It also gives you total control of AirPlay-connected devices (with a highly intuitive user interface), and you can search for things by typing on a pop-up QWERTY keyboard right on the display. It quite literally turns your iPhone into an oversized touch-panel remote. For free.

Another Reason to Consider AirPort Express

As if you didn't have reason enough to spring for Apple's prior-generation AirPort Express (remember how useful it is in spreading a single hotel Ethernet connection to all of your Wi-Fi travel companions?), it also acts as the cheapest, most seamless way to send a signal to an audio system you already own from the iPhone. And yes, that includes wired audio systems. The AirPort Express has a 3.5mm minijack that supports analog and optical audio cables (shown in Figure 7-2). Connect this jack to an existing A/V receiver or speaker input, and that's the last cable you'll need to run. From there, your iPhone can send audio from the Music app directly to the AirPort Express with no wire in between, allowing whatever speaker system is attached to have the tracks and volume dictated remotely and wirelessly right on the phone.

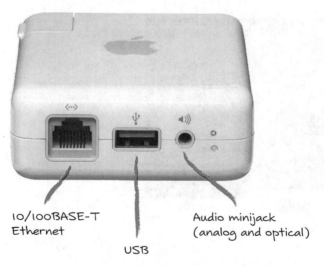

10/100BASE-T Ethernet

USB

Audio minijack (analog and optical)

FIGURE 7-2: Three ports on the bottom of the "old" AirPort Express. So little, doing so much.

AirPort Express is easily one of Apple's most awkwardly named and universally understated products. But then again, I'm not really sure there even exists a succinct way to name a product that does so much. Sure, it's a mobile broadband router that can be plugged into any home outlet. But the audio jack on the bottom is extremely powerful in conjunction with AirPlay. You can connect your AirPort Express to your home stereo or powered speakers using a digital fiber optic cable, analog mini-stereo-to-dual-RCA cable, or mini-stereo to mini-stereo cable (depending on what type of connectors your stereo uses) connected to the Line Out port. Better still, you can stream iTunes music to more than one AirPort Express at a time by choosing Multiple Speakers from the Speakers pop-up menu (assuming, of course, you actually *have* multiple AE base stations installed). In other words, you can place an AirPort Express in every room where you have a receiver or speaker set up, and then broadcast music to each of those rooms from a *single* iPhone. House parties just became entirely more feasible.

CONFIGURING YOUR AIRPORT EXPRESS

Setting up AirPort Express is as simple as tapping into the AirPort utility on your Mac, or the like-named app on your iPhone (it's available as a free download from the App Store). But there are litanies of possible configurations, which are worth going over in detail here.

▶ You can use an AirPort Express exclusively as a wireless streaming liaison, without ever tapping into its other powers in the networking space. Simply connect your speakers to the 3.5mm jack, plug the device into a nearby AC outlet, and select it as an AirPlay-compatible streaming device within iTunes or on the iPhone's AirPlay menu.

▶ If an AirPort Express is your primary wireless router, you'll need to ensure your speaker system and Internet modem are near enough to both reach the device. Then, in AirPort Utility, ensure that Enable AirPlay/AirTunes is checked in the Music tab when creating a new wireless network.

▶ If your AirPort Express is acting as a music streaming device and an extension of a network that's connected via Ethernet, you'll need to again ensure that your speaker(s) and router are both within reach. Once the Ethernet and 3.5mm cable are connected, you'll need to use the AirPort Utility to configure AirPort Express as part of a roaming network, and ensure that Enable AirPlay/AirTunes is checked in the AirPort Utility Music tab.

(continues)

(Continued)

▶ If you're connecting your AirPort Express to your wireless network in client mode—in other words, only for its wireless printing and audio streaming capabilities—you'll need to join the AirPort Express SSID from your list of available wireless networks. On a Mac, you can use the AirPort status menu in the menu bar; on a Windows-based computer, hold the pointer over the wireless connection icon until you see your AirPort network name.

▶ If you're setting up your AirPort Express as a wireless repeater or extender to your existing wireless network, you'll simply need to ensure that Enable AirPlay/AirTunes is checked in the AirPort Utility Music tab, and connect to it as you would in the first example.

It's important to note that Apple changed the AirPort Express design in 2012. The prior model, which is still available from the online Apple Refurbished Store for $69 (or eBay, failing that), is the one I recommend. The new one requires a lengthy power cord, which makes it less useful for travel.

WARNING If you're planning to use the AirPort Express as a wireless repeater or extender to your existing wireless network, it's worth investigating the protocols supported on your other wireless router. If it's in 802.11b/g mode, switch your AirPort Express to the same. If one is using 802.11b/g/n, allow your AirPort Express to follow suit. Don't mix and match network protocols across devices. I've seen lots of connection problems and interference when various routers on the same network are using different wireless technologies to broadcast.

UNDERSTANDING WHAT CAN BE STREAMED WHERE

With every new iteration of iOS, and every new model in the Apple TV line, the visual map of what can be streamed where gets a little more complicated. In fact, it's so perplexing already, that it's worth taking a look at the specifics. For example, the Apple TV 2 is required to accomplish a few feats that the original Apple TV cannot.

Unfortunately, neither a NAS drive nor a Time Capsule can be used to stream from *unless* a host computer is online and running iTunes. I'm hoping that Apple removes the middleman in a future update, but if you absolutely have to tap into a NAS library of music, Sonos' systems may be a better option.

In any situation, it's important to remember that your iPhone software and Apple TV software (and even your AirPort Express firmware) are up to date. Some of the more advanced streaming functions are enabled only when everything in the streaming family is running the latest software, and if you're still facing troubles, you may want to temporarily disable firewalls (both network and local) as well as security software. Also, ensure that two or more devices aren't trying to connect or stream to a single AirPlay-enabled device. It's also worth disabling your Bluetooth radio (found in Settings → General → Bluetooth) to prevent any unforeseen interference or connection confusion issues.

Widening Your Reach with Home Sharing

Here's a situation: What if you'd like to use your iPhone to stream audio to a wireless speaker setup, but you have only 16GB of onboard storage. Perhaps even more importantly, the bulk of your favorite tunes are stored on your Mac or PC. So, you're left with two options. You can either use your Mac or PC (and the accompanying iTunes library), or, you can take advantage of the Home Sharing library (shown in Figure 7-3).

FIGURE 7-3: Activating Home Sharing from within iTunes

▶ You can also use another Mac or PC (or even an Apple TV 2) in place of the iOS device if you feel like streaming to something other than your iPhone.

Home Sharing is a relatively new technology that's pretty involved to start, but once you're established, using it is simple. You'll need a computer with the latest build of iTunes (one that's logged in using your Apple ID) as well as an iOS device (that's where your iPhone comes in).

The key is to match the Apple ID on your iTunes with the one on your iPhone. To get this squared away, you'll need to visit the Preferences section within iTunes → Sharing → Share My Library on Local Network. Then, on the iPhone, head to Settings → Music and input the same Apple ID and password. From there, ensure that your iTunes computer and phone are both online, and then open the Music app. To switch to a shared library, you'll need to tap More → Shared and locate the library that you just made available. It's not exactly obvious, but it'll be there if the right inputs were given. Apple has a fairly robust startup guide and FAQ on Home Sharing here: www.apple.com/support/homesharing.

> TIP Make sure the iTunes computer that's sharing its library doesn't fall asleep or go offline while you're streaming. None of that library is stored locally on your iPhone; if the host drops out, all you get is silence.

Hacking Extra Functionality Out of AirPlay

Apple, like any for-profit company, cannot reasonably support an aging product forever, and at some point, the updates simply have to cease. The original Apple TV was always dubbed a "hobby" by the late Steve Jobs, but the Apple TV 2 seems to be much more than that. Thankfully, the hacker community has found a way to add AirPlay support to the original, and if you're mildly familiar with coding and have the ability to follow step-by-step directions, there's a solution waiting.

Perhaps unsurprisingly, AirPlay isn't exactly buddy-buddy with Windows, either. But even *more* unsurprisingly, there's a workaround for that, too. Here, I discuss a few hacks that are absolutely out-of-bounds for those who aren't into voiding extended warranties, but pack an awful lot of fun for those who are fond of throwing caution to the wind.

> ▶ Thanks to a clever hack from the folks responsible for the Remote HD plug-in, AirPlay functionality can indeed be shoehorned onto the original Apple TV. Accomplishing this isn't for those who lack courage. It'll take a fair bit of underhanded tinkering, and while the warranty on your original Apple TV has long since expired, meddling with the code inside of one's Apple TV has been known to leave the device unusable. If you're still interested, you can unearth the complete how-to guide at: www.appletvhacks.net/2011/01/05/airplay-streaming-hacked-into-the-old-apple-tv.

- If you already have a Windows-based PC connected to your TV, or you'd simply rather broadcast video from your iPhone to a Windows XP, Vista, or Windows 7-based rig instead of an Apple TV 2—good luck. Apple doesn't natively support it, but an older project dubbed AirMediaPlayer does enable it. You don't have to jailbreak your iPhone to pull this off, but locating download links for the software itself could take a bit of Googling—it's not hosted on a centralized FTP due to its unapproved status. Check here for a how-to install guide: http://compixels.com/8974/enable-airplay-on-windows-pc-to-wirelessly-stream-audio-video-from-ios-devices.

- iTunes for Windows will stream audio from your PC library to any AirPlay-compatible device, but if you want to stream music *to* a PC *from* your iPhone, you'll need a handy piece of freeware called Shairport4w. Ensure you have the latest version of iTunes, download the software from http://sourceforge.net/projects/shairport4w/, and make sure that your PC is on the same Wi-Fi network as your iPhone. If done properly, your PC will show on your iPhone as an AirPlay-compatible device to stream to.

- If you're also dabbling in the world of Android, you can install the DoubleTwist AirSync add-in from the Android Market ($4.99) in order to stream audiovisual material from your Android device to an Apple TV 2. Twonky Mobile is a free alternative, but it lacks the tight iTunes integration that AirSync has.

- AirPlay for Windows Media Center is a free piece of software that enables your iPhone to beam content directly to your Media Center PC. It's perhaps the perfect mix of Apple and Windows, and the install instructions can be found here: http://thomaspleasance.wordpress.com/2011/05/23/airplay-for-windows-media-center-beta-1/.

- If you're comfortable jailbreaking your iPhone and you need to pipe all manners of content *from* your phone and *onto* your Mac, AirServer has you covered. It's a $7.99 app, and can be downloaded from here: www.airserverapp.com/?page_id=182.

SELECTING YOUR NEXT SPEAKER SYSTEM

As explained earlier in this chapter, the purchase of a $99 AirPort Express is all you need to convert *any* wired speaker system or A/V receiver into an AirPlay-compatible speaker. But in that scenario, you're still forced to move your AirPort Express and speaker system together if you want to reposition it. That's probably not a huge deal for surround systems that you've no intention of moving, but for smaller systems that are suitable for moving from room to room based on your current location, asking an AirPort Express to tag along isn't idyllic.

Slowly but surely, a host of AirPlay-certified speakers are rolling out, which includes the wireless AirPlay functionality from the factory. In other words, an Air-Play-certified speaker has Apple's wireless transceiver technology baked right into the device, so no extra accessories are required in order for the speaker to receive audio signals that are sent out from your iPhone. Perhaps not surprisingly, most of these speaker systems are at least somewhat mobile—after all, a wireless speaker makes the most sense when you can easily move it from the outdoor patio to the kitchen, or toss in the rear of the truck for a day at the beach.

In a nutshell, an AirPlay-enabled speaker system—if situated within range of your iPhone—will show up as an AirPlay device in your Secondary Dock bar. Once selected, you'll be able to stream audio from your Music app to it, while also dictating the volume remotely. Speaking of range, AirPlay's usage of Wi-Fi technologies enables it to be effective over a much greater distance than typical Bluetooth speakers, which are limited to around 30 feet. Wi-Fi signals can be sent up to several hundred feet away, so even those with miniature mansions shouldn't have a problem using an iPhone in the kitchen to send AirPlay commands to a speaker in the sauna. Granted, said speaker probably won't last too long in that kind of environment, but when you have a sauna, what's another AirPlay speaker?

> **WARNING** Although Wi-Fi may be superior to Bluetooth for situations like this, it's still not perfect. AirPlay connections take around two seconds, as do subsequent actions, and full-on drop-outs aren't unheard of. Wireless might be convenient, but it's not flawless.

In the next sections, I break down the pros and cons of a few recommended AirPlay speakers, covering everything from stay-at-home options to iPhone-friendly ones.

Stay-at-Home AirPlay Speaker Options

Bowers & Wilkins Zeppelin Air. This is, perhaps, *the* stay-at-home AirPlay speaker. Why? For one, it's on the "somewhat enormous" side, and two, its shape makes it really impractical to carry around without fuss. The upside to this, of course, is that the sound quality is far more impressive than any of those pocket-sized alternatives. B&W is a name oft associated with high-quality aural experiences, and the Zeppelin Air is definitely a showcase piece for the home. There's also a unique docking arm that will hold (and charge) your iPod or iPhone, should you care to take advantage. It's a perfect ornament for game rooms, dens, or patios, but at $600, it's also one of the most expensive AirPlay speakers on the market. You get what you pay for, as the saying goes.

Libratone Lounge Speaker. Say hello to the king. Or, at least the king in terms of price. This high-end AirPlay speaker checks in at a whopping $1,300, but it's the closest you'll get to finding an AirPlay-enabled sound bar right now. It's big, classy, and understated, and will undoubtedly bring the house down (while simultaneously breaking the bank). The Libratone app (available free from the App Store in iTunes) allows you to enhance and customize your FullRoom musical experience. You can input information about the placement of your Libratone Lounge and it then automatically adjusts the sound to fit your room.

Philips Fidelio SoundSphere AirPlay Speakers. If you're looking for AirPlay speakers that involve more than a single, elongated bar, look no further. The Fidelio SoundSphere duo ($800) consists of two separate satellites. The design is certainly worth showcasing, and the 100-watts of built-in power should be plenty to fill the average room. Better still, there are no wires running between the left and right drivers, making it entirely wire-free outside of the power cord. These are also compatible with Philips' free Fidelio app (available in the App Store), which allows you to remotely access over 7,000 Internet radio stations, sound-setting controls, a clock and multiple alarms, and a sleep timer.

Highly Mobile Speaker Options

iHome iW1. In my estimation, this $300 option strikes the perfect balance between a stay-at-home option and a mobile option. It's big enough to produce laudatory sound, but the built-in lithium-ion battery ensures that you can toss it in the car for a spontaneous getaway. (Boy, couldn't we all use one of those right about now?) There's also a convenient carrying handle and a complimentary iHome Connect app for easy network setup.

Audyssey's Lower East Side Audio Dock Air. The only major gripe I have here is the absence of a built-in battery pack, but the remarkably mobile design helps me to forgive that nitpick. The company crams an awful lot of drivers into a tight package, and while the $400 price tag isn't easy to swallow, you'll be hard-pressed to find the kind of audio fidelity here in an enclosure this portable.

JBL On Air Wireless Speaker System. Besides having an omnidirectional speaker design that cleverly doubles as a carrying handle, this is also one of the first AirPlay speakers to tout a built-in LCD. That screen is perfect for displaying album artwork or song information to those nearby, although you can control and shuffle things through your iPhone from afar. It also offers an FM radio tuner and dual alarm clocks, as well as a perfect docking/charging port should you have an iPod or iPhone laying around. At $350, it's also one of the cheaper options—yes, I said cheaper. None of these AirPlay speakers is "affordable" by most definitions.

> **NOTE** Pioneer's X-SMC3-S Music Tap doesn't quite fit in either of the categories discussed here, but it just might be the best bang-for-your-buck AirPlay system, period. Aside from supporting Apple's wireless protocol, it also supports the more universally accepted DLNA wireless streaming technology. There's even a 2.5-inch LCD for showcasing album art, a built-in Ethernet port, an iPod/iPhone charging dock, and a video output to boot. Quite versatile for $400.

AirPlay-Enabled A/V Receivers

▶ The $49 upgrade is merely a firmware update. Consult your individual owner's manual for a how-to on downloading and applying the new software.

Although the simplest route to adding AirPlay functionality to speakers you already own is to purchase an AirPort Express, serious home theater buffs may scoff at such a notion. For those considering something a bit more—shall we say, *robust*—there's the newfangled option of an AirPlay-certified A/V receiver. Apple's been working hard to add partners to its list, but so far there are only a handful of companies that are producing AirPlay receivers. In fact, a few older A/V receivers are being offered AirPlay upgrades, but the unfortunate part of that is the $49 upgrade fee. Apple's not exactly giving away this AirPlay stuff—any partner company that buys in has to pay a stiff licensing fee, and in the case of older units that are being blessed with an update, that fee is being handed down to the consumer. Far from ideal, but then again, it's better than having to buy an entirely new kit.

Denon and Marantz were two of the first companies to bite into the AirPlay agenda, so it's no surprise to see a litany of their devices on the upgrade block. That said, I can't wholeheartedly recommend that the average consumer go out and procure an A/V receiver from either of those firms. Despite producing outstanding equipment, anything with either of those labels is prohibitively expensive—at least, for the average consumer.

AIRPLAY RECEIVERS

You're probably wondering which A/V receivers fall into that "upgrade-eligible" camp. Glad you asked!

▶ Denon AVR-4311CI

▶ Denon AVR-3311CI

▶ Denon AVR-991

▶ Denon AVR-A100

▶ Denon N7 Networked CD Receiver and 2.0 Channel Speaker System

▶ Marantz SR7005 A/V Receiver

▶ Marantz AV7005 A/V Preamplifier

▶ Marantz NA7004 Network Audio Player

▶ Marantz M-CR603 Networked CD Receiver

Thankfully, there's an alternative. Pioneer has introduced a smattering of AirPlay-enabled receivers of its own, all of which are drastically cheaper than the options offered by Denon and Marantz. The $550 Pioneer VSX-1021 is the starlet of the bunch. It's only marginally more expensive than some of the mid-range Air-Play speakers, and it'll also stream content from DLNA devices when your iPhone takes the occasional break. If that 7.1 piece is still too pricey, the VSX-521, VSX-821, and VSX-921 all feature AirPlay as well, and they're priced at $249, $349, and $449, respectively.

▶ With over 250 member companies, DLNA is the de-facto streaming protocol that almost everyone uses. Except Apple.

WHAT'S NEXT FOR AIRPLAY?

Put simply: *plenty*. AirPlay is still in its infancy and Apple is still building out its partner list. Recently, Klipsch and Logitech decided to join in, and both companies have plenty of AirPlay-certified speaker systems en route. And that's just on the audio front. The next logical step is for Apple to license AirPlay video streaming. You can already mirror your entire iPhone experience onto your HDTV if you have an Apple TV 2 in between (video included), so it's clear that Apple's already in possession of the technology. It's only a matter of logistics before that same video support trickles down to A/V receivers and perhaps even rivals set-top boxes.

And then, of course, there's the long-rumored Apple HDTV. It's unclear if the company is actually going to put its name (and more importantly, its software) directly into a television of any kind, but I have it on good authority that huge names in the industry are knocking at Apple's door in order to produce exactly that. Companies have struggled to produce cost-effective, lag-free wireless HD equipment, and tight integration with other products (namely, smartphones and tablets) is all but nonexistent outside of the Apple universe. The iPhone is a fairly powerful controller today. If AirPlay is allowed to sink its tentacles into more than just a handful of speakers, receivers, and the Apple TV, the iPhone could become the world's most multifaceted and versatile universal remote.

Keying In on Video Streaming

To date, AirPlay is predominantly about audio streaming. In fact, the only way to actually stream video content from the iPhone and onto an AirPlay-certified device is to have an Apple TV 2 around—if you're doing things by the book, anyway. But with the introduction of iOS 5 (and continuing with iOS 6), Apple made it clear that video is going to be the next big push with AirPlay, and I have a host of tips for making the most of that initiative. Using your iPhone not only as a video controller, but also as a video *source*, opens up all new avenues of enjoyment, and it brings your phone one step closer to truly being the center of attention in your multimedia universe.

Tapping the Power of Apple TV

Apple did something unique with the Apple TV 2. It opened up the world of iPhone streaming in a way previously only thought possible in the world of jailbreaking. In fact, the capabilities that are given to one's iPhone simply by having an Apple TV 2 connected to a television make it a must-buy accessory in my book. Like the similarly important AirPort Express, the Apple TV 2 is also $99. Not exactly "nothing," but hardly a bank breaker for those already investing in an iPhone.

Although I've alluded to some of the video streaming capabilities earlier in this section, here I focus on taking full advantage of a little thing that Apple calls "Mirroring." AirPlay Mirroring was a completely new addition in iOS 5, and it's this addition—which is only becoming more impressive in iOS 6—that really makes the Apple TV 2 purchase worthwhile.

WARNING AirPlay Mirroring is a fantastic technology, but it doesn't always work… fantastically. Too many walls, flaky routers, and bad karma have all been blamed for sporadic dropouts, so if you're planning to watch a movie or play a game that'll require multiple hours of beaming, I suggest picking up a Digital AV Adapter ($39). That will allow a corded HDMI connection to connect your iPhone and HDTV, and while it's hardly as convenient, the signal will be a lot more stable.

Without any trickiness on your behalf, you can send anything and everything on an iPhone display to your HDTV, so long as there's an Apple TV in between. This has long since been possible with a dongle that protruded from the iPhone's dock connector, but cutting the cable entirely makes a world of difference.

▶ Sadly, older iPhones (prior to the 4S) are left out of the Mirroring fun, as is the original iPad.

What does Mirroring really mean for you? For one, it means that your iPhone can now be used to showcase photo slideshows, stream Netflix, and even show Keynote presentations on a big screen. This is also a cheap way to get out of buying a new game console for the 45-year old kid in your life. How so? Even games are beamed wirelessly to whichever television your Apple TV 2 is connected, so that $9.99 racing app can be more than just a personal piece. In fact, it's not inconceivable to think that single-player gamers wouldn't opt for this type of setup over a traditional console; after all, the average iPhone game is four to five times cheaper than a home console title.

In order to activate Mirroring on the iPhone, simply ensure that your Apple TV 2 and iPhone are connected to the same Wi-Fi network. Then, double-tap the Home button and swipe twice from left to right as the Secondary Dock bar emerges at the bottom. The AirPlay icon should be there in that central row of buttons; give it a press, and select the Apple TV 2 from the list of options. Also, switching from landscape to portrait mode on the iPhone will rotate the image on screen. If you are watching a movie and prefer that things remain horizontal for a bit, be sure to activate the software orientation lock once you're situated.

TIP While Mirroring may focus on video, there's actually much more you can do with an Apple TV 2 connected to an entertainment center. While AirPlay-enabled speakers and receivers work well, those who already have their speaker systems linked to their television can actually skip a step. If your Apple TV 2 is the wireless liaison between your speakers and iPhone, you're able to DJ a party from your phone without having to invest in new speakers or a new A/V receiver. Moreover, with everything tied together, it's one less fragmented portion of your home entertainment setup. Oh, and you can even have a fancy visualizer running on your television as the music pumps. I won't be offended if you take the credit when your new pals drop by and ask.

Making AirPlay (and Your iPhone) Even Better

In most scenarios, adding special functionality to a product that Apple itself doesn't deem "doable" requires a tricky software hack dubbed a "jailbreak." It's a common term that describes the process of modifying certain files on an iPhone in order to let unapproved applications and scripts run free. Naturally, it opens your device up to all sorts of hacker shenanigans, but if you're smart, you'll open your device up to all sorts of functionality that would otherwise be out of reach.

ADDING MIRRORING SUPPORT TO THE IPHONE 4

If you still have an iPhone 4 kicking around and you aren't afraid to jailbreak it, it's possible to enjoy Mirroring. Unfortunately, you'll still need a VGA or HDMI adapter (no wireless!), but outside of that the steps are fairly easy. An easy-to-follow guide can be found here: www.redmondpie.com/how-to-enable-hdmi-video-mirroring-on-iphone-4-ipod-touch-4g-tutorial.

JAILBREAKING, AND WHY YOU'D EVEN BOTHER

I won't go into great detail on *how* to jailbreak your device, for one simple reason—it voids your warranty. Apple has made no secret that it's strongly against the practice, but I'm including this section for a couple of reasons. For one, your iPhone may be out of warranty already. Secondly, there's at least a sliver of chance that you couldn't give two hoots about what Apple is for or against. And finally, the reality of the situation is that jailbreaking is a heck of a lot of fun, and the apps found in those unapproved app stores can be way, way more titillating than the ones certified for distribution in the *actual* App Store.

iOS 6 has been one of the toughest builds yet to crack. Not surprising, given that Apple's likely making it more and more difficult with every release. There are a handful of names that you'll need to know in order to stay up-to-date on the ebb and flow of the jailbreak. Comex, Grant Paul (chpwn), Jay Freeman (saurik), and Muscle-Nerd are the ringleaders, and all of these fine folks can be found on Twitter with a simple search. As for websites? Be sure to bookmark www.jailbreakme.com and blog.iphone-dev.org. Both are go-to sources when it comes to jailbreaking, and you can rest assured that they'll have up-to-the-minute information about the latest cracks.

Once a jailbreak is applied, you'll need to surf over to the Cydia app store. There are a few more repositories, but that's the main one. It's effectively an app store that Apple doesn't approve of, and you should know that any app there is "download at your own risk." Nothing there has been quality-checked by Apple, but if you're adventurous (and you feel like trodding through online forums regardless of the latest and greatest unauthorized app), you can find all sorts of programs that allow you to customize notifications (SBSettings), tweak your lock screen (LockInfo), multitask differently (Activator), and even use your iPhone's Internet as a mobile hotspot—MyWi, Tetherme, or PDANet—without paying carrier fees for tethering.

MAKING ANYTHING AND EVERYTHING AIRPLAY-COMPATIBLE

If you're serious about hacking and you're comfortable coding, there's a program you should know about: ShairPort. It's an unofficial dump of the ROM trapped within Apple's AirPort Express, and now that it's exposed, you can effectively add AirPlay audio streaming support to any piece of software in existence. So long as you can interweave the ShairPort code into an application, it'll register as an AirPlay device. In fact, if you're into DIY electronics, you can even embed this code into your own homegrown AirPlay hardware. Crack your knuckles and download it here: http://mafipulation.org/blagoblig/2011/04/08#shairport.

EXTENDING THE FUNCTIONALITY OF YOUR APPLE TV 2

Surprise, surprise! You can jailbreak your Apple TV 2, too! Unlike iOS jailbreaking, doing so on Apple's nifty set-top box requires some dough, but you (and your iPhone) will appreciate the added functionality. Firecore's aTV Flash is available for both the original Apple TV and the new Apple TV 2, with pricing between $20 and $30 per device. By visiting the company's website (http://firecore.com/atvflash-black), you'll be able to purchase access to a point-and-click update procedure that requires minimal hacking knowledge and no physical alterations.

You can use the Remote HD app—mentioned earlier in this chapter—to give your iPhone control over aTV Flash, which enables robust codec support, NAS streaming, web browsing, Last.fm access, and more. If you're using your iPhone to interact with your Apple TV, and you're just searching for *more* than what Apple's willing to give you, this may indeed be worth an install. It's easy to remove, too, should you decide that the new interface just isn't for you.

SUMMARY

Tapping into the (mostly undercover) AirPlay functionality that's tucked within iOS 5/6 is a surefire way to justify your iPhone purchase. That said, a few relatively easy hacks and tweaks can bring a couple of highly useful features (including Mirroring) to the iPhone 4. All it takes is a bit of searching, clicking, and patience.

On the audio front, you're just a speaker system (or AirPort Express) away from being able to use your iPhone to wirelessly DJ a party. And because AirPlay uses Wi-Fi instead of Bluetooth, the range is far greater. There aren't a plethora of AirPlay-certified speaker options out just yet, but the ones that have made it to market are really impressive—and expensive.

As for video? There are plenty of secrets to learn there, too. The iPhone's Mirroring functionality—unlocked first in iOS 5—gives you the ability to send Netflix, home videos, and even FaceTime calls to the big screen. But if you want to dig deeper, there are plenty of jailbreaking options for extending the capabilities of both the Apple TV and the iPhone. One thing's exceptionally clear: the iPhone is opened up to an entirely new world of control with the purchase of Apple's $99 Apple TV. It's worth budgeting for.

CHAPTER 8

Cutting the Cord: Utilizing Wireless Functionality

IN THIS CHAPTER

▶ Printing sans wires

▶ Sorting out device compatibility

▶ Taking advantage of Wi-Fi sync

▶ Understanding when the plug is superior

▶ Transferring files from device to device

▶ Using Bluetooth to transfer files

If I didn't make it clear enough in Chapter 7, the iPhone is at its best when no cables are involved. It just feels less like a tool and more like a... magic wand. I'm sure Harry Potter would agree. In newer builds of iOS, and in iOS 6 in particular, Apple has granted the iPhone wireless abilities that some may argue it should've had from the start. Wireless printing and syncing everything from contacts to music over Wi-Fi are now included. This chapter covers the ins and outs of the wireless features that are often overlooked on the iPhone, and even dives into the art of wireless transfers between devices. Bluetooth and Wi-Fi will be the driving forces at work, but as always, it takes a little effort on your part to facilitate the connection. Eager to get more done while cutting even more cables? You're in the right place.

CUTTING THE USB CORD

I have to wonder if even Apple knew that its proprietary Dock Connector would end up being the barnburner that it has been. It's quite remarkable, actually. There's a USB port on one end and a Dock Connector on the other, but you'd be hard-pressed to know which one was the "universal" of the two.

Indeed, the proliferation of Dock Connector accessories and compatible peripherals is staggering, and these days, it's the devices that *lack* support for a Dock Connector that are considered anti-compliant. The iPod and iPhone have become so prevalent that the Dock Connector has become standard fare on lots of audio-related gear, but it's now clear that Apple may be planning the funeral of its own socket.

With the introduction of AirPlay and the many, many cloud features in iOS 5 and iOS 6, it's becoming less and less important to have a Dock Connector cable nearby. Of course, until wireless power is implemented (remember the Palm Pre?), we'll still need one for the wall, but the goal after this chapter is to simply unplug it from charging and leave the cable there. Believe it or not, it's feasible in a lot of situations.

▶ Fun fact: Even Sony's newest speaker docks have iPod support. If you can't beat 'em, join 'em?

Taking Advantage of AirPrint

What's most attractive about AirPrint—the ability to send print jobs to a nearby printer without wires—is just how (relatively) easy it is to use. In typical Apple fashion, all of the functionality is baked right into the operating system, so there are no drivers to tinker with, no additional software to install and—most importantly—no cables to connect. You can see an example of just how integrated it is in Figure 8-1. AirPrint can do its thing in the background, too, so once you send out a Print command, you push the dialog aside and get back to whatever it was that you were doing—sifting through e-mail, flipping through a slideshow, or becoming engrossed in that *X-Men* trailer.

Getting started, however, requires a bit of elbow grease. On second thought, it may actually require a bit of hard-earned cash. You see, not every printer is designed to play nice with AirPrint. As nice as it would be for the iPhone to be able to print wirelessly to any printer ever built, part of that "no driver" deal is the inclusion of software on the other end. And that means a new printer, perhaps. To date, only seven major printer manufacturers are producing AirPrint-enabled printers: Lexmark, Brother, Dell, Samsung, Canon, HP, and Epson. The list of compatible printers is certainly growing, though, and there are currently a few dozen options to choose from. The full (expanding) list can be found here: http://support.apple.com/kb/ht4356.

▶ At first, only HP had AirPrint-enabled printers, but the list of companies that support AirPrint has since grown by seven. Expect more to join as the bandwagon forges ahead.

FIGURE 8-1: Have a look at the new sharing menu in iOS 6, including the Print option.

AirPrint Alternatives

If AirPlay was any indication, you may have a sneaking suspicion that there simply *has* to be some way around the aforementioned stipulation. After all, buying a new printer just to print a few documents per month from your iPhone doesn't exactly sound ideal. Thankfully for us all, the third-party development community is coming to the rescue once more.

For those diehard Mac users, there's a phenomenal piece of software called Printopia 2 that enables your iPhone (and any other nearby iOS device with AirPrint support) to send Print commands to practically any printer in the known universe. Assuming it's in your home and in some way affiliated with your Mac, of course. All you need is a printer of any description plugged into (and configured to work with) your Mac. Or, you can have a network printer plugged into a connected Time Capsule or AirPort. A shot of Printopia 2's control panel (seen in Figure 8-2) shows how well integrated it is in OS X's settings.

▶ Apple's Time Capsule ($299+) is an 802.11n wireless router and NAS backup drive that also has a USB port for your shared printing needs.

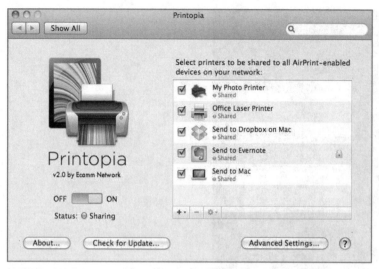

FIGURE 8-2: Printopia 2 blends right into OS X's Settings; no separate app required.

It'll even recognize printers that are simply connected to the same router as the one your Mac is on, be it via wire or wireless. In case you haven't caught on, as long as you have a connected printer that's set up to work with your Mac, the installation of Printopia 2 creates the missing bridge that allows your iPhone to view it as an AirPrint-enabled printer.

The software is available for free on a trial basis from www.ecamm.com/mac/printopia, but the full version costs $19.95. It's important to note that this is software *for your Mac,* not for your iPhone. There's no App Store download required, and no jailbreaking or other tomfoolery necessary. If the program is installed on your Mac, the printers will show up in the exact same spot on your iPhone with no configuration necessary on the device.

> **TIP** Perhaps the most impressive feature in Printopia isn't its printing abilities, but its virtual printing abilities. One of the most difficult things to do on an iPhone is get a document, a photo, a web page—anything—from the iPhone to a computer with little to no fuss. It generally requires some strange third-party app or some mysterious series of clicks to e-mail something to yourself. By enabling your iPhone to print to an unlimited number of virtual printers, you're able to "print" a file directly to your Mac or even send files directly to a Mac app such as iPhoto and Evernote, as well as Dropbox. Talk about seriously cutting the cord on file transfers!

It's also worth mentioning that Printopia 2 works with a shocking amount of legacy Macs. Even Leopard (OS X 10.5) and PowerPC-based Mac users can download the utility and take advantage. Unfortunately, there's no Windows client to speak of, and the company certainly doesn't seem eager to change that in the near future. But, as you'd expect, there's an alternative for those who have Microsoft's OS running the house.

If you'd prefer a workaround with a bit more of a multi-platform vibe, there's Air-Print Activator (shown in Figure 8-3). It's a subtle, less sophisticated application that effectively does the same (basic) thing as Printopia 2. It allows non-AirPrint printers to be seen by one's iPhone. But unlike Printopia 2, it sticks to rudimentary printing functions. On the upside, it's absolutely free, although donations are obviously encouraged if it ends up suiting your needs. Installing it on a Mac is as easy as downloading the program and tucking it in your Applications directory. That can be downloaded here: http://netputing.com/airprintactivator/airprint-activator-v2-0/.

For Windows users, things are (unsurprisingly) a bit more complicated. But if there's anything I hope you've learned thus far, it's the adage, "If there's a will, there's a way." If you want to enable AirPrint on a Windows XP, Windows Vista, or Windows 7-based machine (32-bit or 64-bit), you need to do a little more manual labor. And by that, I mean manually creating a few file folders, mashing OK through a firewall warning, and feeling extra proud about yourself in the end. The complete

FIGURE 8-3: Flip it to On. Do it!

how-to guide is here: http://jaxov.com/2010/11/how-to-enable-airprint-service-on-windows/. If you're concerned about your ability to follow instructions, or you'd simply rather pay someone $9.99 for the convenience of something simpler, there is *one other* Windows option worth mentioning. Collobos has launched its FingerPrint software—shown in Figure 8-4—for OS X and Windows platforms, and similar to Printopia 2, no jailbreak (or software installation at all, for that matter) is required on your iPhone. That option can be downloaded here: www.collobos.com.

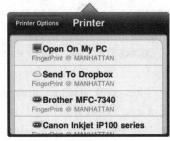

Finally, there's experimental support for printers working in conjunction with Linux. The step-by-step can be found at the following link, but more so than with any other OS, your miles may vary: http://forums.macrumors.com/showthread.php?t=1265049.

FIGURE 8-4: So many wireless print options with FingerPrint

WI-FI SYNCING YOUR WAY TO CORDLESS FREEDOM

Thinking back on it, it's a little crazy that we ever had to connect our iPhones to a computer in order to have very basic and essential information synced between the two. But, as with most things, it was probably easier said than done when it came to putting the necessary architecture in place behind the scenes. Starting with iOS 5— according to Apple—you don't actually need a computer any longer in order to fully operate an iPhone. Of course, what it isn't telling you is that it's still *highly* beneficial to have one tagging along, but at least you don't actually have to physically connect the two with a cable.

WI-FI SYNC'S BEGINNINGS

The introduction of Wi-Fi Sync was an uncharacteristically tumultuous one. If you're looking for a quick history lesson, here goes. Greg Hughes, a university student at the time, submitted an app called Wi-Fi Sync to Apple in May of 2010, where it was subsequently rejected for breaking a few rules in the developer handbook. But, as it turns out, Apple actually pinged Greg, asked for a résumé, and affirmed that it was "impressed" by his app submission. Nothing ever became of that relationship, but after Greg tossed Wi-Fi Sync into the Cydia App Store (for jailbreakers)—selling around 50,000 copies at $10 each—Apple soon launched a like-named service of its own. Curiously, this isn't the first time such a case has cropped up; a gal had an app similar to Apple's own iAds rejected, only to soon be aped by the designers in Cupertino.

As it stands, Wi-Fi Sync isn't an app. It's an innate, built-in feature of iOS 5 and 6, and you see it just as soon as you start your iPhone for the first time.

CROSSREF Specifics on enabling Wi-Fi Sync are discussed in Chapter 1.

I'll make it easy for you: you have two options when it comes time to sync your contacts, Safari browsing data, e-mail, photos, apps, and music. You can go the wired route or you can do the wireless thing. A quick survey has confirmed that the latter of the two is what all the "cool kids" are into. Jesting aside, here's what you need to do if you're interested in syncing things up wirelessly.

TIP I *strongly* recommend running your initial sync with a cable. That first one— where you are most likely to push many, many gigabytes of audiovisual content onto your iPhone—is arguably the most important. It's also the most likely to take the longest, given that so much information is being transferred. Trust me on this one: be wired at first, and then go wireless.

After your initial sync is complete, you'll want to change something in your iTunes settings *while your iPhone is connected* with the standard USB/Dock Connector cable. On the Summary page in iTunes, scroll down to the Options block and look for the Sync With This iPhone Over Wi-Fi box. Check it. Now your iPhone's set up to... sync over Wi-Fi! From there, you can disconnect the cable, grab your iPhone, and begin part two of this operation. See for yourself in Figure 8-5.

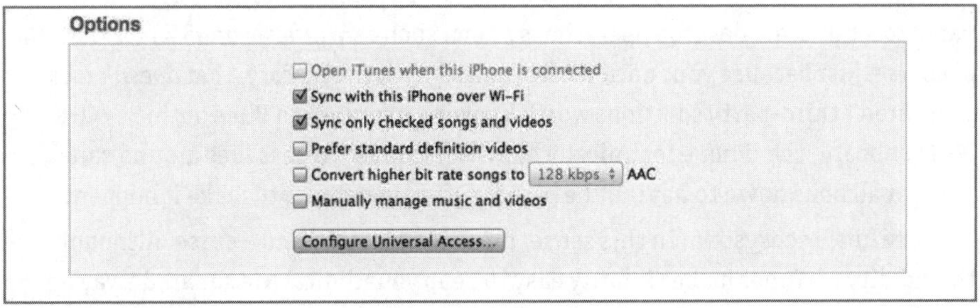

Options

- ☐ Open iTunes when this iPhone is connected
- ☑ Sync with this iPhone over Wi-Fi
- ☑ Sync only checked songs and videos
- ☐ Prefer standard definition videos
- ☐ Convert higher bit rate songs to [128 kbps ⬍] AAC
- ☐ Manually manage music and videos

[Configure Universal Access...]

FIGURE 8-5: Find this option on the first pane within iTunes.

Because it's obvious that you won't be initiating iTunes syncs with iTunes, it *should* be obvious where to initiate it on the iPhone. But, it's not. Here's how to initiate a sync from the iPhone itself—head into the Settings app, then to General, then to iTunes Wi-Fi Sync. The icon up top—if your iPhone and your host computer are online on the same Wi-Fi network—should say Sync Now. Give that a tap to begin the process.

> ▶ Make sure you have at least 10% battery life before starting a sync!

A few words of warning with Wi-Fi syncs. First off, be sure you have two or three bars of Wi-Fi signal before starting one. And then, make sure you have plenty of time. Depending on the amount of new data that's being shuffled around, it could take anywhere from 20 seconds to 20+ minutes for a wireless sync to complete. If only a few files have changed since your last sync, you won't have to wait too long. If, however, you're hoping to add a gigabyte or two of new music, it could take a solid 15 minutes for it to complete.

In testing that I've done, particularly with larger syncs, Wi-Fi syncing takes between 8 and 15 times *longer* than USB cable syncs. That's fairly significant from a percentage standpoint, but when you're talking about 6 minutes versus 20 seconds—well, as long as you aren't in a hurry to make an exit, 6 minutes isn't too awful—particularly if you're in a different room than your host computer or you don't have immediate access to a USB/Dock Connector cable.

The good news, however, is that your iPhone is fully functional while Wi-Fi syncs are ongoing. In other words, you don't have to sit around and wait for a sync to complete before you can browse the web, send an e-mail, or enjoy a round of Angry Birds. That fact alone makes the idea of waiting 10 times longer entirely more palatable.

▶ If your iPhone is set up to sync over Wi-Fi, it will automatically sync whenever it's plugged into power, so you don't have to initiate it in that case. Of course, the host machine you're syncing with also has to be awake.

MASTERING DEVICE-TO-DEVICE TRANSFERS

As I alluded to in prior chapters, one thing the iPhone is actually a bit weak on is file transfers. You can thank the innate limitations of a mobile operating system (compared to a full-scale desktop operating system, such as Windows or OS X) for that. But of course, just because your options are limited from the factory, that *doesn't* mean there aren't third-party solutions worth knowing about. With Bluetooth, 3G/4G and Wi-Fi onboard, the iPhone technically has the hardware to pass files around sans wires; it all boils down to having the proper software in order to make it happen.

The iTunes ecosystem, in this sense, is really a blessing and a curse. Although the rigidity of iTunes makes it fairly easy to keep your digital life squared away on your host computer and your iPhone, it also makes doing anything outside of those invisible bounds a bit of a challenge. Apple hasn't even included native support for e-mailing every file type on the iPhone, so you can imagine how difficult the transfer of material using any other method is. (Although, with iOS 6, you can now add pictures and videos from the Compose menu in the Mail app by long-pressing in the body section.) In this section, I offer up a few tried-and-true solutions for getting things to and from the iPhone.

Using Dropbox

▶ If you need more storage, you can grab 100GB for $9.99 per month, 200GB for $19.99 per month, or 500GB for $49.99 per month.

Dropbox. To all but the technologically misinformed, this term is probably one that's known well. It's a program that actually acts a lot like Apple's iDisk—a feature the company curiously killed as it phased iCloud into existence. But unlike iDisk, Dropbox is about as universal as it gets. The premise is fairly easy to grok: you sign up for an account, which gives you 2GB for free. This 2GB is available on pretty much any platform you can imagine, and so long as you log in to each account with the same e-mail address, you'll find mirrored views of your stash everywhere. The Dropbox iPhone app is shown in Figure 8-6.

FIGURE 8-6: Say hello to Dropbox on the iPhone.

TIP Although it's not wireless (yet), DiskAid is a hugely powerful program for Windows and Mac platforms. When used in conjunction with the FileApp app (available for free in limited form, $4.99 for the Pro version), users can transfer files to and from any app installed on an iPhone.

In other words, if you upload a document on your Windows machine to Dropbox, you'll see it immediately on your Mac, iPad, iPod touch, and Android smartphone within seconds—all without any extra effort on your part. It's pretty fantastic, and it serves an incredible purpose on the iPhone.

If you're hoping to send myriad documents, e-mails, and PDFs to your iPhone for offline viewing—this is important when you travel overseas or into areas where you know that finding Wi-Fi will be a challenge—Dropbox is tailor-made to help you out. My suggestion is to convert (or Print to PDF) documents and messages into PDFs, and then host them all in a named folder within your Dropbox account. Once they're uploaded, your iPhone will be able to open them, and once loaded, they'll repeatedly open without having to ping back to the Internet.

▶ Be careful not to assume that Dropbox will download your files automatically. You need to manually download each file once on the iPhone while connected to the Internet.

TIP One of the biggest iPhone limitations is the one-way street that surrounds cloud transfers. For example, if you open a text document, you can only view it. You can't edit it within Dropbox, and you can't even ask Dropbox to allow another application to open it, edit it, and then save it back to your Dropbox account. There's no universal solution yet, but in apps that support WebDAV (like Apple's Pages), you can tap into the power of the $5/monthly WebDAV app, available on the App Store. DropDAV lets you interact with Dropbox files through a conventional WebDAV connection, which allows you to edit on the phone and then save it back via the same unorthodox channel. It's a bit of a hack job, but it does the trick! You can read more here: **www.dropdav.com**.

If you're not interesting in monkeying around with WebDAV connections, and you only need very basic text-editing capabilities, there are a few app options to consider. Elements ($1.99) and iA Writer ($1), both beautifully seamless, and all are Dropbox-compatible.

Working with Box.net

The similarly-named Box.net does many of the same things that Dropbox does, but it's geared more toward small businesses and IT professionals. In other words, it's not as simple, but the advanced feature set may prove useful for those who have money or resources on the line when it comes to file sharing. Aside from enabling all sorts of business collaboration features, it's also completely free to try.

What's more, Box.net's iPhone app even taps into a few of Apple's most impressive built-in features. Using AirPlay, you can wirelessly stream Box content to an Apple TV for seamless projection of photos, videos, and presentations, and it'll also support video output via Apple's Dock Connector to VGA Adapter.

Multimedia Streamers

Make no mistake; iTunes facilitates the movement of audiovisual content from your host computer to the iPhone. But more often than not, I'm guessing that you'd like to have content magically appear on your iPhone, rather than have to touch base with iTunes. There aren't too many easier ways to get that kind of material onto your iPhone, but it's important to think about alternatives here. Storing content locally isn't the only way, and in most cases, it's actually the least desirable way.

The concept's pretty simple, actually. What if you could use some Wi-Fi device to beam content to the iPhone for easy viewing? A lot of companies have had the same thought, and this section carves out the best of the best for more easily piping music, videos, and photos onto your iPhone. Sorry iTunes—you're about to get circumvented.

CLOUD ALTERNATIVES

Although Box and Dropbox are the file-shuffling mainstays, you have plenty of alternatives. In fact, a new player seems to crop up every other month or so. Here's a short list of solid, oft-updated options should the big boys not tickle your fancy:

▶ **SugarSync**: This highly sophisticated file-sharing app doubles as a backup solution

▶ **SpiderOak**: Enables you to e-mail any file from the iPhone's mail client, and allows access to all of the data you have backed up across your various devices regardless of platform

▶ **Wuala**: While effectively accomplishing the same thing as Dropbox, Wuala offers a native Linux client for those using Linux host computers

▶ **Nomadesk for iPhone**: Designed specifically for unlimited (yes, unlimited) storage and sharing, but requires a $35 monthly payment per file server

▶ **Google Drive**: Now that Google's own cloud-hosting solution has an iOS app, this is a must for anyone that avidly uses Google's suite.

ACCESSING VIA AIRSTASH

If you shoot videos and stills on a camera that uses SD (Secure Digital) cards, you owe it to yourself to consider yet another $99 accessory. The AirStash looks like a beefed up SD/SDHC card reader, and in fact, it is. There's a USB plug on one end and a slot for your full-size or micro Secure Digital memory card on the other. If you simply plug it into a PC, it'll function as a card reader. But that's hardly what's magical about it.

The *real* pizzazz lies within. There's a multimedia streamer, an internal battery, and a Wi-Fi module all tucked inside, which allows any audiovisual content on your SD card to be transferred to your iPhone over Wi-Fi. The accompanying app, not surprisingly, is completely gratis. After all, you need the $99 hardware in order to actually use the software. The app allows users to wirelessly stream movies, view and import photos, listen to music and podcasts, and view documents stored on your AirStash. AirStash+ (that's the name of the app) is an enhanced

▶ Don't try to stream DRM-laced files over AirStash. They won't work, sadly enough. (DRM stands for Digital Rights Management, and acts to keep media files from being pirated.)

▶ For shooters that shoot RAW, you'll be happy to know that format is supported. In-the-field previews are a go!

alternative to the built-in web app and includes features only possible with a native app. You can stream materials into the browser by directing your iPhone to connect to the Wi-Fi access point created by the AirStash, but why bother? It's all about apps at this point.

WIRELESS PROJECTIONS

Although it's highly specific, the free Panasonic Wireless Projector for iOS app (available on the App Store) enables consumers to send PDF files and JPEG images saved to an iPhone, iPad, or iPod touch to a Panasonic wireless projector over a wireless network. You can send PDF files transferred from a PC via iTunes to the Documents folder of this application, and JPEG images saved to the Photos folder of your iPhone, iPad, or iPod touch. You can also project websites with the built-in web browser, and photos taken with the built-in camera on your iPhone, iPad, or iPod touch. In addition, the application lets you rotate the screen, enlarge or reduce the screen with a pinch operation, and flip through pages with a flick operation.

Granted, this works only with a certain class of projector from a certain company, but it proves that interest is there. With time, expect this type of functionality to be baked into more and more devices, enabling even more wireless power to be emitted from the iPhone's antenna array.

HARD DRIVE-BASED STREAMERS

AirStash is a terrific device, *if* you have SD cards full of content. Although a multi-format card would probably serve a greater slice of the population, there is one more alternative to AirStash. Both Kingston and Seagate have hard drive-based solutions, which allow audiovisual content socked away on an external (and yes, portable) hard drive to be streamed over Wi-Fi to one's iPhone. Both of them also have batteries within, so a couple hours of wireless streaming is totally feasible. These devices are fantastic for kids on road trips; just load one up with their favorite movies before leaving, and let 'em stream at will in the back seat without any wires whatsoever.

▶ Seagate's option is also capable of streaming directly to a web browser, so pretty much any device is compatible.

Kingston's Wi-Drive starts at $130 for a 16GB model, whereas a 32GB model is $175. Seagate's GoFlex Satellite is far more sizable, but with 500GB of capacity at $200, it's arguably a far better deal than Kingston's alternative. It also streams to up to three devices at once, and that includes Android devices.

CAMERA-TETHERING SOLUTIONS

You have a couple of options when it comes to transferring photos onto your iPhone. For slowpokes, there's the iTunes sync with your photo galleries on a host computer. For budding hares, there's Apple's own Camera Adapter kit. For wireless aficionados, there's the AirStash method mentioned previously. But there's an even *better* solution for all of the sects mentioned in this chapter, and it doesn't matter what camera you use or what kind of memory card is in your camera.

You'll need a few things in order to make the magic happen: your iPhone, a camera with an Eye-Fi memory card, a wireless network, and a $15.99 app dubbed Shuttersnitch. Never heard of Eye-Fi? They specialize in producing Secure Digital memory cards with built-in Wi-Fi modules. In other words, having one in a camera allows images to be distributed over Wi-Fi as soon as they're captured.

▶ Eye-Fi has stuck to SD cards, but CompactFlash users can always pick up an SD-to-CF adapter.

That's how the chain of events begins. You shoot a photo, and the Eye-Fi card is primed to send it. But to do so, you need a wireless network nearby. The easiest way to create one is to use a Mi-Fi device—I recommended that those who longed for a 3G iPhone opt for one earlier, and now you have yet another reason to choose that option over the integrated 3G service. Once a network is in place, you need to connect your Eye-Fi card and your iPhone to it; having them on the same network is essential for the process to work as it should.

Now, you need Shuttersnitch running on the iPhone. That's a highly specialized app that'll suck down photos passed over through an Eye-Fi card. Seconds after a shot is taken, you'll see it right on your iPhone's display. From there, you can browse, pinch, zoom, and evaluate, and your original shot will remain on your camera's memory card. It also allows users to arrange shoots in albums, lock private albums, resize or watermark shots before sharing (via e-mail, FTP, Flickr, SmugMug, Zenfolio, Facebook, or Dropbox), geotag incoming photos, add a caption and byline to the photos, and much, much more.

▶ There are plenty of wireless tethering options that use a host computer in between, but the Shuttersnitch setup doesn't require a middleman.

If, however, you don't need an advanced program to watermark or significantly tweak the incoming photos, and you don't mind buying a new SD card, there's one more option you should know about. The Eye-Fi X2 (and only the X2) supports Direct mode. That's a short way of saying that it's capable of sending photos directly to the iPhone, without a Mi-Fi or other network in between. So long as your iPhone has Wi-Fi enabled and the free Eye-Fi app is launched, you're in business. In fact, it'll work even if the app is running in the background in iOS 5 or 6.

The app accepts full-resolution images, and it automatically sorts by date captured. You can also send over videos, and you can share select clips or shoots via your favorite social networking program (including Facebook, Flickr, Picasa,

SmugMug, and YouTube). Eye-Fi also has an Android app that allows Google devices to accomplish the same thing, but you have to pony up $99.99 for an 8GB X2 card. You can learn more about the whole operation here: `www.eye.fi/how-it-works/features/direct-mode`.

CREATING AN IPHONE FILE SYSTEM

One of my biggest gripes with the iPhone—a gripe that is shared by many—is that there's no file system. That limits its functionality in a number of ways, but not in a way that can't be at least patched over by third-party development. Air Sharing, an $8.99 app available on the App Store, allows you to wirelessly mount your iPhone as a drive on your host computer. From there, you can create folders and load it up with files—things like Excel documents, PDFs, and so on. Better still, no cable is required; it mounts as a wireless drive, and you can drag-and-drop files as you would on any conventional flash drive.

▶ In other words, tell all of your iOS-using friends to download a copy of Air Sharing if you're looking to easily swap files.

With OS X, the iPhone is found automatically via Bonjour, while Linux users can connect via SSH. Windows users need only download the free Copy FTP desktop app. Beyond the conventional file sharing capabilities, it's yet another facilitator of wireless printing, and it will auto-detect Air Sharing on other devices for tablet-to-tablet (or tablet-to-phone, and so on) sharing.

TAPPING INTO BLUETOOTH

A decade ago, Bluetooth was the go-to protocol when it came to short-range sharing on phones. Everything from ringtones to photos were slung from friend to friend using some of the earliest Bluetooth stacks, but today, Bluetooth has slipped into the background when it comes to file sharing. By and large, most modern-day mobile devices have a Wi-Fi module built-in, and given how much quicker Wi-Fi transfers are... well, there isn't much incentive to stick with Bluetooth.

▶ Bluetooth can be used to link headsets for Skype calls, and to beam music to Bluetooth-enabled speakers, too.

Except, of course, that you may be dealing with devices that have only Bluetooth. You have a few options when it comes to transferring files with Bluetooth, and the only ones worth paying attention to are developed by third parties. For whatever reason, Apple includes no functionality whatsoever for Bluetooth file transfers directly from the iPhone. Thankfully, Apple hasn't ignored developers who figured that some users might be interested in this very functionality.

Without question, the premiere Bluetooth transfer app for iPhone is Bluetooth Photo Share by Nathan Peterson. Best of all, it's free and it doesn't require that your iPhone be jailbroken. It works as advertised for sharing contacts and photos, and better still, it doesn't compress images that are shared. The receiver not only gets the full-resolution image, but also sees a thumbnail of the shot as it's being beamed over. Just remember: you need to keep your iPhone and the other iOS device close to one another. Bluetooth's pretty finicky, truth be told.

Need to transfer something other than a contact or photo? I figured you might. Bluetooth Share HD, available on the App Store for $1.99, allows two iOS devices to share files, photos, and contacts. You can also use your iPhone as a USB disk to store files and transfer them between iPhone and computers.

If you're looking for completely unrestricted Bluetooth file transfer capabilities, there's an app for you. But—and it's a big but—you'll need to jailbreak your iPhone. If you're comfortable doing that, you can head to the Cydia app repository and download Celeste for $9.99. This app enables users to send and receive images, contacts, music, iBooks and just about anything else (using iFile, which is also available on Cydia). But unlike the "approved" options, this one allows files to be transferred between iOS devices *and* between an iOS device and any other Bluetooth device that supports OBEX (OBject EXchange) transfer capability.

Perhaps the best solution is Bump. It's a free app, and it allows iOS devices to share contacts and photos. Your iPhone can also easily transfer contacts and photos to a Mac or PC by having your computer visit http://bu.mp on a web browser. Be aware, however, that photos you take with your iPhone won't be transferred across as full-resolution; they're scaled down a bit to make the transfers quicker. If you need the full-res version, you'll still need to transfer that via iPhoto.

> **WARNING** The vast majority of Bluetooth-sharing applications in the App Store are poor quality, and rarely do what they say they will. But even with the solid ones mentioned in this chapter, you'll be best served by keeping the transferring devices close to one another. Bluetooth transfers are (comparatively) sluggish, and if you stray beyond 20 or so feet, it's likely that your transfers will fail.

SUMMARY

The iPhone's wireless functionality doesn't stop with AirPlay. Given just how adept it is at creating and viewing content, tweaking it for an optimal wireless printing experience is a great place to jump in. Once you've had a taste of just how much is possible without wires holding you back, the possibilities are then only limited by the imagination of the developers pushing apps into the App Store.

Tapping into AirPrint (or just tricking your existing printer into believing that it's compatible) is a great start, but syncing files without a USB cable is where the real magic begins. Keeping the Wi-Fi Sync to yourself just seems rude. Device-to-device transfers are possible through both Wi-Fi and Bluetooth, although the speed and ubiquity of the former is making the latter less of a go-to solution. There's an entire stash of cloud-based apps designed to make hosting and viewing files a cinch, but I've shown a few tricks that'll allow you to edit things on your iPhone, too.

PART III

DIVING INTO SOFTWARE

Game On with Game Center

In May of 2010, Nintendo of America President Reggie Fils-Aime said that Apple was their primary "enemy of the future." That was stated shortly after Nintendo's CEO Satoru Iwata said that the battle with Sony was "already won." A decade ago, Apple was the laughingstock of the gaming universe. The company's platforms were so underutilized by the mass market that the vast majority of developers didn't even bother porting their Windows and console titles to Mac. 'Twas a sad, sad state of affairs. Now, iOS has completely transformed Apple's position in the gaming universe, and in many ways, Apple is now the company to catch. Mobile gaming has shifted dramatically in recent years, with mobile phones and tablets becoming powerful enough to handle the gaming that was once reserved for portable handhelds. Game Center is Apple's first major foray into the gaming universe, but the company doesn't go to great lengths to publicize its features. This chapter discusses the ins and outs of Game Center and shows you the ropes to getting connected, staying engaged, and keeping tabs on your progress. Yes, I show you how to be vain. Only kidding.

GETTING JACKED IN

Although Apple has received a stunning amount of praise and credit for its innovations of late, it doesn't do everything right. In fact, the company has missed seriously when it comes to social networking; its Ping music network went nowhere after popping up in iTunes. But unlike Ping, Game Center has traction and all of the pieces are in place for it to see the kind of growth that people expect from Apple. Check out the app's understated motif in Figure 9-1.

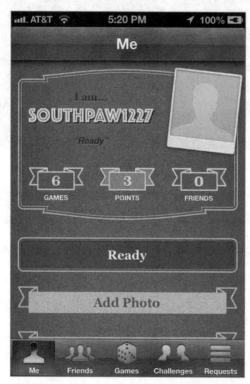

FIGURE 9-1: A look at Game Center on the iPhone

NOTE Apple recently soared past 130 million Game Center users. For a service that just recently came to the platform, that's pretty impressive, and it's proof that iOS device owners are interested in gaming. It's also more than a newsstand for games; instead of just housing your games, it's a place where your profile lives and thrives, your achievements are stored, and your next multiplayer game is just a click or two away.

In a nutshell, Game Center is a gaming social network. If you're familiar with console gaming, it's most akin to Xbox Live or the PlayStation Network, but only for iOS devices. Game Center, in a way, is like a newsstand, acting as a unified portal for your Game Center-enabled titles. Furthermore, it allows users to locate and track friends, start or join a multiplayer game, track achievements, see where they stand globally, and easily find new titles to try.

> **TIP** As you might expect, there's a way to override Apple's limitations in regards to using Game Center with older iOS versions. In theory, the iPhone 3G just isn't powerful enough to handle some of the more advanced multiplayer titles now available in the App Store, so rather than providing limited support (which, let's be honest, could lead to huge frustrations), the company decided to simply not offer it at all on that device. Turns out, some iPhone 3G owners wanted in anyway, and if you're willing to jailbreak your device, you can bypass Apple's stipulations and join in for a little underground gaming fun. Within the ModMyI repository (found in Cydia), search for HDR/GameCenter Enabler. That app does exactly what you'd expect—once it's installed, Game Center is just a tap or two away. Be warned, however, that the app is only approved to work in iOS 4.1; your miles may vary when using it with any other build. Full instructions can be found here: www.machackpc.com/how-to-install-gamecenter-app-on-iphone-3g-running-ios-4-1.

Understanding the Setup Process

Game Center is quite unlike any other built-in app on the iPad, or within iOS 5/6 as a whole. It's one of the few places where Apple actually asks you to register; for the most part, an iTunes ID is enough to get you around in iOS. Although I do recommend using your iTunes ID to sign up for Game Center, you can create a different username than the associated e-mail address—useful for privacy reasons. As you can tell, my birth name and my gamer tag are different in almost every respect.

I strongly recommend creating a username that's nothing like your e-mail address and reveals nothing about your personal identity. I've never been one to don a tin foil hat, but there's just no compelling reason to let strangers in multiplayer game sessions know precisely who you are.

▶ Friends can still find you via username or e-mail, even if your full name is kept private.

After you've created a username, you can click the stock Photo icon to the right of your username in order to select a new avatar (see Figure 9-2). That's shorthand for a photo that represents your online profile; you can either select a shot from your image gallery or use the iPhone's camera to capture your mug on the spot.

Of course, you can use the Change Photo button to do the same. Just above that, there's a space for you to input your status. Oddly, Apple provides no predetermined lines—messages like Online, Away, BRB, or Ready would make a lot of sense. At any rate, a tap of that button will pull up the iPhone's virtual keyboard, where you can input any status you want. Folks who have you in their friends list will see your status as you update.

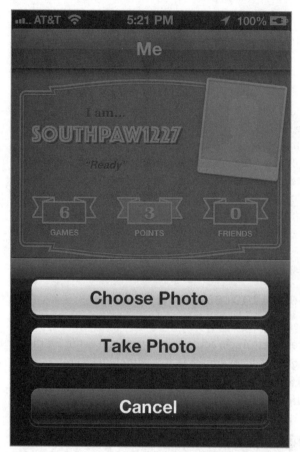

FIGURE 9-2: You can choose a photo of your pup, a photo of your mug, or anything in between.

New to iOS 6 and Mountain Lion over on the desktop side is Challenges. Now, you can challenge opponents on their Macs to play against you on your iPhone, assuming the title is available for both platforms. Fancy!

Navigating the User Interface

Apple includes but four main tiles to sift through: Me, Friends, Games, and Requests. I'll start with the third. The cluster of icons dotted across the top isn't there just for show. Tap 'em and they'll take you into a windowed view of the App Store page for the respective apps. Basically, these are game recommendations based on rankings and ratings from Game Center users. It's a great way to get your feet wet when you're overwhelmed with possible options. These selected apps tend to be highly played, polished, and well regarded, making them great no-brainer options if you're unsure where to start. Not every one is free, however, so be careful about jumping into each one and installing.

Moving back a notch, you should visit the Friends tab as soon as you get a couple of titles in the stable that you're interested in playing. If you're online (and you're *always* online, right?), the iPhone will scour your Contacts list in order to find acquaintances that also have a Game Center account. Given that Game Center accounts are assigned by e-mail address, it's pretty easy for the system to put two and two together. This is a good reason to ensure that your Contacts app is stuffed with e-mail addresses, and not just phone numbers.

▶ It's highly important to have your Contacts in order. They impact more than just your daily forwarding list.

FIGURE 9-3: It's the App Store... inside of Game Center.

▶ The final main pane—Requests— couldn't be simpler. You can respond to any requests from folks to add you as their friend. Easy!

Start by tapping the Recommendations banner at the top; in there, you'll find recommended additions. Once you've sent all the requests you'd like from in there, the + button enables you to manually search for new pals via e-mail address or username. (See the interface in Figure 9-4.)

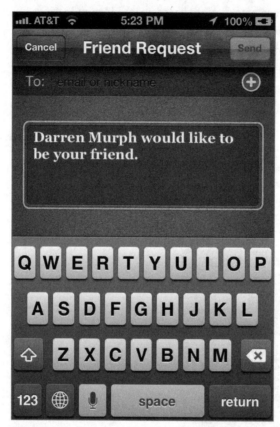

FIGURE 9-4: Got a friend? Add 'em!

NOTE Up top, you'll notice an A-Z button, a Recent icon, and a Points button. The Points button showcases your friends (or enemies) in order of most points to least; naturally, this is the place to go if you need a little motivation in getting your scores up.

Keeping Notifications in Check

Starting with iOS 5, Apple completely overhauled its notification system. In fact, it was one of the most notable, visible, and fundamental changes to iOS since the platform's inception. Aside from taking a few cues from Google's Android, Apple has also enabled some fairly specific controls for notifications. Rather than just giving users the option of having them on or off, or giving users the option of customizing how they appear, Apple has enabled *both* of those for pretty much every major (and in some cases, minor) facet of the system.

Regardless of how you have your Notifications arranged for other portions of the operating system—be it Messages, e-mail, FaceTime, Reminders, Facebook, Twitter, or Calendar—you can tweak your Game Center notifications to make them more useful and less annoying. How? Simple. Head to the Settings app within iOS. Tap the Notifications icon and select Game Center. From there, you can toggle the Notification Center, choose how many notifications to show (I recommend five or ten unless you're a hardcore gamer), and choose an alert style.

The alert style is the most important. I recommend using Banners. Alerts are the typical pop-up notifications that troubled so many users in earlier builds of iOS, interrupting whatever it was you're working on and forcing you to respond immediately in some form or fashion. The three options beneath that (Badge App Icon, Sounds, and View in Lock Screen) are most useful if left on, but those who'd rather disable Sounds can certainly take a hint via the visual cues available in Alert Style. Have a look at what you should be seeing in Figure 9-5.

> **NOTE** With iOS 6, Game Center added Challenges and Facebook Connect. Challenges is a way to quantifiably track victories and losses specific to people you send them to. Facebook Connect enables you to pull in friends from your existing Facebook friends list.

If you end up amassing a load of friends—and given just how stunning you look, why wouldn't you?—notifications can easily get out of hand. In that situation, head to Settings → Notifications, and turn the Alert Style to None and Sounds to Off. That'll leave only badges on, which are the least invasive way to keep track of other events going on within Game Center.

▶ Check out Android's pull-down notification window, and then do the same in iOS 5 and 6. See any similarities?

FIGURE 9-5: Tweak Game Center's notifications before they tweak your nerves.

DISCOVERING AND DOWNLOADING NEW GAMES

▶ Take a deep breath: Angry Birds is compatible with Game Center.

Truth be told, Game Center is nothing without games that are compatible with it, and the functionality is severely limited without an Internet connection. Remember, this is a social network for games. Without the social aspect, it's just another hub for games. The Games icon along the lower edge is where I recommend starting. Tap Game Recommendations from there. The games that tend to be most addicting (and rewarding) are those with Achievements. If you're unfamiliar with the term, Achievements are any number of accomplishments that toss "points" into your account once you reach a certain goal. The more you play—and the better you are—the more points you acquire.

Not all Game Center games support Achievements. It's pretty easy to spot, though. When you click into any title in the Recommendations grid, you'll spot a Leaderboard and Players tab; on occasion, you'll see an Achievements tab in the middle. By tapping there, you can see what goals lie ahead, and you'll know ahead of time what you need to strive for in order to rule the roost. As you play a particular game and hit those achievements, you'll see them "unlocked" in this panel. The great part about having your entire account tied to the cloud is that those achievements translate between iOS devices; as long as you're signed in with your iTunes ID, you'll have all of those statistics saved and visible.

Given the "social" aspect, it's no surprise that Apple provides a way to invite your best buds to download (and hopefully play) any title that you're fond of. But as of now, the suggestion feature is a bit spartan. Rather than being able to tap into your address book, invite via iMessage, or just send invites to folks who are already in your Friend list within Game Center, you're given the option to send an e-mail. Thankfully, you *can* pull addresses from your Contacts here, and with iOS 6, you can pull 'em from your Facebook friends list.

In an effort to quell any confusion from hopping in and out of apps, I want to point out that downloading games from within Game Center isn't *exactly* the same as downloading one from the App Store. Let's say you tap the price (or Free) icon; from there, you're taken to a windowed App Store, where you then have to tap the price or Free icon again. If you aren't signed in to your iTunes account, you'll need to type in a password. Then, the app will download to a home pane on your iPhone, effectively exiting your Game Center session. Once you hop back in, however, your new title should be sitting there, desperately longing for attention.

If you're looking for a broader range of apps, or perhaps a more simplistic way to find games that the masses deem awesome, you can do so within iTunes. Once you've opened the program, pay a visit to iTunes Store ➜ App Store, and gaze over at the right rail. There's a box there entitled App Store Quick Links. A few lines down, you'll spot the Games Starter Kit, an oft-updated catalog of the highest rated, most played Game Center titles on the entire App Store. If you're the type who prefers a higher power making decisions for you, this is absolutely the place where your discovery should begin. (And don't worry, it's okay to get ideas of what you might or might not like using a total shortcut like this.)

▶ Farmville is Game Center-compatible, too. Take another deep breath.

▶ You can easily wade through your games by using the Search box in the top right of the Games pane.

▶ iMessage is an iOS-to-iOS communications protocol seen first in iOS 5. It's like BBM—the messaging protocol adored by BlackBerry users—but for iPods, iPhones, and iPads.

PROTECTING YOUR PRIVACY

Given that we live in a world full of connected devices, GPS hounds, and location-based deals, it's not surprising to hear of a privacy outrage related to this app, that program, or [*insert company here*]. Apple has certainly been at the center of a few of those, and although there's nothing tremendously worrisome about Game Center, I do want to point out one recommendation that most folks would probably never see without a fair bit of digging.

By default, your Game Center profile is "public." What that really means is that your profile—including your real name—is visible to other players. The upside to allowing this is that Game Center will recommend you to other players using your real name, and your nickname will be used on public leader boards. Not surprisingly, I'd strongly recommend disabling your public profile.

In order to do so, hop into Game Center, visit the Me pane, and click your Account banner. Once you enter your password, your full account pulls up; the Privacy slider should be set to Off, disabling your public profile. Once this is complete, only your added friends will be able to see your real name, although keep in mind that Game Center will no longer recommend you to other players and your nickname won't be shown on public leader boards. My opinion on this is clear: I'd rather not be on a leader board if it means my full name is widely available to the entire iOS universe.

▶ While we're on the topic of removing things, it's worth noting that you can't "remove" a game from Game Center unless you delete the app entirely.

KEEPING A HANDLE ON RESTRICTIONS

Game Center's a joyful place, sure, but the fees can add up if your youngster gets in there and starts purchasing in-app additions at will. If you're planning to allow your children to tap into Game Center in order to pass the time (or keep 'em quiet on the long trip to grandmother's house), you should absolutely set a few boundaries beforehand.

I recommend heading to Settings ➔ General ➔ Restrictions. From there, you need to create a Restrictions PIN code, which allows only the owner with that four-digit code to make changes. Once you're in, you can scroll down to Apps in order to disable access to apps that are rated for a certain age category (or disable apps altogether), and beneath that, you can disable in-app purchases altogether. If In-App Purchases is flipped to Off, you and yours will be unable to ding your linked credit card from within an app. Plenty of games offer in-app purchases; if you aren't careful, it's quite easy to slip a game update into your iPhone with a subtle charge.

▶ In-app purchases can quickly turn a "free" app into a very costly one. Many new programs are using this free-then-fee structure.

If you'd rather your kids keep the gaming to themselves (but you still want to allow them to track achievements), glance down to the Multiplayer Games section and flip that toggle to Off. Not a bad idea if you're not keen on having perfect strangers play games with your own offspring. (Yeah, this may sound extreme to some, but it's great that Apple has included the option here for the overly paranoid.) Taking things a step further, you can disable the Adding Friends option if you'd rather your kids not be able to accept unsolicited friend requests.

▶ If you'd like to take things to the extreme and remove Game Center as a whole, you'll need to jailbreak your iPhone and download an app called Poof!

GOING BEYOND THE GAME

You may be wondering if there's a second level to Game Center, or if beauty truly is skin deep. Without getting into any philosophical conversations, I'd like to point out that app developers are making Game Center into something much more robust than Apple likely intended. In fact, the name "Game Center" may not even be applicable if the trend continues. Fact is, there are quite a few titles in the App Store that tout Game Center compatibility, yet aren't games at all. These apps simply tap into Game Center's use of achievements and social networking, but aren't "games" in the slightest.

One of my favorites is 100 Cameras in 1, a $1.99 app that acts as a cross between Instagram and Foursquare. In essence, this camera app allows users to add filters and tweak photographs taken on their iPhones, as well as unlock certain achievements based on the location of their photos and which filters they use. It's a clever way to encourage the continual use of an app, and sure enough, it aids in the discovery of the app's sizable feature set.

The honest truth is that the vast majority of Game Center titles available today are indeed games, but there's a burgeoning market out there for non-games. Even if you aren't into gaming, it's worth keeping an eye on new apps that land with Game Center support. Every so often, one filters in with a category *not* named "Games."

NOTE If, for whatever reason, you aren't satisfied with Game Center, there actually is another option for gaming-related social networking on the iPhone. OpenFeint is a third-party network that serves a similar purpose, and there are a growing number of compatible games popping up in the App Store. Moreover, OpenFeint is also supported over on Android, enhancing the potential for critical mass. It's worth checking into if you're a serious gamer: www.openfeint.com.

SUMMARY

Perhaps surprisingly, gaming has become not only an integral part of iOS, but the iOS has actually become a leader in the portable gaming space. Companies like Sony and Nintendo are now paying attention to a new enemy, and the introduction of Game Center acts as proof that Apple is taking this initiative seriously. Before you dive into Game Center too deeply, it's best to set up your account, establish your privacy limits, and set any restrictions on in-app purchases. If the idea of downloading new, unheard-of titles sounds daunting, don't worry—Apple's Recommendations portal helps you ease into what'll likely become the addiction.

Unlike most other apps on iOS, Game Center is prone to tossing out dozens—if not hundreds—of notifications, particularly for those who have a significant amount of friends. Calming that storm is fairly easy if you know how, though. Game Center is most beneficial (and enjoyable) when you take advantage of the social aspects; tracking achievements, watching your friends move up and down the leader board, and inviting contacts you haven't touched base with in a while to a few friendly bouts of Touch Tanks.

Game Center is primarily used for games today—not surprising given the title. But there *are* non-game titles being published with Game Center support. Even users with little to no interest in gaming can find something useful in Game Center, with 100 Cameras in 1 being an excellent example of how the Game Center functionality can spread to other genres in the App Store.

Useful Productivity Apps

Apps. They make the world go 'round. And no matter the problem you have, "There's an app for that." It's pretty astounding to think that when iOS launched originally as iPhone OS, there was no App Store whatsoever. Trying to envision a successful iPhone today sans a market place for apps is nigh impossible, and it's clear that Apple's mobile stable of devices has seen skyrocketing adoption largely due to the creativity and determination of its third-party developer community. Today, apps aren't just a part of iOS, they are iOS. Apple has done a phenomenal job making beautiful, desirable hardware, and it has also done a laudatory job optimizing its hardware and software in order to provide a world-class, rock-solid user experience. But the rest of the equation is filled in by people who aren't even employed by a company in Cupertino. Apple's biggest strength in the smartphone and tablet market is its App

Store. One of the first questions that people ask me upon purchasing an iPhone is this: "Which apps should I download?" With well over 300,000 apps on the App Store, it's a huge chore to wade through those in order to find a worthwhile handful. In this chapter, I cover a wide array of genres and categories, dishing out my favorites and a few off-the-wall inclusions that you may not normally hear about through the proverbial grapevine. Everything from reading to traveling to learning is covered, and even if you're not a bookworm, there's no harm in using your iPhone to increase your productivity.

CALENDARS, MAPS, AND TO-DO TOOLS

▶ An iPhone is the perfect replacement to that pen-and-paper method you've relied on for way too long.

When it comes to being productive on the iPhone, there are few tools more essential than a solid, trustworthy calendar. Apple has improved its built-in Calendar app quite substantially with the introduction of iOS 5 and 6—and those new notification options go a long way to making it more useful. But with hundreds of thousands of apps at your disposal, you can rest assured that more options are out there.

Keeping those appointments tied to the cloud is an even wiser move. Self-contained calendars haven't been useful for years, but a shocking amount of people still have their events tied to one single device, inaccessible to any other device (or even to a web browser). In the age of dumbphones and PDAs, that was forgivable; in today's world of hyperconnectivity, your calendar can be everywhere at the same time.

NOTE   Even grandmothers and infants have heard the term "app" by now. After all, that's half of the phrase "App Store." But what's in an app, really? Best I can tell, app is shorthand for application, but over the years, it's been slanted for use in the mobile realm. Recently, with the introduction of the Mac App Store and confirmation that a similarly styled shop will open in Windows 8, app has also been used to refer to desktop software. Apple actually doesn't hold a trademark on app; Google Apps were around in 2006 and the Amazon Appstore obviously uses it right in the title. But, Apple does own a trademark for "There's an app for that." The good news in all of this for iPhone owners? When a company gets a trademark for something, there's probably some amount of truth behind it; sure enough, you'll have no issues finding more iPhone apps than you'll ever have time to explore in Apple's App Store.

Benefits of Using Apple's Calendar App

I have to imagine that folks eying a brand new vehicle ask themselves a similar question—do they opt for the built-in factory navigation system, or do they simply pick up a $99 Garmin unit to serve that purpose? The former is sleek, form-fitting, and beautifully integrated. Every morsel of it is able to interact with the vehicle's buttons and triggers, and no aftermarket tinkering is necessary. The latter, of course, is inexpensive. It's also more customizable—you can opt for any size or shape, with just about any feature set to serve your needs.

Two highly compelling options that, in the end, will serve the core need. But both options will get you there in very different ways. I recommend giving Apple's built-in option a go, at least initially. Not only is the layout quite pleasing to the eye (judge for yourself in Figure 10-1), but it's also fairly easy to tweak it so it works with any existing Google Calendars you have.

▶ In truth, even a $99 Garmin could be replaced by Google Maps Navigation on Android or by an inexpensive app on an iOS device.

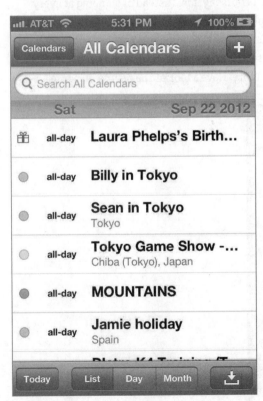

FIGURE 10-1: Calendar: making an impossible schedule seem a bit less daunting.

Referring back to the "well-integrated" bit, there's no calendar in the App Store more tightly integrated than the one Apple provides. In fact, this aspect is the strongest selling point for it. What does integration entail? Three things, primarily.

SPOTLIGHT SEARCHING IN CALENDAR

First off, the Spotlight Search feature I detailed earlier only works with Apple's built-in Calendar app; no third-party calendar app can be added. It's unfortunate that Apple doesn't provide Spotlight APIs to developers in order to add that, but as of now, it's just the way it is.

If you're wondering why this matters, allow me to queue up an example. Let's say you know you have a meeting with Alexander at some point this month. Your mother asks if there are any evenings coming up that wouldn't work for a surprise house-warming party. You immediately remember that you've blocked out a Thursday evening with Alexander, but you've no clue as to which Thursday it is. Instead of glancing at every Thursday in your calendar, you can simply double-tap your iPhone's Home button and type "Alexander." So long as Alexander's name is in that meeting notice, Spotlight will pull up the exact date and time in mere seconds. If you use any other calendar app, you won't get this kind of quick-search capability. Have a look at the results in Figure 10-2.

▶ In fact, Spotlight won't search for anything in a third-party app.

FIGURE 10-2: Lookie there—finding an appointment is just a search away.

Furthermore, Spotlight works *frighteningly* well. Even if you can only remember the first couple of letters in someone's name, it'll do its best to locate upcoming events that match whatever letter combinations you can muster. In many cases, it'll pull up invites that you were searching for with a shockingly low amount of information. It works so well, in fact, that it has become my go-to way to search through my calendar events.

If you're already inside the Calendar app, head over to List view to search from within. As you can see in Figure 10-3, it's also pretty elegant.

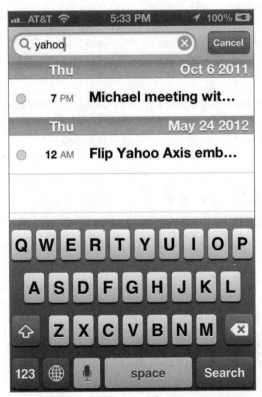

FIGURE 10-3: A look at Calendar's built-in Search function

CROSSREF You can learn more about customizing Spotlight for your needs in Chapter 5, "Multi-Tasking Magic".

▶ It's worth perfecting your notifications; without that pestering, your appointments might go unnoticed.

NOTIFICATIONS AND DROP-DOWN REMINDERS

Apple is giving developers the tools they need to add notifications to apps within iOS 6. In other words, third parties can now create programs that allow for notifications to be pushed to users, and for those alerts to even show up in the new notification pull-down menu. Of course, just because the APIs are there, doesn't mean developers will use them.

As it stands, Apple's built-in Calendar app supports push notifications (which can be tweaked and customized in Settings ➔ Notifications). Whenever you set an iPhone event or a synced Google Calendar event (as examples; other calendars work, too) to ping you before an appointment, you'll get a note that appears in and remains in your pull-down menu until you tap it away. It's a fairly beautiful way to stay abreast of what's coming up; just glance at the pull-down bar, and anything you've asked to be notified of will be sitting there.

On top of all that, there's no extra cost to using Calendar, and as easy as it is to chide Apple on this, you can't delete it, either. In other words, it'll be hanging around on your home pane regardless, so you'll need a really good reason to use something else.

> **NOTE** It's worth mentioning that Apple's built-in applications, including Calendar, are doubly useful when you throw in Siri integration. Just hold down your Home button and tell Siri when to make an appointment, how long it'll last, and who needs to be invited. Adding appointments via voice is a huge reason to stick with first-party programs.

Third-Party Calendar Apps

Wouldn't you know it? There actually *is* a good reason to try something else. If you fit a certain set of criteria and you're willing to spend a little cash, that is. Apple's built-in Calendar app may be superb, but it's hardly a one-size-fits-all solution—particularly for hardcore Google users. As I've stated before, the iPhone and Google's suite of applications don't always get along, and neither company is particularly inclined to help the other in making the compatibilities seamless. Thankfully for us all, there's a market outside of Silicon Valley that actually yearns for tighter integration, and they have the apps to prove it. The following list describes calendar apps that are worth looking into, and the reasons behind them. Just search for each within the App Store to pull up their information and purchase pages.

> ▶ **Readdle Calendar** ($6.99; also works with iPad)—What makes this option special is the *even tighter* integration with Google Calendars. It allows you

to manage your calendars online and offline, and it supports the "drag-and-drop" functionality that has become a staple of using Google Calendar in a conventional web browser. In fact, the biggest selling point here is just how much the entire thing mimics the actual Google layout; if you're more comfortable with the Android environment, this is a great option. The real kicker is the support for Google Tasks; for those who make constant use of Tasks, losing them in Apple's default Calendar can be a serious buzz kill. In addition to all that, this app supports SMS alerts to upcoming events, the ability to search events/tasks, and the ability to undo additions you accidentally make.

▶ **Pocket Informant** ($9.99)—Calling this "just a calendar" probably does the app a disservice. This is one of the most elaborate, sophisticated calendars available for the iPhone, and indeed, it does far more than just keep track of events in nondescript squares throughout the year. It's more of a digital datebook, with pages to flip and sections to comb. You can view year and month views simultaneously, with a detailed task and filter system helping you to keep tabs on which events and duties are coming due, which are overdue, which are in progress, and which are completed. It's more like a life organizer, but the calendar function alone is truly exceptional.

▶ **Calendar+** ($1.99; also works with iPad)—It's drop-dead simple and not nearly as full-featured as the others mentioned here, but it's also among the cheapest in the App Store. The primary selling point here is the multi-colored view and the automated syncing with built-in calendars that you've already set up. It also accepts new events while you're offline, and then syncs them back to the cloud as soon as you're connected.

▶ **Agenda Calendar** ($0.99; also works with iPad)—The apps described so far generally add something *more* to what Apple's built-in Calendar app offers. This one strips features away. It's aimed at consumers who don't want extras cluttering up their calendars, although there's a surprising amount of advanced functionality hidden just underneath. It's designed to give you "at a glance" views at what's hitting you next—during your workday, that's the most important, anyway. It works best if you set everything up in Apple's Calendar first, and then allow Agenda to pull things in from there. This app also supports notifications in the pull-down ("Notification Center") and on the Lock Screen.

ALTERNATIVE CALENDARS

Naturally, the App Store is home to all sorts of alternative calendar apps, but what if you're in need of specialized calendars? To borrow a line from Apple's vault: "There's an app for that." Here are a few quirky, highly specialized calendars that just might strike your fancy.

► **Moon Calendar** ($0.99)—View the phase of the moon for any month, in any location, as well as rise and set times for both the sun and moon.

► **Pampers Hello Baby Pregnancy Calendar** (free)—Week-by-week guide of what to expect during weeks 4 to 40; great reference guide for new moms.

► **GW Calendar** ($4.99)—A far snazzier interface than what's offered through Novell's stock GroupWise WebAccess portal.

► **WomanLog Pro** ($1.99)—Yes, it's a menstrual and fertility calendar. No, it's not "a great gift idea" for husbands, boyfriends, girlfriends, or any other "friend."

► **Sports Free** (free)—Perfect for keeping tabs on schedules from every major sporting league.

► **Baby Countdown** (free)—Counting down the days to delivery? Don't get it wrong!

Navigational Guidance

Things have changed a lot on the navigation front from iOS 5 to iOS 6. In iOS 5, the factory Maps app relied on data from Google, and while it did give you routing instructions from one place to another, it wasn't a turn-by-turn solution. To fill that void, apps from Garmin, TomTom, Navigon, and a host of others emerged in the App Store. With the introduction of iOS 6, however, vehicular turn-by-turn guidance is included for free.

As the tensions rise between Google and Apple, Apple chose TomTom to provide the mapping data used in the new Maps application present in iOS 6. Because it's TomTom, turn-by-turn guidance for automobile transportation is included in select regions (the USA is obviously accounted for). This means that Google will now be able to submit its own standalone Maps app on the App Store, much like it has done with YouTube.

Of course, the question now is this—because Apple throws in a free navigational app with iOS 6, do you need to look any further? The answer is "yes."

The new Maps app on iOS 6 currently supports turn-by-turn directions only with personal vehicles, as well as walking instructions. If you need mass transit directions, train directions, or bus directions, the app becomes less useful. That said, it's still my go-to app when using a car; I can simply speak my destination to Siri (for example, "Directions from current position to the Empire State Building in New York City") and it will automatically begin the routing. This hands-free approach is brilliant, and will no doubt be safer than hunting and pecking to input a destination while trying to dodge traffic.

Speaking of traffic, the new Maps app also shows accidents and takes traffic flows into account when routing you, all for free. If you'll be actively using a navigation app while on motorcycle, bicycle, foot, or mass transit, I recommend a combination of apps. First, spring for Telenav's Scout guidance app. It's a great turn-by-turn backup that won't cost you a dime to download, but it also provides the ability to operate *offline* for just $2.99 per month or $9.99 per year. (It also recognizes voice input, separate from Siri!)

Wrangling Reminders

There are a nearly endless number of ways to keep tabs on what you need to keep tabs on, digitally. Some folks just create reminders in their calendar app, but if you're looking to keep appointments and your to-do list separate, there's a very real need to utilize Reminders. Clearly, Apple realizes this. It has included a dedicated app within iOS 5 (yes, it's called Reminders) that cannot be deleted—just like Maps, Messages, Calendar, and so on. There's definitely a good deal of value in using what's tightly integrated with the operating system, but for those yearning for more, the third-party world seems to have the to-do-list app market completely satisfied. I'll discuss both sets of options here.

BENEFITS OF APPLE'S REMINDERS APP

The usual lead-in applies here: when using a built-in app in iOS 5 and 6, you gain certain advantages that apply only to apps that are actually built into the fabric of the OS. Reminders is a fairly simple app, but it does what it purports to do. Upon launching the app, you can create or delete new reminder lists, as well as create actual things you need to be reminded of. From there, you can sort them into lists, which is useful for keeping your repeating to-do items categorized somewhat. Have a glance at the interface in Figure 10-4.

▶ Despite your hunches, Reminders and Calendar are separate apps, and there's not too much interplay between them.

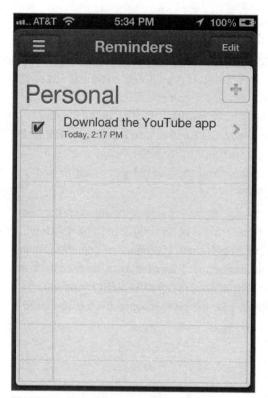

FIGURE 10-4: Apple's Reminders app is simple. Maybe too simple for some users.

▶ iPhone owners can set up location-based reminders, and can also input reminders via voice thanks to Siri. Just toggle Siri and start your request with "Remind me...."

Reminders can also be synced to the cloud—the iCloud, that is—if you enable it in Settings ➔ iCloud ➔ Reminders. (Have a peek in Figure 10-5.) This may not strike you as particularly beneficial, but those who also carry any other iOS device will certainly benefit from this feature. The iCloud sync feature enables you to view a reminder you created on an iPhone on your iPad, and vice versa.

CONSIDERING THIRD-PARTY TO-DO APPS

Truth be told, there's really only one third-party reminders app to be concerned with. That app, as you may have heard, is Remember The Milk. RTM is actually a full-featured website, and it enables you to interact with your account and manage your profile from any web browser on any machine. There just happens to be apps to access the same service, with the iPad, iPhone, and iPod touch being supported. The app enables you to add and complete tasks on the go, while having it all synced to the cloud. You'll have access to priorities, due dates, time estimates, repeating lists, tags, and more, and you can even see tasks nearby and plan the best way to get things done. You can be reminded

▶ Try to use to-do/reminder apps that support push or SMS notifications. Without these alerts, you're apt to forget!

via e-mail, SMS, and instant messenger, and amazingly, the basic version of the app is free. For $25 per year, you can upgrade to a Pro account, which unlocks unlimited syncs (instead of one per day), usage on multiple devices, and push notification reminders.

FIGURE 10-5: Toggle Reminders to be synced across iCloud on or off here; but mostly on, if you want to remember your appointments on any device.

In the interest of expanding your horizons, I list a few slightly off-beat alternatives that may be a better fit for your specialized reminder needs:

▶ **BugMe! Stickies Pro** ($1.99; also works with iPad)—If you're a fan of Stickies on OS X, you'll love this. You can craft alerts and pin them to a virtual corkboard within the app, and if the traditional reminder alert isn't enough, the visual board might be.

▶ **Due** ($4.99; also works with iPad)—This is a highly rated, frequently updated app that's overly simple in design and is engineered to handle short-term reminders with poise. I love the contrast with a calendar; use the Calendar app for long-term, repeating appointments, and use Due to handle the random to-dos that pop up during the course of the average day.

- ▶ **Task Pro** ($1.99; also works with iPad)—It does everything that Reminders does, but the multi-tiered approach to tasking makes it more flexible and easier to organize than most other options.

- ▶ **OmniFocus for iPhone** ($19.99)—Don't even bother diving in here if you aren't serious about organizing your digital life. At nearly $20, this is easily one of the most expensive apps you'll find in the App Store, but there's a ton of value here for those who need a sophisticated, robust to-do app for handling their personal and business lives. Cloud-based syncing is supported, and free e-mail and phone support is thrown in, too.

- ▶ **Corkulous Pro** ($1.99)—A clever name for a clever application. If you're coming from the School of Old where reminders were scribbled on scraps of paper and pegged to a corkboard, this app is most certainly for you. It allows you to place photos and notes on a virtual corkboard, and multiple boards are supported in order to help you segment your tasks and reminders.

OBLIGATORY OFFICE APPS

You spent hard-earned money on the iPhone, so it might as well pay you back in some form or fashion. It's true that most Office-style programs were designed for inputs from mice and keyboards, but now that the iPhone has been out for a few years, app producers have tweaked programs to accept multi-touch inputs. There's no question that working on documents with the iPhone is typically slower than using a full-fledged notebook or desktop, but toss a Bluetooth keyboard into the mix and the playing field levels somewhat. Of course, hardware's just half the battle. In this section, I touch on a handful of world-class Office apps that handle documents, spreadsheets, and presentations.

> **CROSSREF** Look for accessory and peripheral suggestions in Chapter 17, "Ace Accessories".

Believe it or not, Microsoft doesn't make a version of its Office suite for iPhone. Only heaven (or perhaps Bill Gates) knows why. It'd clearly sell like hotcakes based on brand name and familiarity alone, but it's probably for the best. Instead, there are a number of third-party alternatives jousting for your bucks, and that intense competition makes 'em all better.

▶ **Quickoffice Pro** ($14.99)—It's the preeminent Office-compatible document app for iPhone. It takes full advantage of the extra screen space, masters the art of input via touch, and boasts a multi-edit tool that enables users to quickly format text, numbers, colors, paragraphs, backgrounds, and cells, minus the multiple menus. It's also dead simple to navigate to files, and the built-in integration with cloud services (Dropbox, Google Docs, Box.net, Huddle, SugarSync, Evernote, and Catch) ensures that any files you create or documents you edit can be pushed back onto the web as soon as you're done with them. It allows you to create, edit, and share Microsoft Word, PowerPoint, and Excel files, and the extensive amount of shared functionality (Find and Replace, as an example) makes it easy for Office addicts to adjust to.

▶ **Documents To Go** ($9.99; also works with iPad)—The primary advantages of this guy over the first option should be clear—it's cheaper and it also works with the iPad you probably own. It allows you to open, edit, and create Microsoft Word, PowerPoint, and Excel documents, not to mention RTF, iWork, PDF, text documents, and more. The real kicker is the gratis desktop version that comes with your purchase, enabling users to two-way file sync with a Wi-Fi connection.

▶ **Apple iWork suite** ($29.97; also works with iPad)—Strangely, Apple doesn't sell a discounted bundle of its three homegrown Office apps, but you can still pick up Pages, Keynote, and Numbers separately for $9.99 apiece. These are Apple's document editor, presentation editor, and spreadsheet editor, and not surprisingly, they're amazingly intuitive. Apple clearly built these specifically for multi-touch, and they're undoubtedly the most elegant, easy-to-use Office apps for iPhone. Toss in iCloud integration, and I'm finding a hard time not recommending this trio *strongly*.

▶ **Documents 2** ($1.99; also works with iPad)—Can you really go wrong? It's a full-fledged document suite editor for under two bucks. It lets you store, manage, print, and share all your photos, documents, spreadsheets, and recordings in one place on your iPhone, iPod, and iPad. Furthermore, the user interface is very "File Explorer" like, so it should be quite familiar to anyone who has used a computer in the last decade. You can also view, edit, e-mail, and share (using Google Sync, AirPrint, Wi-Fi, or USB) whatever you open or create.

PRESENTATION IS EVERYTHING

First impressions go a long way, and if you're pitching a startup or just showing off your analytical wizardry in a staff meeting, having a beautiful presentation setup can go a long way. These days, lasting through a conventional PowerPoint presentation is a feat in and of itself, but using the iPhone to present with has been scientifically proven to both maintain interest while leading to higher projected earnings from future promotions. Okay, I confess, I made most of that up, but anyone who stares at slides for a living probably understands the point. Not only does AirPlay give presenters an even sexier way to showcase their pitch, but the iPhone as a whole is far easier to connect to a projector, far less likely to crash halfway through, and way more tailored to "present" than any work-issued laptop you have laying around.

> **CROSSREF** AirPlay functionality is addressed extensively in Chapter 7, "Streaming Your Multimedia Without Wires: Airplay".

Contrary to popular belief, presentation applications are actually useful for more than just business. Avid travelers can easily showcase trips with jazzed-up presentations, and parents who are entirely too active in their local PTA meetings could use this to petition for new band uniforms. Best of all, most of these apps make it possible to concoct a presentation right on the iPhone itself, and even if you create a Keynote or PowerPoint presentation on a full-fledged computer, it'll format beautifully for use on the phone. Here are a few of my favorites in the category:

▶ **Apple Keynote** (9.99; also works with iPad)—Yes, I already recommended you pick this up in the Office category discussed earlier, but in case you took that suggestion lightly, it's here again on its own. Keynote is a splendid iPhone app—largely thanks to it being built in-house at Apple for use on its own devices. If you own a Mac with the desktop version of Keynote, all the better. The most outstanding aspect of this is that it was built specifically to be controlled 100 percent by touch. It's also worth pointing out that Keynote works with iCloud, so your presentations stay up to date across all your iOS devices—automatically. It ingests PowerPoint files with no fuss, and you can import files from Mail, the web, a WebDAV service, or your Mac or PC using iTunes File Sharing.

▶ **Wooji Presentation Remote** ($7.99; also works with iPad)—You're probably wondering why you'd consider paying $8 for a presentation remote, but if you've ever priced out dedicated presentation remotes, you understand that the price point here is actually a bargain. The only major downside is the incompatibility with PowerPoint, but for avid Keynote users, it works like a gem. You can tap anywhere on the screen to spotlight your slide, with a choice of graphics and colors.

TRAVEL MUST-HAVES

There's just something about the iPhone that seems tailor-made to travel. Perhaps it's the "I never leave home without my phone syndrome?" All joking aside, most iPhone owners who I've talked to purchased one with the intent to travel with it—have iPhone, will travel, as it were. And it makes sense. It's easy to wrap your entire digital life around the iPhone, and being that it fits in your pocket, there's really no reason to hit the open road (or the friendly skies) without it.

Evidently, I'm not alone in that line of thinking, as the App Store is chock full of travel-related apps that make getting from Point A to Point B way easier than it should be. All hail technology, eh? Here's a look at my favorite iPhone travel apps— coming to you from a man who has proudly (and safely!) driven a motor vehicle in all 50 U.S. states.

▶ **Kayak** (free)—Going somewhere? No? That's a problem. You'll know the travel bug has bitten when you can't rest easy if your next trip isn't somewhere on the calendar, and there's no better way to plan ahead than with Kayak. This app is a beautifully designed portal into the famed Kayak.com website, which searches hundreds of flights in order to find you the best prices, and even gives you the opportunity to expand your search backward and forward a few days in the effort of cost savings. Why use this? Airlines have a nasty, nasty habit of keeping track of your flight searches when you search directly on their websites; if they *know* you're interested on a certain route on a certain day, they'll jack the price up the second time you search for it. Kayak searches anonymously, helping you to avoid targeted price hikes.

▶ **TripIt Pro** (free app; $49/year service)—Travel is complicated. It just is. But the journey is half the fun, and keeping those journeys organized makes things even more fun. TripIt is a fantastic free app, and I recommend trying the free version first. However, avid jet setters will appreciate the $49/year

Pro service. TripIt monitors your travel-related e-mails and automatically builds and updates itineraries as changes fly in, and you can automatically share those details with folks who need to know. You even get flight refunds on fare drops, and it helps you find an alternate flight if something gets in the way of your existing one. (*Remember to avoid the ad-free $3.99 app if you're going Pro, anyway.*)

▶ **TripAdvisor** (free; also works with iPad)—TripAdvisor's website is still an absolute catastrophe of design, but the app is surprisingly *soigné*. It's worth signing up for an account. Within the app, you can search for reviews and ratings to nearby hotels, day trips, activities, and attractions, and better still, the highly valuable forums portion of the site can also be accessed here. It's the easiest way to look for "top things to do" in any locale, but be warned: reviews aren't always what they seem. People *jump* at the chance to post a negative review, but the *vast* majority of satisfied customers will never take time to leave a positive remark. (*In other words, always leave a good review when you have good experiences!*)

▶ **Travel Interpreter** ($4.99; also works with iPad)—Here's the thing—Google's language translate app is *amazing*, but it requires data. If you haven't heard, you *do not* want to use roaming data overseas. International roaming—particularly on data—is impossibly expensive. To put it in perspective, looking up 10 words using roaming data will probably cost you between $5 and $10. This particular app has popular terms and phrases for 28 languages, and all are available offline. More than 2,200 illustrated phrases and words with audio tracks are included per language, and although it checks in at a hefty 692MB, that's a small price to pay for offline access.

▶ **National Parks by National Geographic** (free)—If there's any place in America where you can count on spotty connectivity, it's in our beautiful National Parks. Having offline access to maps and trail maps is hugely helpful, and if you haven't been taking advantage of your parks, there's no better time than now. iPhones love nature too, you know.

▶ **AllSubway** ($0.99)—Hundreds of cities, thousands of subway lines. Tough to manage on your own, particularly if you don't speak the language. This oft-updated app provides a look at subway stops in the world's most popular city centers, and if you're able to grab an Internet connection, you can also look up schedules and revised fares.

FIDUCIARY RESPONSIBILITY

If you're looking for a way to justify your "investment" in an iPhone (and in this book, while we're on the topic), you'll probably need an app or two. Good news for you—there are plenty to choose from. In fact, I've been downright shocked with how many finance-related apps are popping up in the App Store, and a handful of them are just wonderfully polished. Steve Jobs spoke of a "post-PC world" shortly before his passing, and once you start doing taxes on an iPhone (instead of a computer), you sort of feel like that future has arrived. Here are a few of my favorites for keeping finances in check:

▶ *If you haven't done so already, creating a Finance folder for all these apps is a good idea.*

- ▶ **Mint** (free)—This app allows you to track, budget, and manage your money all in one place, so you can see where you're spending and where you can save. The app is beautiful, and the web interface gives you another way to manage the same profile when your iPhone is away. It's actually pretty astounding that this service is completely free. I highly, *highly* recommend this for college-age folk or users who are just starting to build their financial foundation. If you open an account, add your bank, credit, loan, and retirement accounts, Mint will automatically pull in and categorize your transactions. Keeping things in order from the get-go makes record keeping all that much easier.

- ▶ **Compoundee** ($2.99)—You might balk at the idea of toting around a financial calculator if you aren't a CPA, but in truth, you'll know and understand a lot of these financial calculations. Money makes the world go 'round, and understanding how the decimal falls is vital to grokking mortgages, loans, and everyday negotiations. Best of all, it doesn't take a Masters in Mathematics to use.

- ▶ **Expensify** (free; also works with iPad)—What's the first thing you think of when I say "expense reports?" Thankfully, the rest of this paragraph will still be here when you return from hurling. Managing expenses is one of the most dreadful experiences for avid business travelers, but having this app around makes it significantly less so. Not only does it pull in e-mailed receipts and keep 'em in a tidy list, but you can use your iPhone's camera to snap photographs of paper receipts in order to keep track of new expenses as they happen (and before you lose said receipt). If your company allows it, you can even be reimbursed directly to a checking account.

- ▶ **iDonatedIt** ($2.99; also works with iPad)—Charitable donations are good. Fact. But keeping track of 'em is a massive headache. This app nixes a lot of the frustration with that, enabling you to keep detailed records of thrift store drops and the like as they happen. A $2.99 app just made it easy to both help folks and whack a few dollars off of your taxes. That's progress.

▶ **Square** (free; also works with iPad)—This is easily one of the most innovative, game-changing applications in the past decade. The app is free, but you need to sign up for an account at www.squareup.com. A free card reader—which sits in your iPhone's headphone jack—is shipped to you, and it allows absolutely anyone to start receiving credit card payments immediately. The fees aren't any worse than what you probably see in PayPal, but Square is a *far* more customer-friendly company. No monthly fees and no contracts. For small business users who simply have to accept credit cards in order to gain business, this is undoubtedly the best way. It even e-mails receipts immediately to those you do transactions with.

▶ **Time Master + Billing** ($9.99)—Freelancers who need to keep track of billable hours should stop here. This is absolutely the most comprehensive time-keeping app on the iPhone, and the real kicker is the included invoicing capabilities. Consultants, attorneys, and contractors (among others) can finally keep track of who owes 'em what, and yes, this tracks time right down to the second.

CALCULATORS AND TRANSLATORS

▶ *You can find calculators for nearly anything in the App Store: pregnancy, finances, weather, graphing, and more.*

Look, math is hard. Scoff if you want, but even common multiplications are a struggle when the world's crumbling down around you, you're tired, or you're just feeling lazy. Thank heavens for calculators, right? The App Store is chock full of 'em, but finding the *good* ones is a challenge. There are also a slew of highly specialized calculators and translators, and in this section I cover a smattering of my most trusted.

▶ **Soulver** ($2.99)—If you're still into the idea of doing math on paper, this app is a godsend. It's a masterfully designed program that allows you to use words alongside your numbers. It's ideal for comparison shopping, couponing, figuring out margins, or just keeping track of which numbers correspond to which data.

▶ **Digits Calculator for iPad + iPhone** ($1.99; also works with iPad)—All of these basic calculators start to run together, but the one major standout here is the ability to enter a long series of calculations and then e-mail it all to yourself for import into Numbers or Excel. You can also quickly calculate a few different scenarios by editing any previous entry to automatically update the total.

▶ **MedCalc Pro** ($4.99; also works with iPad)—It may only apply to those in the medical field, but having a full-on medical calculator at your disposal is a huge boon. Better still, this particular app is designed in a way that even the everyman could appreciate and use. Plus, it's cheaper than becoming an actual doctor.

▶ **Weight Watchers Mobile** (free; also works with iPad)—If you're already entrenched in the program, this is a full-featured app that works right alongside your program. The fitness calculator is the standout aspect, but having an app at your side can help you stay focused on reaching your goals, even while away from your desktop web browser.

▶ **Google Translate** (free; also works with iPad)—It's the quintessential translation app, supporting a staggering 60+ languages. It also translates spoken words into a foreign tongue, and you can actually listen to spoken translations for 20+ languages. Best of all, it's free; the only downside is that a live Internet connection is required.

▶ **Jibbigo** (price varies by language)—These guys started with a Spanish/English spoken translation app, but they're building out their language app library. Just search their name in the App Store and you might find the language you need; it allows two people speaking different languages to speak into the iPhone, and *without an Internet connection*, it speaks aloud the translation. Pure magic.

APPS FOR KIDS

Try as you may, you'll probably fail at keeping your iPhone out of entirely reach from your offspring. It's the whole "kids these days…" thing. Apple's touch interface is among the easiest in the industry to understand, and thus, the iPhone is almost instantly attractive to kids with wandering hands. Thankfully for you, the App Store is bursting with options for young minds.

▶ **Interactive Alphabet** ($2.99)—This one is obviously designed for the youngest of the young, but the colorful nature and masterfully designed user interface makes it a real winner in the minds of parents. It's a great first step to convincing your young one that "alphabets are fun!"

▶ **Grover's Number Special** ($2.99)—Again, this one hits at the younger-than-young crowd, but hey—it's Grover! Learning about numbers has never been so enjoyable, but I recommend this app with one word of caution—budget for lots of Grover toys. You can bet your kid will start asking for 'em.

▶ New to iOS 6 is Guided Access. Although originally designed for accessibility purposes, its ability to disable the use of the Home button lets parents enter a specific app and keep their kid there. Talk about peace of mind.

▶ For loads of amazing reading experiences, search for omBook selections in the App Store.

- **WeetWoo!** ($3.99)—A brilliant video viewer showcasing curated, tasteful, educational content for kids. Many youngsters learn better from watching videos, and the options here are endless. Better still, the app supports AirPlay so that these videos can be beamed to a connected HDTV so long as it has an Apple TV 2 connected to it.

- **Sums Stacker** ($0.99)—More than just a math app, this multifaceted learning tool integrates Roman numerals and even Spanish. It's the ultimate gamification of mathematics, and it's useful for kids of all ages.

- **Star Walk** ($2.99)—It's the next best thing to being shot up into space... maybe, anyway. This app is sure to educate both the young and old, enabling users to point their iPhones at the sky and see which stars, constellations, and satellites are above in real-time. It's a beautiful way of marrying augmented reality with education, and support for AirPlay mirroring and AirPrint make it even easier to use in group or classroom settings.

- **Fish School** ($1.99)—Letters, numbers, shapes, colors, matching—just about anything you can think to teach your budding whiz kid is here. It's an under-the-sea themed title that brushes up on the most basic of basics, aimed at "early learners" and chock full of activities. It's honestly one of the more elaborate learning titles for the iPhone targeting this age bracket. I'm guessing they'll be spent long before they plow through every last game.

- **Math Bingo** ($0.99; also works with iPad)—It's inexpensive and it teaches a tough subject using a game that just about everyone understands. You can select from addition, subtraction, multiplication, and division, and push your youngster with three different levels of difficulty.

- **Color & Draw** ($0.99)—This one's probably fun enough for kids ages 3 to 103; it invites users to draw, color, and decorate drawings or photographs with voiceover artistic invitations. In short, it's an interactive coloring book, and there are letter/number tracing tools to enhance learning as well. The only downside? Your offspring will never be excited about a conventional coloring book after experiencing this.

- **The Cat in The Hat** ($3.99; also works with iPad)—What would a kids' section about iPhone apps be without a tip of the (cat) hat to Dr. Seuss? Not much. This particular app is a real standout, featuring professional narration, background audio, and enlarged artwork for each scene. To promote reading in young children, individual words are highlighted as the story is read and words zoom up when pictures are touched.

▶ **Any app by PBS KIDS** (price varies)—These guys have a model that just works; games are inexpensive, colorful, and full of replay value. There's a variety to choose from to cover a wide array of ages, and I've yet to be let down by any that they've developed.

> **NOTE** The definition of "kids apps" varies widely depending on the age of your kid(s). I highly recommend a look through **www.bestkidsapps.com**. This site is routinely updated and does an excellent job of showcasing the best of the best.

READING AND RE-READING

Early on, pundits suggested that the conventional LCD on the iPad and iPhone would render them nearly useless as e-readers. As the market has unfolded, there's obviously still a niche being filled with E Ink-based products such as the Kindle, but many consumers have decided that an iPhone will serve just fine as a digital reader when they don't feel like carrying a second device.

The only major knock is the glossy display, which glares uncontrollably when placed in direct sunlight. That said, it's clear that Apple's positioning both the iPhone and iPad as reading devices—iOS 5 saw the introduction of Newsstand and iBooks (a free download) is another Apple-created app for fetching books. Outside of those two, here are a few others that digital bookworms shouldn't miss:

▶ An anti-glare screen protector from BoxWave or Zagg works well to quell reflections.

▶ **GoodReader for iPhone** ($4.99)—I've already extolled this app enough, but seriously, if you're attempting to open massive TXT or PDF files, there's no better option than this. It's also highly useful for things outside of just reading complex documents, making it a shoe-in for inclusion in your app library.

▶ **Kindle** (free; also works with iPad)—Funny, right? One of Apple's archrivals in the e-reading space actually has a highly sophisticated app in the App Store. The best part about the Kindle app for iPhone is the cross-compatibility. You can buy an Amazon book on your Windows machine, open it where you left off on your iPhone, make a few notes in it on your iPad, and lend it to a friend on your MacBook Pro. That's powerful stuff.

▶ **Nook** (free)—It's pretty much the same story as the Amazon Kindle app, but works well for those already invested in the Barnes & Noble ecosystem. Cross-compatibility and sharing are both here, and the layout couldn't be finer.

▶ **Stanza** (free)—If you're okay with having an app folder stuffed with e-reader apps, add this one to the pile. It doesn't hurt the wallet, and it offers better-than-average "sideloading" capabilities, meaning that you can load your own ePub, e-reader, PDF, Comic Book Archive (CBR & CBZ), and DjVu books from your Mac or PC by dragging and dropping the files into the File Sharing section of the Apps tab of your device in iTunes.

NEWS AND REFERENCE MATERIAL

▶ While I'm referencing The Beatles, I should note that those guys are finally in iTunes!

I'll confess—news is one of my passions. By day, I'm a news hound. I track and report stories, investigate leads, and bury my nose in the App Store looking for the sexiest, most seamless ways to consume the absolute torrent of news that flows from the Internet each and every day. Ingesting news on the iPhone is one of the most lovely and enjoyable experiences surrounding the entire device. There's nothing quite like kicking back after a Hard Day's Night, grabbing a cup of Joe, and catching up on whatever it is you missed.

- ▶ **Zinio** (free; also works with iPad)—This is a downright beautiful app that enables you to shop for and read a slew of great magazines—things that were seemingly built to be showcased on the iPhone. You can read full-color, high-fidelity pages, or switch to enhanced text mode and resize text for simpler reading. It also supports offline reading, and you can buy subscriptions or single issues using your existing iTunes account; no extra sign-up is necessary.

- ▶ **Flipboard** (free)—Two things make this app great. One, the layout is stunningly beautiful. Two, it can ingest any content as it sits on the Internet right now, so long as there's an RSS feed, and turn it into something gorgeous. In other words, you don't even need to find new favorites; simply pop the RSS feeds that you visit routinely into Flipboard, and it instantly converts those articles into magazine-like modules. It's really not doing much more than beautifying RSS content, but it does it *so well*. And, it's free.

- ▶ **Pulse News for iPhone** (free)—Pulse works in a similar fashion to Flipboard, but the layout is better suited to handle vast, vast quantities of news. In a nutshell, it takes your favorite websites and transforms them into a colorful and interactive mosaic. Not only does it do an excellent job of visually segmenting stories, but it also enables users to save particular articles for later reading across all platforms, or sync them with Instapaper, Read it Later, and Evernote. Sharing a story via Facebook, Twitter, and e-mail is as easy as two taps, and truthfully, the hardest part is putting it down.

▶ **Google Currents** (free; also works with iPad)—Similar to Flipboard, Currents pulls in stories from your favorite websites by way of RSS. It then reformats them to look absolutely beautiful on a smaller screen, and in my opinion, much more readable.

▶ **Instapaper** ($2.99; also works with iPad)—This is the de facto application for reading online articles at a later point in time while offline. It's tailor-made for underground subway rides, where you'll load up a few longer articles here and then read them when there's no connection available. Well over 150 iPhone and iPad apps support direct integration with Instapaper already, and that list is growing by leaps and bounds. It does a commendable job stripping down complex articles to ones that are easily saved and read, and you can adjust a dizzying amount of settings to make reading all the more comfortable for your two eyes.

▶ **Engadget** (free): A shameless plug? Yes, but if you're even remotely interested in keeping pace with the world of consumer technology, this app provides access to news, opinions, and reviews from the author of this book and his wonderful colleagues.

WIZARDING WEATHER APPS

It's hard to explain, but there's something tantalizing about checking the weather on an iPhone. Maybe it's the feeling of having your own "green screen" of sorts, or making yourself the meteorologist with those oh-so-easy swiping movements. Perhaps it's just the kid in me, but a super sophisticated, ultra-nerdy weather app just makes the iPhone that much better. Googling forecasts for a certain area just feels boring; throw in interactive maps, webcam feeds, and historical data, and you have the forecast of the future. Here are a few of my favorites:

▶ **swackett** (free)—It's a new take on weather apps. Aside from sending you push notifications for alerts in customizable places, giving you a glance at the forecast, and displaying the current temperature, it also uses an edgy graphical interface to display what kind of clothing you should wear out for the day. Useful!

▶ **Weather+** ($0.99; also works with iPad)—The only compelling reason to actually pay for a weather app on the iPhone is the visual awesomeness baked into this one. The layout is simply stunning, and dare I say, looks a pinch like elements of it were borrowed from HTC's Sense Android overlay. It also offers full-screen video feeds from select locales, wind direction and speed details, and a plethora of customization options.

▶ **Living Earth HD** ($0.99; also works with iPad)—Half weather app, half Google Earth(ish), this app nicely mixes 3D simulations with up-to-date forecasts. It's less of a tool for figuring out your local weather and more of an exploratory app to discover weather patterns across the globe, but if you're in the education sector, it's a good way to get your kids to pay attention to a topic they may otherwise tune out.

▶ **Fahrenheit** ($0.99; also works with iPad)—There's really only one reason to consider this app over the others: The icon itself dynamically changes to show the current temperature, so you never actually have to enter the app to know how warm (or frigid) it is in the area surrounding you. Should you do so anyway, you'll be greeted with a lovely user interface that shows forecasts, radar screens, and the usual complement of extras.

ALTERNATIVE BROWSING OPTIONS

Safari just so happens to be the web browser that Apple built (shown in Figure 10-6), and in turn, is planted front and center on the iPhone. For years, developers of third-party browsers watched in vain as their handiwork was rejected from the App Store, but Opera Mini for iPhone broke that ice back in April of 2010.

FIGURE 10-6: Safari is simple and understated, but well refined at this point.

Since then, a handful of other finely tuned alternatives have filtered in. There's absolutely nothing wrong with Safari—particularly now that it has native tabbed browsing—but there's also nothing wrong with taking a look at the other options out there. This section covers a few of my recommendations.

Skyfire

Skyfire's a potent enough rival to deserve its own space, so its own space it has. The browser app can be purchased for $2.99, and although it certainly has a few laudatory features—including a robust bookmarking system, private browsing and mobile/desktop view switching—there's one feature in particular that puts this app on the map. Apple and Adobe have long feuded over the inclusion (or exclusion, I should say) of Flash on iOS products, and now that Flash development on the mobile side has been killed, I'm guessing it's just a matter of time before web-based video transitions entirely away from Flash. That said, thousands upon thousands of websites and web videos still use Flash, and not being able to view "the whole web" on an iPhone just feels... wrong.

▶ Did Apple catalyze the death of Flash on mobile? Let's just say Cupertino's non-support definitely didn't help matters...

Skyfire adds back that crucial missing feature with just a click. There's a built-in transcoding feature that converts Flash video to HTML5, and although it's a bit clunky when trying to stream over 3G, it's certainly better than staring with an error message. Any Flash video that shows up while using Skyfire can be initiated by clicking a small pop-up icon. A few seconds later, assuming the transcode goes smoothly, it starts playing back.

Google Chrome

During Google's annual developer conference for the year 2012, the highly touted Chrome browser was finally ported to iOS. Both the iPhone and iPad now have access to Google's acclaimed web browser, and with that comes Google Sync. In other words, those who use Chrome religiously on their home computer and/or Android device can sign in across all platforms. That way, their bookmarks, saved passwords, and open tabs are synced across every device that uses Chrome.

Unfortunately, the lightning fast speed that Chrome's desktop browser is known for has been hamstrung by Apple's policies. As of now, the only browser in the iOS universe capable of using Nitro—an engine that has proven to be wicked quick on mobile platforms—is Safari. All other third-party browsers, Chrome included, are forced to use a pre-Nitro alternative (called UIWebView), which isn't as quick. Apple claims it's for security; I think it's partly to keep Safari in the lead in terms of speed.

Opera Mini

It wasn't too long ago that Opera had its own fingers crossed, waiting and praying that Opera Mini would be accepted into the App Store. It was quite the precedent-setter when Apple allowed it, effectively giving third-party developers the green light to produce and distribute apps that directly and unequivocally compete with software that was born and bred in Cupertino. Now, it stands as one of the best alternatives to Safari, and it's absolutely free to download and enjoy.

Not only is the interface polished (see for yourself in Figure 10-7), but it also includes an amazing compression feature that truly sets it apart. In a world constrained by data tiers, usage limits, and overage charges, the reality is that mobile Internet users have to be mindful of how much data they're consuming. It's a drastic change in mentality from even five years ago, when unlimited data was the norm and "usage" was not a consideration.

FIGURE 10-7: Opera Mini is a bit flashier than Safari.

Opera Mini takes web page requests and redirects them to its own servers, where pages are compressed by up to 90 percent before they're shot back to your iPhone. The result? Slightly lower quality images, but huge data usage savings. Even if you're unconcerned with usage (those who are still holding onto unlimited data plans, I'm looking your way), you'll probably be interested in faster browsing. Given that so much less data is transmitted when browsing with Opera Mini, pages load more quickly. On crowded networks, this could be the difference between a low-fi version of your favorite website loading, or a page time-out. Furthermore, the Visual Tabs feature enables users to see all of their open tabs at once and hastily switch between them, whereas the Opera Link allows those who use Opera at home to pull in their bookmarks with just a couple of taps.

▶ Keep an eye on its Data Usage Meter to see exactly how many kilobytes you're saving. Take pride in frugality!

iCab Mobile

This particular browser doesn't do any zany Flash tricks or completely wipe the floor with Safari, but there are enough unique features here to justify the $1.99 price of admission. It allows users to search within web pages, save passwords and form-fills, and there's even a customizable Filters function that enables you to toggle images off completely in order to save bandwidth. Fullscreen mode gets rid of the border and toolbar areas, whereas the homegrown Scrollpad function allows a three-finger tap lead to anywhere-on-the-page finger scrolling. There's also native Dropbox support, which allows you to import/export bookmarks as well as transfer downloads, images, files, and web pages to your cloud account. AirPrint is naturally supported, and there's even a way to customize how multi-finger gestures control the browsing experience.

▶ iCab Mobile also supports page compression, similar to Opera Mini, to save you precious kilobytes while browsing.

SEARCHING FOR GREAT APPS

This chapter closes by giving you a few tips on searching that tend to work quite well, regardless of what you're looking for. It's quite likely that you'll find yourself interested in related apps after diving into the laundry list shown here. The question is, how do you even begin? Apple has segmented the App Store as best it can, but with well over 300,000 apps, there's just no corralling them all.

Start by opening iTunes, venturing into the iTunes Store, and looking for the App Store button along the top edge of the program. Besides that, you'll spot a drop-down arrow. Give that a click, and a lengthy list of app genres and categories will appear.

Apple seems to be fine-tuning this list as the App Store blossoms and evolves, so you should definitely expect the list of categories to grow over time.

> **TIP** While in the App Store, keep a close eye for the Hall of Fame section. It's a great overall place to start cherry-picking proven apps, and in my experience, apps found here are frequently updated. In other words, bugs are squashed nearly as quickly as they're found, because developers stand to lose a lot if their offerings aren't flawless.

▶ In most sections, you can search by Featured or Name, while some sections include Release Date.

From there, I suggest clicking into a category that you're interested in; you'll be brought to a portal page that features only applications from whatever segment you selected. From here, the search options really get useful. New apps are plastered across the top, and this is a great place to hop into if you're religiously checking the store from week to week in order to see what new and exciting software has arrived since your last visit. If you're just looking for the best of the best regardless of age, the What's Hot and Top Charts sections generally list the highest rated apps.

▶ You should peruse the Great Free Apps area, in the right rail of any iTunes category portal, weekly. It's like window-shopping at the $0.00 Store.

Best of all, a quick scroll down the page enables you to look only at paid apps or only at free apps. I generally recommend a peek in the free section first; if you can find a suitable app without having to spend any money, go for it. If you come up empty there, the paid section will usually present you with a far more robust, polished array of options. After all, the developers here know that they have to offer something quite exemplary to encourage users to buy their app over a free alternative.

If you simply have no idea where to start, I suggest rereading this chapter on a day when your brain is a bit less frazzled. I also suggest visiting the iPhone Apps Starter Kit option, which is located in the App Store Quick Links section of the App Store in iTunes. To get there, open iTunes, click iTunes Store ➜ App Store and look in the top-right rail. Within, you'll find a stout collection of universally adored applications from just about every major genre.

Unfortunately, there's no direct way to force the Search box within iTunes itself to narrow a query to the particular segment that you're viewing. In other words, each search within iTunes scans the entire marketplace for results. You can, however, narrow these down somewhat. If you're on the hunt for apps—querying something like "biology app"—be sure to click the Apps line over in Filter by Media Type, a box floating along the left edge after each search. If you're after something else—perhaps Music, Podcasts, Books, or Movies—simply aim for the corresponding filter.

That said, there is a separate way to fine-tune your results. Once you search, you can click the Power Search button that sits atop the aforementioned Filter by Media

Type box. The resulting box—assuming you already filtered by apps—enables you to search specifically by keyboard, developer, free/paid, and even by device compatibility. It takes a bit of poking around to find this feature, but it's worth it for occasions when the traditional search just isn't helping.

It's also worth downloading Chomp. It's a free app in the App Store, and acts as a super customizable search engine to find the kinds of apps you're looking for. Think of it as the Power Search version of Apple's own app search.

▶ If you snag a universal app such as Apple's GarageBand, one purchase gets you the app for your entire stable of iOS devices. Nice!

SUMMARY

It's an app-filled world, and the iPhone is just living in it. In all seriousness, the iPhone would be a lot less useful without apps. Every ounce of its functionality is unlocked by the power of developers, and although it'd handle phone calls and texts just fine without a suite of apps on its home screen, it's actually a potent productivity device if you have the right software.

Everything from highly specialized web browsers to educational and instructional apps are available, but wading through the 300,000+ apps in the App Store can be a huge chore. Apple has done a solid job in creating Best Of portals within iTunes, and I recommend frequenting those weekly in order to see what's new and improved since your last visit. Digging into the productivity side of things is also the perfect excuse to finally buckle down and create a folder system that works for you, and generating a reliable and seamless workflow on your iPhone can end up creating a new world of free time.

It's important to remember that while the apps listed here are surefire winners, development is forging ahead each and every day. New coders are designing more intuitive ways to be productive on the iPhone, and unless you develop masterful searching skills, you'll miss out on apps that are just around the bend. Keeping your toes dipped into the New section in the App Store is a great way to discover future hits before they hit the mainstream, and keeping the Chomp app nearby is a great way to search for and discover new programs that fall into your favorite categories.

The Best Not-Exactly-Productive Apps

The previous chapter focused almost entirely on apps to make you more productive, or perhaps just more informed, while using your iPhone. But as any good foodie knows, the meal is only as good as the dessert that follows. The indisputable success of the App Store hinges largely on its ability to provide fast and cheap thrills (the legal kind), and if you're buying an iPhone for play, this is the chapter to hone in on. Even the most dedicated of businesspeople need to blow off steam every now and then, and there's certainly nothing wrong with earmarking a home screen or two just for non-business related apps. There's a litany of programs designed to do nothing more than kill time, but some of these pull double duty by mixing education and information into good old-fashioned fun. I'm guessing you can barely contain yourself at this point, so fire up the App Store, cancel all of your meetings for the next 24 hours, and let's get down to business. And by "business," I mean "everything but business."

MINDLESS FLINGS

Is there anything more fulfilling than opening up a folder worth of apps that you know serve no purpose whatsoever outside of mindless entertainment? No. It's with that beautiful, wonderful thought in mind that I tackle one of the most difficult sections of this entire book. (Difficult in part because it's so hard to close the title shown in Figure 11-1.)

FIGURE 11-1: Angry Birds will undoubtedly make you less productive, but more happy as a human.

You laugh, but I'm tasked with narrowing down thousands upon thousands of incredible time-wasters into a subset that I feel best exploits the powers of the iPhone. In truth, it's hard to go (*too*) wrong with time-wasters, but I encourage you to get your collection started with a few of my favorites:

▶ **Angry Birds Space** ($0.99)—Cliché? Yes. But let's be honest, Angry Birds didn't reach its level of acclaim by simply being overhyped. This is easily one of the most addictive, rewarding, and interactive time-killers on the iPhone.

If you've somehow missed out on the craze, it's a (conceptually) simple title that allows users to fling birds at other objects and animals, with the goal being to destroy all enemies with a very limited amount of flings. Despite its cleverly plain overview, it does a fine job of teaching the impact and importance of angles, trajectories, and physics. Fancy that!

▶ **Minecraft** ($6.99; also works with iPad)—This particular title took the long route to iOS, but it's having just as significant an impact here as it did on Android. It's a rather obscure-looking app, demanding that users take building blocks and construct "randomized worlds." You literally construct your own dream world, and if that's not a perfect method for killing time, I don't know what is. Furthermore, you can sync with other Minecrafters on a local area network in order to invite and play with friends in your own little world. Linguists may refer to this process as "extreme escapism." I prefer "awesome."

▶ **Tiny Tower** (free; also works with iPad)—Just in case you aren't getting enough building action in Minecraft (or you're hankering for a free alternative), this one will fill whatever void is left. It's another low-fi construction game (shown in Figure 11-2), allowing iPhone owners to erect a tower and then manage the businesses and digital citizens that live within. Game Center integration ensures that you know just how weak your tower is compared to the competition, and if you're sensing a bit of "Sims" inspiration here...well, let's just say you're probably onto something.

▶ **Cut the Rope** ($0.99)—Let's set the scene: you're responsible for cutting a rope in order to drop candy into the mouth of a green alien. Period. This widely adored title epitomizes mindless entertainment, but the Game Center integration keeps you coming back for cut after cut. There's also a Lite version that costs absolutely nothing; you can try it before investing your $0.99. I'll save you the trouble and confirm your greatest fear: you'll be unable to resist the full edition.

▶ **Fruit Ninja** ($0.99)—Over ten million enthralled, totally occupied gamers can't be wrong, can they? This title is the top paid app in myriad countries, and I'll confess: it's a lot of fun for under a buck. It's an action title that involves ninjas slicing fruit, with multi-fruit combos racking up major points. Throw in multi-player support through Game Center, and you've all the reason you need to exhaust your vacation days just to improve your overall rank.

FIGURE 11-2: Tiny Tower is ultra cute and ultra addictive.

NOTE "Productivity" is an interesting word. To some, it means inching ever closer to achieving a financial goal. To others, it simply describes the art of feeling accomplished. Most of the apps discussed in this chapter aren't engineered to help you nail a boardroom meeting, but there's something to be said about firing up an app that brings a smile to your face and gets your synapses firing. Unlike handheld gaming consoles, the iPhone can wear multiple hats. The Nintendo 3DS is really only good at entertaining; the iPhone, on the other hand, can entertain for hours on end, and with a folder switch, converts into a masterful presentation tool. It's that multifaceted nature—and the truly unlimited potential in the App Store—that makes chapters like these so enthralling to write.

BRAIN BOLSTERERS

Looking for a few titles that you actually need both eyes open and at least 20 percent of your brain active to enjoy? The App Store is home to a great number of exciting titles that also act as brain benders. Mixing education and entertainment takes a delicate development hand, but I have a handful of sure bets for those looking to expand their horizons.

▶ **Carcassonne** ($9.99; also works with iPad)—It's a classic board game title, but the execution on the iPhone is just beautiful. Game Center integration enables users to play along with friends and family, or you can play with up to five locals by simply passing your iPhone around. Make sure you stay sharp, though!

▶ **Contre Jour** ($0.99)—This is one of the more challenging physics-based titles, and the otherworldly graphics and audio don't hurt its appeal. The game demands constant interaction, and there's Game Center integration to keep you pressing for more. As an aside, this is the perfect game to use with AirPlay Mirroring; not too many titles look this good displayed on an HDTV.

▶ **Brain Challenge 2** (free)—Here, you'll find 40+ mini-games, all of which are designed to test your mental aptitude. Five categories are covered—visual, memory, logic, math, and focus—and if you're into puzzles, you'll be at home playing this one.

▶ **Conundra** (free; also works with iPad)—Scared of mental commitment? I recommend starting here, given that noncommittal price. You'll be tasked with solving anagrams that are from six to ten letters long, with a total of 1,000+ puzzles to work through. The design isn't anything to write home about, but it's tough to kvetch given the gratis admission.

▶ **Brain Trainer Unlimited** ($49.99)—Sick and tired of apps "attempting" to "challenge" your "amazing cranium?" Plop 50 bucks down on this one, and you'll have unlimited access to Brain Trainer's entire suite of scientifically designed exercises for life. Lumosity.com has worked closely with leading neuroscientists from Stanford, UCSF, and Berkeley to create a cutting-edge and clinically proven cognitive enhancement program, and that research is being brought over in this wildly sophisticated brain-training program. I can't promise that it'll improve your memory and generally enhance your life, but it'll certainly feel like a never-ending challenge if that's what you're after.

PUZZLING PROGRAMS

Puzzles may perhaps by the oldest form of brain entertainment as it pertains to games, but the following are decidedly modern iterations. We've come a long way since the crossword.

▶ **Unblock Me** ($0.99; also works with iPad)—If Jenga, Tetris, and that peg game at Cracker Barrel got together and decided to combine DNA, you'd end up with this. It's a beautifully simple puzzle game that requires you to get the red block out of danger in the most efficient way possible. With four levels of difficulty, the replay value is remarkably high. A free version is available for those terrified of buying anything without a trial.

▶ **World of Goo** ($2.99; also works on iPad)—One of the bigger, more immersive and thoroughly unorthodox puzzle games in the App Store. It's a monster of a download, but it'll reward you with hours on end of new game footage. You can compete in Game Center to craft the tallest tower of goo. Yes, I realize that sounds a bit nauseating.

▶ **Words With Friends** ($2.99)—If you're Scrabble'd out, this is an excellent alternative for wordsmiths to get wrapped up in. The turn-based design lets you play up to 20 games simultaneously, and you're able to engage in multiplayer games with friends or perfect strangers. There's even support for push notifications for alerting you as to when it's your turn. (Just don't try using it while on an active runway—right, Alec Baldwin?)

▶ **Moxie 2** ($1.99)—It's one of the more relaxing word games, with no timer hanging over your head. You get five different game selections, a daily challenge mode, and a global leaderboard. Not like you care about *winning* or anything.

MUSICAL ENDEAVORS

There's nothing quite like using an iPhone to enhance your musical aspirations. It's hard to imagine that Apple planned for the iPhone to become a musical powerhouse, but I've seen dueling iPhones used to DJ entire parties. And that's just the half of it. Third-party hardware dongles and adapters allow just about any instrument to be connected to the device, and there's an entire industry being created around music-related apps and peripherals. I touch primarily on applications here, so be sure to peek at Chapter 17, "Ace Accessories," for recommendations on the hardware side.

Music Creation

We currently live in a world where it's possible to create, edit, and produce music on one's phone. After you're over the shock of that realization, feel free to load your iPhone up with these music-minded programs.

▶ **GarageBand** ($4.99; also works with iPad)—It's one of the few apps that Apple designed, but this one's probably the most underpriced of them all. Anyone familiar with the desktop version of GarageBand will feel right at home here. Even if you're a musical newcomer, there's plenty of instrument sounds to tinker with here, and given that recording/tweaking tracks is so easy, it's the perfect way to blow off steam. Tap out drumbeats, tickle the virtual ivory, mix up to eight tracks per song, and e-mail completed projects right from the app.

▶ **AmpliTube** ($19.99)—What if you had hundreds of guitar effects in a pedal board that weighed less than two pounds and cost less than $20? In a way, that's precisely what this app is. Rather than spend hundreds (or even thousands) on multi-effect pedals, you can use this one app to connect guitars to have their input mutilated and tweaked to sound like just about anything—from an acoustic to a baritone metal axe. You need an iRig interface adapter (www.amplitube.com/irig) to connect your guitar or bass, but if you've been looking for an inexpensive way to track riffs, look no further.

▶ **A Noise Machine** ($0.99)—This isn't your grandmother's music app. It's tailored for music geeks who salivate at the mere mention of "sequencing" and "bloops," but it's a wild ride in experimentation that will undoubtedly lead to the creation of music you never knew you had in you. You use your fingers to move dots to various spaces, with movements bending and tweaking outputs, rhythms, and tempo multipliers. It's a ton of fun, even if you have absolutely no idea what you're doing.

▶ **Future DJ** ($3.99)—Quoting the developer, "this is not a toy." If you're looking to DJ a party using an iPhone or two, start here. Be prepared to deal with a steep learning curve, but the amount of underlying power is really incredible.

NOTE SoundHound, which is free, is a must-have for any iPhone owner. It analyzes songs (on the radio, from your pal who is humming in the corner, and so on) and then informs you which track it is. Once it pulls up, you also get access to lyrics and related YouTube videos.

Streaming Radio and Concerts

It used to be a huge chore to keep track of which band was going where, but now there are apps that go so far as to notify you when a favorite artist is coming to a town near you. Furthermore, that FM radio of yours is now outdated, with plenty of apps bringing the radio right to your phone.

- ► **BandMate: Concert Tipster** ($1.99)—Keeping up with which bands are playing where can be a royal pain. This app notifies you when a band in your iTunes library will be swinging by, and takes it one step further by alerting you to nearby shows from *similar* artists that you might like based on what you have on regular rotation. From within the app, you can listen to an artist's music, watch his or her videos, purchase tickets, share via e-mail, Facebook, and Twitter, and view all upcoming shows at a venue. The only negative? Currently, it only works with major cities in the United States, Canada, Europe, Australia, and Japan.

- ► **JamBase** (free)—Similar to BandMate, but this one's free. It not only gives you easy access to upcoming tour dates for bands you like, but it also lists all shows in your surrounding area, sorted by date (you know, in case you just need to see any ol' show while on vacation).

- ► **Pandora Radio** (free; also works with iPad)—This one needs no introduction, a fact that will simply have to serve as its introduction. It's the app that put streaming radio as we know it today on the map, allowing users to build their own customized radio stations and hear music from related artists that they'd probably never discover otherwise. You'll find plenty of ads and limitations if you don't pony up a monthly fee, but some of those limitations can be removed for as little as $3.99 per month. If you're already a Pandora subscriber on the web, all of your stations will show up when you're logged in on the iPhone; if you create stations on your tablet, they will show up elsewhere too. Thanks, Mr. Cloud.

- ► **Rdio** (free; also works with iPad)—It's an app that's quite similar to Pandora in most regards, but I tend to prefer the user interface of this one; plus, Rdio makes it remarkably easy to share what you're listening to on Facebook or Twitter. It's a social network itself, allowing users to follow friends and take suggestions from whatever they're listening to. If you grow tired of ads and limitations, you can subscribe within the app for $14.99 per month. My suggestion? Subscribe on Rdio's website, where it costs $9.99; the in-app subscription is presumably to make up for Apple's cut of the deal.

- **MOG** (free)—This is my music-streaming app of choice, ahead of Spotify and all the rest. The basic streaming service is free, but for $9.99 per month, I have multi-platform access (iPhone, Mac, PC, and Android), and I can download all of the playlists I create at home onto my mobile for offline listening elsewhere. The Radio function enables you to pick a band you like and then hear similar music—it's great for discovering new artists.

- **Slacker Radio** (free; also works with iPad)—This one has been redesigned from the ground up to look beautiful on the iPhone, and yes, it's eerily similar to Rdio and Pandora. I will say that those who prefer to put less effort into music discovery should admire Slacker, as it has over 150 expert-programmed radio stations alongside the ability to craft your own. Per usual, a $9.99 monthly subscription fee unlocks the full potential. Slacker Premium Radio subscribers can also cache stations, playlists, and albums to their device to listen without a network connection, which is probably this guy's biggest strength.

PLAYING WITH PHOTOS

The camera on the iPhone has quickly become one of the most universally used. On nearly every photo hosting/sharing site on the web, the iPhone camera makes up over half of the posted photos. Why? It's just so easy. Photographers have been known to say that the best camera is the one closest to you, and beyond that, Apple has gone to great lengths to make the camera on its latest iPhone devices laudatory.

▶ Looking to get a little editing done on an upcoming flight? Sync over a recent photo gallery from your PC before you leave.

- **Adobe Photoshop Express** (free)—Free? Really? Sure enough, you can get a pinch of one of the world's most highly acclaimed photo-editing programs for absolutely nothing on the iPhone (shown in Figure 11-3). You can choose from a variety of one-touch effects, or simply drag your finger across the screen to crop, rotate, or adjust color. A few filters are here as well, and if you have a Photoshop.com account, you can upload your finished masterpieces.

- **Snapseed** ($4.99; also works with iPad)—This is my photo editor of choice. It's insanely easy to use, and the implementation of gestures to gently tweak photos is terrific. No, it's not free, but it's frequently updated and enhances your photos without using gimmicky filters. Also, there's a 1:1 crop mode that preps your photo for a perfect fit when sharing to Instagram.

▶ **PhotoPad** (free; also works with iPad)—With a price like this, it's hard not to recommend having a secondary editing application around. It's a bit simpler, but the red eye reduction tool does well when tweaking photos from cameras with harsh flashes.

FIGURE 11-3: It's Photoshop, but on the iPhone. And it's free!

▶ **Facebook Camera** (free)—Avid Facebook users, this may soon become your default camera app. There are also built-in filters, and since Facebook purchased Instagram, I wouldn't doubt if some of those frequently used filters are eventually integrated into this app. It's also a great way to keep tabs on photos added by your closest Facebook friends.

▶ **iSwap Faces** ($1.99; also works with iPad)—I can't think of too many more ways I'd rather kill time than this. Put simply, this app makes it easy (way *too* easy) to crop and swap faces of people in a photo. Feel like tossing Marcus' mug on Jane's face? Here's your app, and I'm guessing the belly laughs you'll get from it will more than justify the entry price.

▶ **FaceGoo** ($0.99)—Think of this as the perfect complement to iSwap Faces. It allows creative users to stretch and distort mug shots of whatever photos they take or pull in, putting a whole new spin on airbrushing someone's face "in post." The only downside? You can share your creations immediately on Facebook or Twitter, leaving plenty of opportunity for regret.

▶ **Photogene² for iPhone** ($0.99): This is one of the more sophisticated photo-editing apps available for iPhone, and although it's obviously more of a financial burden than Photoshop Express, those who heavily edit images will likely find the additional filters and RAW support worth the money. It also allows you to export several photos at once, and it supports a wide selection of export destinations, including Flickr, Dropbox, Facebook, Twitter, Picasa, FTP, and e-mail.

▶ **100 Cameras in 1** ($1.99)—As one of the few *non*-games in Game Center, this is absolutely the paid camera app to get if you're splurging on only one. Not only can you add a hundred effects to photos you take, but you can "compete" on a global leaderboard based on photos taken, filters applied, and so on. Making a game out of mobile photography? It's more intriguing than you might think.

▶ **PhotoShake!** ($1.99)—Got a few photos? Got a few minutes? You can have a collage. This app enables users to work a half dozen or so photos into an impressive looking collage print, and the actual construction couldn't be more enjoyable. Just select the photos you're after, shake the iPhone, and watch how it all... erm, *shakes out*. It also supports Wi-Fi import and export, social network sharing, and image filters. "Shake it like a Polaroid" has taken on an entirely new meaning.

SPORTING GOODS

You can definitely find your fair share of sporting news in one of the news apps listed in Chapter 10, "Useful Productivity Apps," but the sophistication of sporting apps in particular warrant a breakout section. From following scores in real-time to streaming events right to your iPhone's display, there's a plethora of options to keep you locked into the sporting world. I will say, however, that most of the more spectacular sports apps are limited in functionality unless you have a pay-TV subscription that includes ESPN. Cord cutting comes at a cost, but you can square up by installing these apps.

News and Viewing

Keeping up-to-date on your favorite sports has never been easier. Rather than grabbing a newspaper, just pull out your iPhone and load up one of the apps below.

- ▶ **WatchESPN** (free; also works with iPad)—Here's the good news: this app provides access to live streaming feeds from ESPN, ESPN2, ESPN3, and ESPNU. *Impressive*, no matter how you slice it. Here's the bad news: you need a pay-TV subscription on Bright House Networks, Time Warner Cable, Comcast, or Verizon FiOS TV. There's no way to simply "pay" for access through the app. It's an awful ploy to keep people locked into an arcane, outdated pay-TV ecosystem that people are peeling away from, but until à la carte programming emerges in America, we're stuck with two options: pay up or don't watch.

- ▶ **ESPN ScoreCenter** (free)—The best part of this app is the newer, lower price tag, which is $0.00. ESPN has proven to be a go-to source for breaking sporting news as well as up-to-the-minute scores across just about every league you can imagine, and all of the web-based content is wrapped up in an easy-to-digest format (shown in Figure 11-4). Better still, no pay-TV subscriptions are necessary to enjoy any of the material here.

- ▶ **Yahoo! Sportacular** (free)—If it's not ESPN breaking sports-related stories, it's Yahoo! I simply prefer the layout of this app when digging up game scores and following moment-by-moment updates on the fly, and there's a nice array of push notifications that you can enable, too. As for your fantasy teams? If you set 'em up with Yahoo!, there's a delightful amount of integration to be found.

- ▶ ***Insert Your Favorite Team Here***—Most, and I emphasize *most*, major professional teams have their own dedicated iPhone app. Some of them are nothing more than schedules, whereas others have news updates, player profiles, and message boards. It's worth a search in the App Store for your team's name. And if their app isn't up to snuff, it's probably about time to reevaluate your loyalty.

Sports Games

Sporting games are easy to find in the App Store, and they're tons of fun for those who have grown fond of a particular team. No need to buy a dedicated gaming handheld just for these titles; chances are, you'll find everything you need below.

- ▶ **Madden NFL** ($4.99)—Every year a new Madden game comes out, and every year it's worth a purchase. This game, if nothing else, takes full advantage of the iPhone's touch panel and graphics processor. It looks amazing and the controls are shockingly accurate. And for just $4.99, it's markedly cheaper than the console variants.

▶ **Tiger Woods PGA TOUR for iPhone** ($0.99)—It's the de facto golf title in the App Store, and Electronic Arts has been improving accuracy in the controls. Bonus: it's cheaper than a round of nine at your local club.

▶ **NBA JAM** ($0.99)—BOOMSHAKALAKA. KABOOM. HE'S ON FIRE. One of gaming's classics is back and better than ever on the iPhone, and if those three capitalized remarks above didn't convince you already, it's definitely one of the best basketball games around. Just don't forget your headphones; the audio is half the fun.

▶ **Real Tennis** (free)—Perhaps more so than any other sport, tennis is just built for the iPhone. Swiping and swinging go hand-in-hand, and even if you're not the biggest fan of the sport on television, it's a pretty exciting title to pick up for zilch.

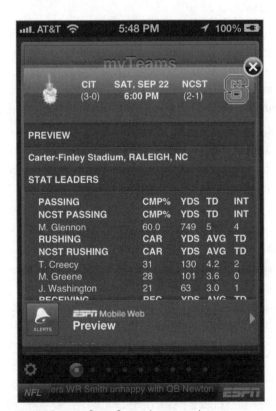

FIGURE 11-4: ScoreCenter keeps you in every game, especially NC State games. (Go Pack!)

NOTE   Sports games are a dime a dozen in the App Store, but if you're going to pay for any, I recommend looking to Gameloft and Electronic Arts. Both of those development houses have excellent reputations for producing polished, robust games.

FITNESS AND TRAINING APPS

For as long as the iPod has been around, runners have been strapping them to their arms in order to keep music rolling with each passing step. Soon, Apple realized that there was an entire niche waiting to be served by something more official, and over time, they developed a partnership with Nike. The Nike+iPod arrangement has led to all manners of peripherals, sensors, and trackers, and the iPhone has reaped a number of those benefits. Here are a few surefire downloads for those who can't wait to put this chapter to bed and start another set of quad lifts.

- **Fitness Pro** (free)—This one won't do the sit-ups for you, but it'll handle just about everything else. It's loaded with over 700 suggested exercises; think of it as a personal trainer, without the obscene monthly fees. You'll find exercises for men and women, Yoga activities, a calorie counter, and the ability to tap into live support from real humans should you need to up your level of devotion.

- **Calorie Counter by MyNetDiary** (free)—If you're willing to be honest with yourself, this is a great way to track your calorie intake. It stores data offline, and once an Internet connection is available, you can sync data to MyNetDiary. com. The real power here is the overwhelmingly large food database, which is updated daily; just punch in what you're having, and the calculations handle themselves.

- **WebMD** (free)—The good news here is that the app is free; the bad news is that you'll need a live Internet connection to access most of its features. The app is more of a website wrapper than a self-contained knowledge program, but if WebMD attempted to shove all of the information on its site into an app, the iPhone probably couldn't hold it. Still, its fitness and medical database is world-class, and it's amazingly easy to browse using the iPhone-tailored interface.

- **Pocket Yoga** ($1.99)—Thinking of starting up your own Yoga routine? Not keen on heading to the park and breaking it down in front of tourists? Fret not—this one gives you workout tips, showcases different difficulty levels, and guides you through 27 different workouts. You even get detailed voice and visual instruction that guides you through every pose, including each inhalation and exhalation. Toss in AirPlay support and you can pipe everything to your HDTV, making it even more useful for living room workouts.

> **NOTE** If you don't mind ponying up for extra hardware, Wahoo Fitness has a bicycle and heart rate apparatus that sends information to accompanying iPhone apps.

ELEMENTS OF ENTERTAINMENT

Despite the iPhone's inability to play Flash videos (natively, at least), there's a cornucopia of content available for it. Essentially, the iPhone has proven to be such a force in the market that content overlords and programming providers have had little choice but to make the necessary changes in order to support distribution on the device. Streaming is clearly the way of the future when it comes to video distribution on mobile platforms, and the iPhone handles a dizzying amount of them. Rather than continuing to spin uncontrollably, grab some control back by focusing on the following apps:

▶ **ABC Player** (free; also works with iPad)—Unlike a slew of other apps, this one doesn't require you to be a pay-TV subscriber to access full-length shows. So long as you're willing to watch ads, you'll have access to full-length episodes of *Modern Family, Grey's Anatomy, No Ordinary Family, Desperate Housewives*, and so on. There's also a built-in schedule, an episode guide, and a viewing history pane. For whatever it's worth, the user interface is about as nice as they come.

▶ **Hulu Plus** (free*; also works with iPad)—Need I say more? The platform that largely started the modern-day Internet programming revolution has a gorgeous iPhone app, but it's not worth much if you aren't paying $9.99 per month for a Hulu Plus subscription. A full season pass grants you access to every current season episode of top TV shows from ABC, Fox, and NBC.

▶ **Netflix** (free*; also works with iPad)—Similar to how Hulu Plus operates, you'll need a streaming account at Netflix (currently running around $8 per month) in order to view any of the content within the program. Best of all, video out is supported, so you could technically load a movie on your iPhone and enjoy it on the big screen. That's the future, folks.

▶ **i.TV** (free; also works with iPad)—You can't actually view content within this particular app, but it's a lovely TV guide program that'll clue you in as to what's coming on the tube. Moreover, it shows what's available on Netflix, Hulu, and iTunes, and it gives you the power to schedule your TiVo DVR, and look up show information on IMDb and Wikipedia.

HIGH-END GAMING

Traditional handheld game consoles are certainly reeling at the thought of touchscreen-based devices (yes, like the iPhone) eating their lunch. Games are easier to get (they're just a download away), they're cheaper (most are $9.99 or less), and they work on a device that folks are already toting around. There's the obvious limitation of not having a physical game controller, but Apple has done a magical job of making the touch response on the iPhone worthy of praise. And, in fairness, app developers have done an incredible job developing programs with impressive control mechanisms.

The iPhone's graphical engine is fairly potent, and while apps like Angry Birds look just fine, there are a few higher-end titles that *truly* show off its prowess. If you're looking to see just how far your jaw can drop while gaming on the iPhone, pop these into your Games folder:

▶ **Mirror's Edge** ($0.99)—It's an action title with a slew of levels, and while the controls are challenging at first, it's an engaging and rewarding title to get wrapped up in.

▶ **Rage** ($0.99; also works with iPad)—It's incomprehensible that this game is only $0.99. Developed by the same company responsible for Doom and Quake, this action-shooter is widely regarded as having the most impressive graphics of any app in the entire App Store. Just try to avoid playing it while alone in the dark.

▶ **Infinity Blade** ($5.99; also works with iPad)—If you're looking for an epic action adventure title with drool-worthy graphics, this is your safest bet. It was built on the Unreal Engine—a platform well-known for producing visually stunning titles on a PC—and the fact that it even runs on a device as mobile as the iPhone is almost unbelievable.

▶ **Real Racing 2** ($4.99)—Not only is the iPhone perfectly made for racing games (*thanks, accelerometer*), but there's something extra baked into this one that makes it worth a purchase. There's split-screen multiplayer support via HDMI or AirPlay, so if you have friends with iPhones (and an HDTV nearby), you can bypass the whole "game console" thing. If you play online, it supports up to 16 gamers at once.

▶ **Dead Space** ($6.99)—It isn't for the faint of heart, but if the idea of blasting through zombies that look entirely too real interests you, this one's the one to get. The graphics alone are worth seeing, and the storyline is engrossing regardless of the platform. It might convince you to delay that impending console purchase, though.

▶ **Broken Sword: Director's Cut** ($2.99)—It's a classic title re-envisioned, and although it's not as graphically impressive on a technical level, it's one of the most astonishingly artistic titles available. The storyline is also gripping, but it's probably not worth picking up if you're fearful of gaming-related addictions.

▶ **Pocket Legends** (free*; also works with iPad)—It's the prevailing choice for an MMO-like (Massive Multiplayer Game) experience on the iPhone, and although it's free to download, you'll need to pony up $4.99+ via in-app purchases to pick up elements that enable you to move through the game.

SUMMARY

If you're overwhelmed by just how many apps are available to turn your iPhone into a productivity powerhouse, you'll be floored when you start peeling back the other side of the proverbial onion. When it comes to gaming, entertaining, and just goofing off, the iPhone has thousands upon thousands of choices. Of course, the cream of the crop can be tough to find, so I've segmented my top choices in a variety of non-business related categories here.

It's important to note that wasting time and productivity aren't necessarily mutually exclusive. Many of the iPhone's best games have some sort of learning aspect to them, and the built-in accelerometer adds a pinch of physics into otherwise mindless titles. More impressive than that, however, is the iPhone's ability to act as a digital cutting board; there's a wealth of audio- and photo-editing programs out there, and being able to touch, pinch, and zoom the content that matters to you most adds a personal feel to perfecting your work.

It's an iPhone. It's fun. And it's worth spending time (and a bit of money) selecting a library of non-business apps that'll keep you coming back. After all, you purchased a product that can kill time, enhance your brain, help you plan a backpacking excursion, and remove red eye from your birthday party photos. You might as well take advantage of it!

iMessage and the Wide World of Push Notifications

A decade from now, I have to wonder: Will the world remember BBM or iMessage? BBM is short for BlackBerry Messenger, and since early 2008, it was the crown jewel of RIM's software suite. Even today, there are millions of RIM loyalists who refuse to jump ship from BlackBerry, and routinely, I hear "BBM" as one of the primary factors. If you aren't familiar, BBM is effectively a supercharged SMS system. But rather than simply enabling two people to send short bursts of text to one another, BBM allows for group conversations, picture messages, voice note messages, read receipts, and a wide variety of emoticons. And trust me, the world would be a much :-('er place without those. The biggest reason for using BBM, however, just might be its ability to function over any flavor of data—3G, 2G, 4G, Wi-Fi, you name it. The downside? It's a closed network, and only those with devices that link into the BlackBerry Internet Service can indulge. Three years later, and up pops iMessage. There's no question that Apple's following the lead of services before it—BBM most notably—but iMessage has one thing going for it that similar services don't—hundreds of millions of installed users. This chapter explains how short-burst messaging fits into the iPhone's usage profile, how to manage multiple users, and how to put conventional text messages (mostly) to bed.

WHAT *IS* IMESSAGE?

Now that Apple has hundreds of millions of iOS products in the hands of users across the globe, it has a wide enough audience to launch something as closed as iMessage. Without critical mass, this service would be nearly useless. But given just how many people already own an iPod touch, iPad, iPhone, or Mountain Lion-equipped Mac, it's markedly useful. With the introduction of iOS 5 came an all-new messaging service, and it's even more powerful with the launch of iOS 6 and OS X 10.8. It's built right into the "Messages" app in iOS—don't bother looking for an app dubbed iMessage—and seamlessly integrates with standard text message threads that reside there.

In addition to being able to send text-based messages as you already can through SMS (to iPhone owners), iMessage supports the sending of photos, location, contacts, and videos. As with BBM, this service also offers optional read receipts and delivery receipts, and as with AIM chats, you can see when the person you're corresponding with is typing a message back to you. I'll dig into the specifics of accounts in a bit, but because this is all tied to a single e-mail address, you can actually start an iMessage chat on your iPod touch and pick it up on your iPhone. Moreover, that conversation can be continued on an iPad or a Mac with OS X 10.8 (Mountain Lion). So long as each of those is linked to your singular Apple ID, the conversation threads will appear across all Messages platforms.

So, if iMessage is so much like BBM, why the fuss? Messaging is clearly possible through Skype, Google Voice, and other non-core apps, but you still have to be engaged in an app to communicate. iMessage is built into the fabric of iOS. It's always on and it's always able to send and receive messages (via "push") if an Internet connection is present. And if a data connection isn't there, it's still possible to send messages through SMS and MMS on the iPhone. (On the iPad, which doesn't have a phone number tied to it, you'll need data 100 percent of the time.)

The other huge boon here is how much it can save those who are still paying for text messages. Rather than texting your best pals, sending out iMessages to those with iPhones can drastically cut down on how many texts that are billed to them. Friends don't let friends text when iMessage is available, you know?

▶ You can send an iMessage to a cell phone number attached to an iPhone only. If you try to send to a number on a non-iPhone, it'll send as a conventional SMS (text message).

▶ Don't bother looking for iMessage in iOS 4 or earlier; it's available only in iOS 5 and newer.

▶ iMessage works regardless of carrier or data source; if you can load Apple's homepage on a connection, you can send an iMessage.

NOTE In a world suddenly fixated on the cloud, it's becoming more and more apparent that data—not conventional voice communications—will be the leading protocol of the future. Already, VoIP services are seeing skyrocketing usage, and iMessage does a fantastic job of stealing the thunder of SMS by eliminating the requirement of a voice plan. iMessages are sent and received using data bursts—regardless of whether you're using cellular data or some other form of Wi-Fi, your messages can be sent. Even in areas where no traditional cell coverage is available, all you need is a coffee shop with a wireless signal that you can borrow, and the doors to communicate are wide open.

TIP Sharing is caring, is it not? Back in the day, Bluetooth transfers were all the rage, with the short-range wireless protocol called upon often in order to beam images and ringtones from one handset to another. That's still possible, mind you, but using iMessage is a drop-dead simple way to share photos and videos between iOS devices. Sure, you could do the same with e-mail, but if you're already living your life one iMessage at a time, why not spread a little visual love, too?

CROSSREF VoIP apps on the whole are described in frightening detail within Chapter 6.

UNDERSTANDING THE DEPTHS OF IMESSAGE

On an iPhone, the messages you receive in the Messages app will all be sent over data so long as the recipient is an iMessage user; otherwise, it sends over traditional SMS/MMS channels. But because iMessage is a platform with many homes, the possibilities of communication are far greater than the text messages you may have grown up with.

First, you need to ensure that you're connected to the Internet in some form or fashion. On an iPhone, you can just flip on your cellular data radio in order to make contact; otherwise, you need to find a Wi-Fi signal to latch onto. From there, you need to ensure that iMessages are enabled. Just pop into your Settings app, and then head to Messages. That top icon (iMessage) will have a toggle to the right of it; flick that to On and the journey begins. Have a look at the aforementioned pane in Figure 12-1.

▶ You can start a conversation on your iPhone in the airport, and once you're on Gogo's in-flight Wi-Fi, continue that conversation on a Mountain Lion-equipped Mac. That's the real beauty of iMessage—it works with all data sources, even in places where text messages cannot be sent.

FIGURE 12-1: iMessages are active. Your social life can now commence.

> **TIP** Even if you aren't paying for an MMS plan with your cellular carrier, you can send photos to other iMessage users in the Messages app. So long as they're iMessage users, it'll send over your data connection without charging you for a pay-per-use MMS. If you're paranoid, you can turn MMS off entirely in Settings ➔ Messages.

While you're in the Settings pane, take a look at those other three options. I recommend leaving Send Read Receipts off; if you flip that on, others will be notified when you read their messages. Or, when looked at through a slightly more negative tint, this enables obsessive texters to know that you've read a message but haven't replied. *Tsk, tsk.*

Beneath that is perhaps the most important field. It's the Receive At field, and it should contain your Apple ID or your e-mail address. Your life will be made infinitely simpler if you align these two, and I recommend popping in there and adding any

▶ Yep, FaceTime also uses an e-mail address to register and verify. If you've done that, iMessage verification is no different.

alternative e-mail addresses you have as well. For example, whereas many people might know your primary e-mail address, those who matter most know your work e-mail address. If you add your work e-mail address as an extra Receive At address, you'll be able to receive iMessages from peers who write to you at either address. Think of this way: the more e-mail addresses you include, the more likely it is that someone will be able to contact you. Of course, those who prefer *not* to be iMessaged by colleagues can casually ignore this otherwise heartfelt advice. Naturally, your cell number will also be listed here.

Finally, the Show Subject Field should be toggled if you plan on using iMessage as more of a rapid-fire e-mail service than a short messaging service. It simply adds an extra field to each message sent, giving you the opportunity to preface whatever you're about to write with an overarching subject line. (My personal suggestion is to leave it off; if you really need a subject line, you need to head to your nearest e-mail app.)

> **NOTE** If you want to add a photo or video to a message, just tap the circular camera icon to the left of your iMessage text box. From there, you have the option of capturing a photo or video, or choose an existing shot from your Camera Roll or synced photo library.

Switching Accounts

Apple never seemed entirely devoted to MobileMe, and the sudden announcement of its death when iCloud hit the scene all but confirms that it never really had staying power. But if you and your family picked up a couple of MobileMe e-mail addresses, yet you share an Apple ID for iTunes purchases, things are a bit complicated. Since the launch of iCloud, those accounts were spun off into separate ones, but there's still a way to automatically download accounts that were linked by legacy. Just pop open the Settings app on your iPhone and venture down to Store. In there, you can toggle the Automatic Downloads feature for Music, Apps, and Books. Off means that you'll manually sync whatever content you want to a device, although you'll still have access to materials in iTunes that were purchased in the family. On will add any purchase that your spouse makes to your iPhone, and vice-versa. Have a look in Figure 12-2.

It's probably worth explaining why Apple had to break this out. If it didn't, family members would have each other's contacts, e-mail, Photo Stream, and calendars, thanks to iCloud syncing. That might end in tears—*or worse!*—so the Settings app was equipped with Store (mentioned previously) and iCloud, where you can toggle what you want shared. Be careful when flicking those toggles mindlessly, though. If you are the only person who uses your iPhone, it's safe to flip any of these to On. But, if your significant other has a thing for grabbing it, signing out of your account and into theirs, and then picking up their own iMessage conversations, make sure you leave all of those switched to Off. Why? If you toggle 'em on, the Apple ID is locked to your device for 90 days (chalk it up to anti-piracy measures), and furthermore, sharing across a family of devices is now restricted to only five.

FIGURE 12-2: Keep these off unless you're okay with your Apple ID being locked to your iPhone for 90 days.

Group Messaging

Sure, going back and forth with that cute someone you met the other day on the subway is enjoyable, but what if you're looking to converse with a gaggle of your besties—ahem—a group of colleagues all assigned to the same project. Either way, iMessage can make easy work of linking up on the fly, without everyone having to be near a computer and able to jump into an AIM conference room or the like. So long as everyone in your group has an iOS device (the mix matters not) or access to a Mountain Lion-equipped Mac, you can start a group conversation by simply starting a new message within Messages and pressing the + button in the top right for as many folks as you need to add.

> **WARNING** When engaging in a group message session, be sure to choose the right folks from the start. Once a conversation gets underway, you can't bring a new person into it without starting an entirely new thread.

MANAGING YOUR MESSAGING CONTACTS

As mentioned, you can start iMessage conversations by shooting a note to someone's iPhone number, and if they have Receive At set to an e-mail address, the conversation will then move between two e-mail addresses. The easiest way to manage your contacts is to ensure that each and every one of them registers their Apple ID as the e-mail address with which you're familiar. Of course, that's not apt to happen, so there's a trick to figuring out whether someone is or isn't ready to receive iMessages based on the addresses you have stored in your Contacts.

▶ If you try a friend's work e-mail and it shows as unregistered for iMessage, try their personal account. If that fails, call them and ask. Nicely.

> **TIP** Once you've successfully initiated an iMessage conversation, you can keep returning to that thread to avoid having to remember which e-mail address was the correctly registered one. If, for whatever reason, you need to delete a thread, it's as easy as swiping right on a message thread and tapping the Delete icon that appears. Be careful, though—once a thread is gone, it's gone!

KEEPING NOTIFICATIONS UNDER CONTROL

One of the beautiful aspects of using iMessage is the built-in notification factor. True, you can activate similar messages for Skype and other communication apps (and I encourage you to do so!), but it's important to select the right notification options for you with any app—*particularly* an app that specializes in back-and-forth messaging. iMessage is useful only if you check it religiously (not recommended) or mind your alerts (recommended). Here's what I recommend.

▶ Try setting different alert mechanisms for FaceTime, Skype, and Messaging to help you differentiate among these types of messages.

Head to Settings ➜ Notifications, and then tap into Messages (as shown in Figure 12-3). Make sure that Notification Center is toggled On up top. I suggest showing 5 to 10 items in the option pane just below it. That way, older replies aren't thoroughly buried by new ones. I'm a huge fan of Banners as the alert style. One of my biggest gripes with iOS builds prior to iOS 5 were those pesky pop-up alerts, which are still available as an option for those who prefer to keep tradition.

FIGURE 12-3: Manage your Messages from here.

If you're actively using an app, a banner-style alert will simply emerge at the top of the display, shuffling the pixels just enough to momentarily grab your attention, but not completely sidetrack you from whatever it is that you were doing. I also strongly encourage you to flip the View in Lock Screen option to On. If you do, you'll see who is messaging you even if your iPhone's display is off.

SUMMARY

iMessage, in a way, is teaching an old dog (SMS) new tricks (sending iPhone-to-iPad or iPhone-to-Mac messages). It's nothing that hasn't already been done in some form or another by Skype and other Voice Over IP applications, but the built-in nature of the program—and the fact that you have over 200 million potential friends to chat with — makes it a juggernaut in a world that's clearly in love with real-time chat. For all intents and purposes, iMessage is Apple's version of BBM, a closed messaging service made wildly popular by the maker of BlackBerry handsets.

The key to getting contacted is to add multiple Receive At e-mail addresses in Settings, and although there's no way to scan your entire Contacts list to see who is or isn't registered with iMessage, the app (which is simply titled "Messages," oddly enough) is smart enough to check with Apple's servers each time you add a new recipient. And, yes, adding multiple recipients is all that's required to start a group chat—great for working on group projects.

Once you've started to use your iPhone as a chat tool, your life is nearly complete. All that's left to reach pure and unadulterated nirvana is to set up notifications to best suit you. Thankfully, Apple provides a fair number of options, and with each beautiful bloop, you can take pleasure in chipping away at the price-prohibitive SMS market. It's the small things, you know?

PART IV

BECOMING A DIGITAL GENIUS

CHAPTER 13

Utilizing the iPhone's Camera

IN THIS CHAPTER

▶ Understanding camera jargon
▶ Digging into the settings
▶ Touching up your photos
▶ Replacing your point-and-shoot
▶ Taking advantage of geotagging
▶ Sharing your photos

Apple's iPhone range has set the bar for phone cameras.

Apple's phone is oftentimes cited as the most popular camera in global photo sharing sites like Flickr, and for good reason. Not only is the best camera the one you have on you (and in the case of the iPhone, it's the one you'll almost always have on you), but Apple has also gone the extra mile to ensure that its sensors are second to none. Particularly with the iPhone 4S and iPhone 5, Apple has created a smartphone camera that produces stunning pictures in terms of sharpness and quality. Natural limitations exist, but there's a reason many people are leaving their point-and-shoot cameras at home in favor of the iPhone. This chapter dives into the particulars for making the most of your phone's shooter.

SPEAKING THE CAMERA'S LANGUAGE

Not surprisingly, Apple makes using the iPhone's camera quite simple. Point and tap, or point and click if you're using the Volume Up button as the shutter depression mechanism. But understanding some of the basics of photography goes a long way to ensuring that your photos look their very best. (And in the event that they don't, you'll know how to correct it.)

DEFINING PHOTOGRAPHY

Here's a quick-and-dirty guide to photography terms, and a description of how each situation impacts your imagery:

▶ **Shutter lag**—Occasionally, your iPhone will be too busy to capture a photo exactly when you want it to, and you may have to wait up to a full second between the time you push the button and when your phone captures the picture. The 4S and 5 are much quicker, but sometimes you just need patience.

▶ **Lighting**—Bright, natural lighting leads to the best shots. If you're looking to avoid harsh shadows, try to shoot in the day with clouds overhead. At night, expect added blur or grain unless you add a flash.

▶ **Aperture**—You can't tweak the aperture on the iPhone, but in general, the closer your f-stop (aperture) is to zero, the less light a camera needs to take a blur-free image.

▶ **Bokeh**—Ever taken a picture where the foreground is sharp and the background is blissfully blurred? That effect is called *bokeh*. You can encourage this behavior by getting your iPhone dangerously close to the subject (but not too close—it won't focus at all!).

▶ **ISO**—Sadly, Apple won't let you adjust this either. In general, however, a higher ISO enables you to take more crisp images at night, albeit with increased grain and noise as the ISO figure climbs higher.

▶ **HDR**—Apple's built-in HDR mode grabs a couple of shots at different exposures and overlays them on top of one another for a fairly edgy result. Generally speaking, these images "pop" more than standard images.

▶ **Panorama**—It's a built-in mode within iOS 6 that works on the iPhone 4S and 5, but in general, it's the art of taking several images as you pan around, and having them stitched together for one massively wide photo.

UNDERSTANDING THE CAMERA'S SETTINGS

Apple's built-in Camera application pales in comparison to apps available on Android. It's a bit strange that Apple equips its phones with such amazing sensors, but so severely limits your control over them. You can't tweak the ISO, shutter speed, or aperture within the Camera application. All you can do is turn the flash on or off (or set it to Auto), and flip the viewfinder so that it takes a photo with the front-facing camera.

> **WARNING** Although it may be tempting to use the front-facing camera to line up a self-portrait, resist the urge. The front-facing camera is of exceptionally poor quality, and is useful only for video calling. The only respectable sensor on the iPhone is the one on the rear of the device.

It's worth noting that there's a wonderful shortcut to accessing the camera in iOS. After you press your Home button or Power button and pulled up the lock screen, just slide the camera icon in the lower-right corner up (seen in Figure 13-1). It'll peel back the lock screen and reveal the camera. Note that this works even if you haven't entered your four-digit access PIN, but you can't do anything after capture without that code. Apple included this so that users who lock their phones won't miss crucial shots while fiddling with an unlock PIN.

> **NOTE** When holding your phone horizontally, you can use the Volume Down button as the shutter button. Also, if your Apple EarPods are connected, their Volume Dock rocker switch will also press the shutter.

You'll also notice a slider once you're in the application; to the left, it acts as a camera. If you flip it to the right, it records video. That small thumbnail icon in the lower left will take you directly to your photo gallery, where you can flick through images that you've taken in the past.

> **TIP** When in Image mode (and not Video mode), you get an Options bubble. In it, there's a Grid selector and an HDR selector. I leave Grid on, as it helps frame my shot, and HDR off. Why? I prefer to edit my shots in Snapseed, a separate iOS application, and using HDR also creates additional lag between shots. To its credit, Apple does a fantastic job with its HDR mode, and those who don't want to mess with editing apps should feel free to use it.

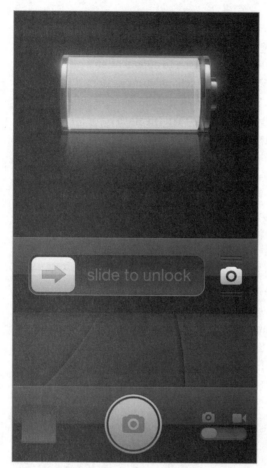

FIGURE 13-1: Slide up to reveal the camera.

Generally, the iPhone does a fairly decent job of determining the focal point of the shot. But every so often, you might want to tell it specifically what to focus on. Thankfully, that's as simple as framing the shot, and then tapping your screen at the point where you want your camera to focus (and in turn, how you want it exposed). From there, you can tap the onscreen shutter button to capture the image, or press the Volume Up button along the phone's edge.

The video mode is exceedingly simple to use. Once you flip the lower toggle from still to video, your onscreen shutter icon will switch to a more familiar red record button. Tap that once, and you'll see a timer begin to count; tap it again, and it'll stop recording and save the video in the Photos app. Curiously, Apple doesn't have a way to easily sort through videos and still images in the Photos app. You'll just notice a small camcorder icon in each video thumbnail.

TIP In an album, you can also select numerous items to e-mail, send via iMessage, or print, but each one has its own hidden maximum. When in doubt, try deselecting an image or two and see if your desired action becomes available.

Notice in the Photos app that things are sorted by albums by default. If you've synced any albums over using iTunes, they show up here. The images you take on your phone are automatically filed in the Camera Roll album. In order to generate a new album on your iPhone, just tap Edit while in Albums view, then tap Add and give the new album a name (see Figure 13-2). It's generally more tedious than just organizing photos into albums on iPhoto and then syncing over, but at least you have this option when you're on the run.

FIGURE 13-2: Go ahead, add a new album. Or three. Or more!

▶ While in the camera screen, just swipe to the right to quickly glance at the photo you just took. Swipe to the left to get back to the camera.

To move photos from the Camera Roll to a new album, just hop into Camera Roll, tap Edit, and select the photo(s) you want moved. Then, tap Add To and select an album that you've created (shown in Figure 13-3).

FIGURE 13-3: Organizing your photos is worth the effort. Trust me.

Available exclusively on the iPhone 5 (which ships with iOS 6) and iPhone 4S (which can be updated for free to iOS 6) is Apple's Panorama mode. To select it, visit the Options bubble while in the Camera app, and tap the Panorama icon (shown in Figure 13-4). Unlike most panorama apps, this one allows you to hold your phone vertically as you pan it; obviously, you'll want to try to hold it as steady as possible, but the results I've seen are really impressive. If you're using an older iPhone, download the free Photosynth app to take your own panoramic photos. (Don't tell anyone it's made by archrival Microsoft, though!)

> **NOTE** Annoyingly, the Email option will only load Apple's Mail app. Users of Sparrow, Gmail, or any other third-party app cannot force the iOS system to use a different e-mail application as the default.

Another nifty way to view your photos is Places, which is a tab found to the right of Albums within the Photos app. If you've enabled geotagging on your phone, photos will populate on maps based on the location that they were taken, as seen in Figure 13-5. Instagram has also added a similar photo-map feature in its latest build.

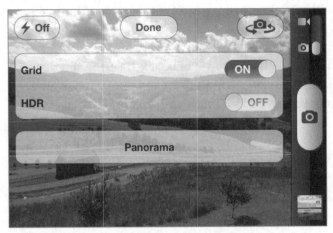

FIGURE 13-4: Life just looks better when viewed panoramically.

FIGURE 13-5: Ah, fond memories of travel destinations. And bad ones of bouts with the TSA...

EDITING YOUR PHOTOS

Yes, you can edit photos without having to dump them onto a laptop and fire up Photoshop or Lightroom. I can't promise that your results will be as stunning, but most iPhone users want to quickly add a bit of tender, loving care to a photo, save it, and upload it to a social network. If you want to take more time, the best way to offload full-resolution images from your iPhone is to connect it to your computer, load iPhoto, and drag photos into an album. If you e-mail a photo, it is a compressed version of the image.

> **NOTE** Toned-down versions of Apple's own iMovie and iPhoto apps are available in the App Store for $4.99. They're certainly well made, but probably only worthwhile for those who routinely assemble slideshows and trailers to showcase their jaunts.

You have a few free options. Facebook's Camera application has some built-in editing tools (as well as seamless integration with the Facebook app), and Instagram's well-known filter selection is there as well. Of note, it's possible to use Instagram just to tweak photos and save the result to your Camera Roll; you don't necessarily have to upload your works of art to its social sharing network.

> **TIP** If you want to use Snapseed for editing, but Instagram for sharing, make sure you take advantage of Snapseed's 1:1 crop mode before engaging in any tweaks. That way, your photo is pre-cropped for Instagram.

I recommend a $4.99 download of Snapseed, shown in Figure 13-6. It's a beautifully designed, easy-to-use editing app that does a fantastic job of using gestures to make your photos look genuinely superior. The app's parent company was recently purchased by Google, so it remains to be seen how much longer iOS development will continue. I have a hunch that most of the Snapseed improvements from here on out will impact Android first and iOS second.

DITCHING YOUR POINT-AND-SHOOT CAMERA

There's a lot of truth to the adage of the best camera being the one that's accessible. The quality of iPhone images has become so good that many people think there's really no need to carry a conventional point-and-shoot camera anymore. Yes, a mirror-less alternative or a DSLR still has attractive merits, but the iPhone's quality and ease-of-use makes it difficult to justify spending $200+ on a typical compact.

FIGURE 13-6: Snapseed makes it quick and enjoyable to spruce up your shots.

The only real drawback to relying solely on your iPhone as your only camera is this—the zoom. Yes, the iPhone has digital zoom, but the results are awful. Without an optical zoom, or a lens that physically moves to zoom, you're left only with the ability to take very wide shots. This might not impact you, but it's something to consider. Furthermore, those who shoot routinely on their iPhone may want to invest in a 64GB model. Don't underestimate just how much space thousands of photos and videos can take up. Because there's no storage expansion slot on the iPhone, there's no way to add extra space once it's filled up.

NOTE Select cameras are now shipping with Wi-Fi (and even Android!), but there's still no better "sharing" camera than the iPhone. Snap a shot, edit it quickly, and upload it to a variety of social networks. These days, it's not just the shot you take, but who you share it with.

GEOTAGGING YOUR PHOTOS

As someone who adores travel (yes, even the frequent headaches that come along with it), I have a particular love for geotagging. In short, geotagging is a process by which a camera looks at your GPS information, and then stamps that data onto the image that you've taken. In other words, a shot taken at the Statue of Liberty includes your exact longitude and latitude coordinates stamped on the metadata of the image, so that you can look at the photo years later and remember exactly where you were when you snapped it. Yes, it's nerdy, but it's also a fantastic way to journal your trips by location over the years.

So long as you're outdoors, have a solid 3G or 4G data connection, and have GPS enabled in your Settings, the Camera app will attempt to find a GPS fix fast enough to associate your location with your image automatically. Moreover, those who use Foursquare, Facebook Camera, or Instagram can use the location features in those apps to tag photos with a locale or landmark. Again, this might seem frivolous in the here and now, but over the course of many years, it's really impressive to look back and see where your life has taken you by way of geotagged images.

To ensure that you have Location Services enabled for your geotagging apps, go to Settings ➜ Location Services and flip the toggle to On (shown in Figure 13-7). Then, make sure that Camera, Facebook, Foursquare, and any other photo-related app you use has its own toggle flipped to On.

SHARING IS CARING

As I alluded to earlier, sharing is a huge part of taking a video or photo on the iPhone. Whereas most apps—including Twitter, Facebook, Foursquare, and Instagram—allow you to open the camera from within the app itself, I recommend a different approach. I generally start all of my photo expeditions from within Camera. That way, I know for sure I have a copy of the photo in my Camera Roll album that I can find and tinker with however I see fit. It gives me more control over what happens to my images.

Then, I open my sharing app of choice, and pick the photo from my Camera Roll. It's possible to start with Instagram, and have that app linked to your Facebook, Foursquare, and Twitter accounts. In other words, you can share a photo on Instagram, and also have that app push your share to three other social networks—pretty handy, no? I've found Instagram to be the most platform-agnostic app out there, as it's the only major sharing app that has no qualms whatsoever playing nice with the others. Have a look at how the multi-platform sharing works in Figure 13-8.

FIGURE 13-7: Keep Location Services on for photo-related apps if you want to geotag your shots.

> **WARNING** With few exceptions, any image shared over a social network app will be heavily downsized. Facebook's Camera app has a setting that allows high-res uploads even over mobile networks, but otherwise, you need to save the high-res version on a machine back at home. It's the cost of sharing in a world where bandwidth is tough to come by.

Thanks to iCloud, sharing has also taken on a different life with iOS itself. Photo Stream, if you have it enabled, allows any photo you take to automatically be uploaded to your photo galleries on other iCloud-enabled products. So, a shot taken on your iPhone 5 will automatically appear on your iPad and Mac back home, so long as they're all logged into your personal iCloud account. Unfortunately, Photo Stream works only with your most recent 1,000 photos, so don't rely on this as a permanent sharing/storage solution.

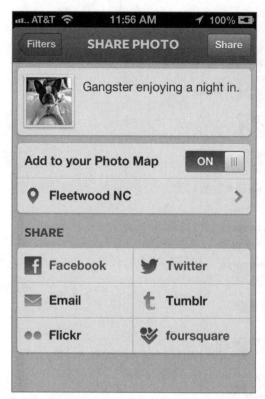

FIGURE 13-8: Instagram shares with everyone. What a well-mannered app.

Shared Photo Streams are perhaps even more enjoyable. Here, you simply select the Shared Photo Streams tab within the Photos app (seen in Figure 13-9), select the images you want shared, and then input the people that you want to share them with. They'll even get a standard URL, enabling them to open the folder in any web browser, regardless of platform.

SUMMARY

There's no question that the iPhone is a formidable camera, and it's being used in place of point-and-shoot cameras already. You'll miss out on the zoom capabilities, but I recommend using the iPhone to complement a mirror-less or DSLR camera. Apple has also limited the amount of tweaking you can do with the Camera app, but thankfully, the App Store has plenty of software to make editing fun and easy.

FIGURE 13-9: Share your Photo Streams, won't you?

Programs like iPhoto, iMovie, Lightroom, and Snapseed should be in any photographer's toolkit, and those who fancy sharing will want to download Instagram, Foursquare, and Facebook, or utilize Shared Photo Streams. Geotagging is also an art that's coming of age, enabling users to tag pinpoint locations to specific photos. Years down the road, you'll enjoy looking back at where life took you by way of photos.

Utilizing Your Personal Assistant: Siri

You've seen the commercials. You might even know the voice by heart. But have you really put in the effort to conjure up a real relationship with Siri? Siri is Apple's personal assistant, who debuted on the iPhone 4S and has since found a home on the new iPad and its most current iPhones. Unbeknownst to most outside of the technology field, Siri wasn't actually created within Apple's labs. The company that built Siri was acquired by Apple in April of 2010, and the rest—as they say—is history. Siri was billed as a "personal assistant" from day one, rather than a run-of-the-mill voice recognition system. The difference? You can talk to Siri like a real person, instructing her to do things. She does more than simply convert spoken words into text on a screen; she's capable of actually accomplishing chores for you. The trick, of course, is understanding how to speak to her, what she can and can't understand, and how to work around her flaws. Oh, and I refer to her as "her" throughout the chapter. Yes, she's an inanimate robot, but it's just so much more fun to think of her as a bona fide confidant.

COMMANDING A ROBOT

If you let yourself be persuaded by the ads on television, you might believe that Siri is *exactly* like a human in your phone. Just talk to her, and she'll respond to anything without issue. That's actually pretty far from the truth. Siri may be wise, and she may possess a freakish amount of language processing skills, but she's not all-knowing. If you've ever used any of Nuance's Dragon Dictate software, you may be familiar with having to tailor your delivery to suit the program. Basically, you have to talk to the robot on the other end in a way that you know it'll understand.

> **NOTE** Unfortunately, Apple has limited Siri to its newer devices, despite the fact that older units clearly have the oomph to power her. If you're still running iOS 5, you can get Siri onto the iPhone 4, iPhone 3GS, and older iPads thanks to a piece of software called Spire. The process is a bit lengthy though, but there's a full walkthrough (video included) here: www.huffingtonpost.com/2012/01/05/spire-install-siri-on-iphone-4_n_1186551.html.

In my opinion, there's really no reason to leave Siri off. She doesn't have a negative impact on battery life, and she stays well out of your way unless you call on her. Unlike other Apple-installed applications like Mail and Safari, Siri is not a standalone "app." There's no "icon" to access her. To make sure she's enabled, simply visit Settings ➔ General ➔ Siri. You'll find an On/Off toggle switch there at the top, which you should slide to On. You also need to select the language that's most closely associated with your own. The Raise to Speak option is an interesting one; with this flipped on, you can simply raise the phone to your ear as if you're about to converse with someone, and it automatically puts Siri into a listen mode. This is designed so that you can talk to Siri while looking "natural" on the phone, and presumably, no one will know you're talking to a robot instead of a real person.

> **TIP** Make sure you double-check the Language setting. If you buy your iPhone in Australia, it defaults to listening for an Australian accent; if you speak British English, Siri has an insanely hard time understanding you. Conversely, if you're a native UKer living in the United States, change the default from US English to British English.

The primary method of activating Siri is simple—just hold down the Home button for a couple of seconds. Notice a small microphone icon surface from the bottom, indicating that Siri is active and listening for spoken commands. Also notice a "What can I help you with?" line, but it's the shadowed "i" to the right of that phrase that's important. Tap that to gain instant access to the growing list of things that Siri can do. If you ever forget what Siri can do, this is where you come to look. You can see what the list looks like currently in Figure 14-1.

FIGURE 14-1: Forget what Siri can do? Here's a handy reminder list.

NOTE Even if you have a screen lock/passcode enabled—and you should!—you can activate Siri. Just hold down the Home button and speak, and if she needs to access the inner workings of your phone (to open a map, for example), she'll remind you to enter your passcode in order to proceed. Still, you can at least start the conversation without having to first unlock your handset. If you want Siri to be available only after your iPhone is unlocked, visit Settings ➔ General ➔ Passcode Lock and flip the Siri switch to Off.

Like most great tools, you need to use Siri frequently to appreciate her. Frankly, it's easy to forget that Siri exists. She doesn't pop up and annoy you, so you need to get in the habit of leaning on her. It's especially unnatural for those who have used the iPhone since 2007; suddenly, there's a new way to input text and commands. You just have to remember to hit the toggle!

Take a look at a list of things Siri can help you with in iOS 6:

- Calling: say "Call [*contact name*]"
- Launching apps: say "Launch [*app name*]"
- Sending a text or iMessage: say "Text [*contact name*]"
- Playing music in Apple's Music app: say "Play [*album, artist, or song name*]"
- Adding a Calendar entry: say "Set up a meeting at [*time and place, with details*]"
- Adding a reminder: say "Remind me [*details*]"
- Using the maps: say "Find [*name or place and location*]"
- Getting directions: say "Directions to [*destination*]"
- Checking the weather: say "What's the weather like in [*location*]?"
- Setting the alarm clock: say "Wake me up at [*time and date*]"
- Using the Address Book: say "What's [*contact name*]'s address?"
- Using Notes: say "Note that I [*details*]"
- Using Safari: say "Search the web [*query*]"
- Using Stocks: say "What is the stock price of [*company*]?"
- Using E-mail: say "E-mail [*contact*]"
- Using WolframAlpha: Ask any generic question and see how it shakes out!
- Checking the movies: ask "Is [*movie title*] playing nearby?"
- Using Facebook/Twitter: say "Post to Facebook or post to Twitter"
- Checking sports' scores: ask about any professional team score
- Checking for restaurants: say "Make a reservation at [*eatery name*]" or "Find [kind of eatery] near [location]"

As for what Siri can't do? If it's not on the list, don't expect her to work miracles. For example, if you use MOG as your primary music app, you cannot tell Siri to "play artist Everember in MOG." She knows only how to play music in the Apple Music app. The same is true for any other third-party app—in fact, that's the biggest flaw of Siri as she stands today. There are no APIs distributed to developers to enable Siri to access third-party apps. Although you can ask the built-in Maps app for directions, it would be better if you could instruct Siri to "open Navigon and route me to Boone, North Carolina." Hopefully, Apple will let Siri converse with third-party apps in the future, but for now, it's a (mostly) closed door. The only major exception is third-party programs that work via CalDAV; for instance, you can make Siri use Remember The Milk instead of its own Reminders app if you program your RTM information from Settings ➜ Mail, Contacts, Calendars ➜ Add Account ➜ Others.

> **TIP** Don't take no for an answer. If you ask Siri, "do I have anything at 2PM tomorrow?", she'll be unable to answer. If you tweak that to, "do I have appointments at 2PM tomorrow?", she'll look into your Calendar and respond. You'll spend a lot of trial-and-error time working on the best ways to state your questions.

INTEGRATING SIRI INTO YOUR DIGITAL WORKFLOW

As you spend a week or two with Siri, you begin to notice what she's good at, and what she's not so good at. Each time I pick up my iPhone, I make a decision as to whether to use Siri, and it all hinges on time. Remind yourself to ask this question: "Can I do this faster myself, or can Siri do it faster?" One of the things that Siri is wonderful for is a reminder. Whenever you're out and about and a thought pops into your head, just toggle Siri and ask her to remind you of something at a later time or place. This is almost always quicker than pulling out your phone, opening Notes, and pecking a reminder in there with your thumbs.

Moreover, the Reminders app becomes infinitely more useful if you have a Mountain Lion-equipped Mac at home. In fact, the iPhone is a lot more useful when you have the other half of the ecosystem—a Mac computer—waiting at home or work. Reminders that you input on your iPhone (or iPad, for that matter) automatically sync with your iCloud account. So long as your Mac's Notification Center is also synced to that same iCloud account, reminders will flash on your Mac even if you're away from your phone.

If you need something deeper than a casual reminder, Siri can create Calendar appointments. If you have integrated your Google Calendars into Apple's Calendar app, I recommend visiting Settings ➜ Mail, Contacts Calendar and cruising down to Calendar. Look for the Default Calendar option and ensure that it's selecting your Google Calendar of choice (it'll default to iCloud). This way, any appointment that Siri makes will also show up in your Google Calendar. It's a behind-the-scenes way to get Siri to add something to Google Calendar.

▶ Reminders are not integrated into Calendar; use Reminders for short-term, one-off things, while reserving Calendar entries for more elaborate appointments that have time schedules and locations.

> **WARNING** You can't use Siri to add appointments to third-party calendar apps. That said, if you configure Calendar (Apple's built-in app) to display your calendar from another source (like Google), you can create a situation where Siri adds an appointment to Calendar, which in turn syncs with your third-party calendar of choice.

Digging a bit deeper into the WolframAlpha integration, it might help to understand what exactly WolframAlpha is. Put simply, it's an information engine. It takes basic questions and produces instant answers. If you ask Siri how many ounces are in a gallon, you'll get a WolframAlpha card displaying the conversion. If you ask Siri how many Euros are in 100 U.S. dollars, you'll get a WolframAlpha card displaying currency conversions. Most generic questions such as these will route through WolframAlpha first, and if no answer can be generated, Siri typically offers to search the web as a fallback.

> **NOTE** One of the bigger bummers about WolframAlpha results is that they display as static images on your phone. This means that Siri cannot read WolframAlpha answers aloud as she can text on the Internet. So, even if you search via Siri without ever having to glance down at your iPhone, you'll eventually have to gaze at the screen to digest the answer.

It's important to note that Siri understands human-like speech much better when relationships are established. In other words, it's worth taking the time to teach Siri that Alice is your mom, Greg is your dad, and Kevin is your brother (hypothetically speaking, of course). That way, you can simply say "make a noon appointment tomorrow for lunch with Mom" and Siri will know precisely which contact to associate with it.

You can establish these relationships in one of two ways. You can toggle Siri and simply tell her "Alice is my mother." Or, the first time you make an appointment using a generic term like "sister" or "father," Siri will ask you which contact to associate with it. Unfortunately, Siri isn't great at pronouncing unusual names. In that case, just have Siri call you "champion" or "master"—whatever makes you feel better in the morning. Have a look at how this conversation typically goes in Figure 14-2.

Although comprehending your tasks is one thing, Siri's also a pretty good dictation tool, too. For instance, if you're composing a new e-mail in your Gmail app, you can simply tap the small microphone button on the lower portion of the onscreen keyboard to make Siri listen for voice input. As long as your cursor is where you want it to be—presumably in the body of the e-mail—Siri will listen for your words, translate them to text, and paste them in.

FIGURE 14-2: Let's talk family, Siri.

But, of course, it's really not as simple as that. Although the process of starting a dictation is the same for everything Siri isn't smart enough to always understand exactly what you mean. For instance, you have to tell her when you want punctuation. If there is to be a comma in the phrase, you literally have to say the word "comma." The same goes for periods, exclamation marks, question marks, quotes, and so on. You also have to be careful when speaking initials, times, company names, nonstandard words, and atypical proper nouns—if it's not in a traditional dictionary, chances are Siri will botch the transcription.

> **TIP** Try to limit your bursts of speech to two sentences at a time. Nothing is more frustrating than being partway through the fourth sentence and having Siri cut you off for processing.

While we're on the topic, it's worth pointing out that dictation is a great safety feature, too. If you're shuffling down a busy city street, being able to keep your eyes up and your senses aware while sending an e-mail or text is a real boon. Even looking down for five seconds can be enough time for you to mistakenly walk out into the street. In a vehicle, I still wouldn't recommend picking up your phone to activate Siri and send a text, but starting with 2013 model year vehicles, BMW, GM, Mercedes, Land Rover, Jaguar, Audi, Toyota, Chrysler, and Honda will include a feature called *eyes free*. Effectively, this feature allows your paired iPhone to have Siri activated via a steering wheel control, where you can then initiate calls, texts, and e-mails to contacts without having to take your focus away from the road.

> NOTE   Siri does an admirable job of hearing your voice even with background noise surrounding you, but it's obviously best to be in a quiet place while speaking calmly and directly. Yelling or whispering tends to confuse Siri.

WHY LOCATION MATTERS, EVEN TO SIRI

Geofencing. Ever heard of it? If not, it's a way of putting a "fence" around your phone based on GPS data. Although GPS data is obviously useful for things like navigation, it's also extremely useful when combined with Reminders and Siri. The iPhone's Reminders app can add location into the mix (as seen in Figure 14-3), in addition to time. If you want to be reminded to drive to the local grocery and grab a bag of oranges after you leave work, you *could* guess what time you'll be leaving and set the reminder for that time. But what if you're a little late leaving the office? Geofencing to the rescue.

If you tell Siri to remind you to grab oranges when you leave work, she'll then ask you if you're at work—or, where work is. Once she has established a link between the word "work" and the location of your workplace, she's able to monitor your position and trigger the reminder just as soon as you're a few hundred yards away from the workplace.

Similarly, this works for "home." If you ask Siri to remind you to check the mailbox when you get home, she'll trigger that reminder as you're pulling into your driveway as long as you've previously established a link between the word "home" and the coordinates of your abode.

It's important to remember that while this feature is useful, it's not bulletproof. If you work in a dense office building in midtown Manhattan, and you ask Siri to remind you of something when you leave work, you may get 8 to 10 blocks away before the reminder is triggered.

▶ Even if you don't want to establish relationships with places, you can ask Siri to remind you to do something once arriving at a specific address.

FIGURE 14-3: See that location field in Reminders? Use it!

I'll wrap this chapter up by mentioning one important thing that touches on everything that Siri does: data. Siri is not only data-driven, she's data-dependent. In order for Siri to comprehend *anything* that you tell her—be it a command or a spoken sentence ripe for dictation—she needs access to the Internet. The reason? None of Siri's speech translations are housed locally on the iPhone. Siri simply takes what you say, sends it out to a cloud-based translation server, and then acts on whatever impulses she receives back. If you remove that middleman, Siri is useless.

Obviously, Siri works best if your iPhone is latched on to a fast Wi-Fi network. She'll work decently if you have a strong 3G or 4G connection, but she'll drive you batty (see Figure 14-4) if you try to use her on a spotty connection or an EDGE (or slower) data connection. In a remote part of Montana, I've seen Siri take three minutes to look up an address. Talk about frustrating. If you notice that your data signal isn't ideal, it's probably best to skip Siri and use the more conventional finger-onscreen method of getting things done.

FIGURE 14-4: If Siri has a lackluster data connection, you'll start getting annoying replies like these.

SUMMARY

Siri has become the heart and soul of the iPhone, and in general, it makes users feel closer to their devices. It's as if she's a real person, able to understand typical human speech and assist you with things like creating appointments, scheduling reminders, and queuing up your favorite tunes.

It's challenging to remember what all Siri can and cannot do, and from there, learning how to best phrase your queries to get the most out of her. Although she's not perfect, she's capable of handling many chores associated with first-party apps, and she's a very suitable replacement to a notepad of to-do items in your pocket.

As great as she is, Siri still requires a data connection to function. This means that rural areas or users traveling overseas won't be able to adequately take advantage of her services.

Social Networking Savvy

Prior to iOS 5, there was no core integration of social networking within Apple's mobile OS. Plenty of third-party apps, sure, but nothing tied into its fabric in the way that Messages, Maps, Facebook, and Twitter are now. To say that the 140-word microblogging site has become a worldwide phenomenon is a laughable understatement, and even Apple knows that it isn't apt to rival The Big Two with anything of its own. (Yes, this is my gentle jab at the now-defunct Ping.) With the introduction of iOS 5, Twitter became not only a recommended app, but an app with links to just about everything else in the system. In iOS 6, that same courtesy was extended to Facebook. Now, sharing just about anything is as natural as e-mailing with the company's own Mail app. In fact, Twitter saw sign-ups increase threefold when iOS 5 was launched, as people found it convenient to register for the service since it was integrated. The iPhone is a highly social tool, and there's plenty to be done with it in the world of sharing and networking. From learning the ins and outs of Twitter to diving into the rabbit hole of location-based deals, this chapter breaks down everything you need to know about "handles," "check-ins," and "Likes."

TAPPING INTO @TWITTER VIA iOS 6 #HOWTO

If you're scratching your head wondering what that heading means, you're in the perfect place to learn. Twitter is not only an entity of its own, but it encourages a jargon and language all its own, too. It's both simple and impossible to explain. You're given 140 characters per tweet in order to make your point, and the sheer nature of that restriction forces you to get creative when thinking about how to best disseminate information.

> **TIP** The Tweet command is always tucked within the generic iOS Share icon, which looks like a rectangle with an arrow emerging and pointing to the top right.

On the iPhone, it makes perfect sense. As a casual browsing tool, built-in Twitter integration makes sharing stories, images, and videos with your "followers" as easy as tapping one or two icons. Interested? Getting started is as simple as opening your Settings app and visiting the Twitter banner (shown in Figure 15-1). From there, you can find a shortcut to download the official Twitter app, and beneath, you can input your Twitter handle or sign up for one. Better still, you can add multiple accounts—useful if you're the social media manager for a brand or a company. The simplistic form, shown in Figure 15-2, is pretty easy to overlook.

> **WARNING** Make sure you're very clear as to which account is sending tweets; a "business" tweeting about Bieber fever might not go over well.

I also recommend tapping the Update Contacts button. With a simple tap, your iPhone will use the phone numbers and e-mail addresses found in your Contacts in order to associate Twitter handles and profile images with your existing list of cohorts. It's worth noting, however, that this feature does *not* scour your Contacts list and then automatically follow them on Twitter. Phew.

Beneath that, still in the Settings pane, you'll notice a section titled Allow. What's curious about this is that a great number of Apple's own apps support Twitter, including Maps, Photos, Safari, and Camera. But it's not until you actually open one of those apps, click the Share icon, and tap Tweet that they show up in the list of apps to allow or disallow access. Have a look yourself in Figure 15-3.

▶ Twitter trouble? Keep a check on updates and iOS change logs at https://support .twitter.com/.

▶ The same person, Jack Dorsey, created Twitter and founded Square, both of which are amazing iPhone-friendly products.

FIGURE 15-1: Setting up Twitter couldn't be easier. You don't even need 140 characters to explain it.

FIGURE 15-2: Punch in your Twitter credentials to add as many accounts as you need. Split personalities are welcome.

FIGURE 15-3: Not interested in enabling Twitter in certain apps? Flip 'em off! Er... switch them off.

NOTE The notion that Apple thinks Twitter integration is so core to the usability of iOS is proof that devices are become increasingly less useful without an Internet connection. I've stated already that many of the iPhone's best features cannot be accessed without a live feed to the web, and it's exemplified here. The discussion in this chapter assumes that you're online. If you're offline, Twitter can't help you. And it's a sad, sad state of affairs to boot.

TIP If, for whatever reason, you need to delete your Twitter account from iOS (if you're quitting the business that owns a Twitter account that you manage, for example), it's easy to do so. Just head to Settings ➜ Twitter, tap on the account that needs to be yanked, and touch Delete Account, while waving goodbye with your free hand.

► Short for "application programming interface," which is code that allows app makers to build certain features.

When apps become "native" to an iOS, this greatly affects what the app developers can do. And soon after, it affects the users. Now that Twitter is supported at an operating system level, developers can program their apps to support the Tweet function that Apple includes in Maps, Safari, and so on. In other words, every third-party app now has access to APIs that allow a Tweet function to be built into it, routing inputs through the official Twitter application. Of course, not all apps will add Twitter support—it just doesn't make sense for some genres—but now that Apple is on board, the floodgates are officially open.

THIRD-PARTY APPS THAT LOVE TWITTER

Developers are still working furiously to add Twitter integration to their programs, but a few choice ones are already trickling out. Here are a few of my favorites:

► **Flipboard** (free)—A magazine-style reader that I recommended a few chapters back. This is one app that makes perfect sense for Twitter integration. As you're catching up on the day's news, being able to tweet out a link you love with one touch is brilliant. One of Twitter's biggest strengths is its ability to spread news; it works wonderfully here.

► **LivingSocial** (free)—If you haven't caught on to the social networking + deals craze, you should. I discuss these in more detail in the section "Checking In for Deals," but suffice it to say, being able to tweet out your favorite deal could make you a local hero.

- ▶ **Groupon** (free)—Same story here; but if you're in the mood to grab apps, go ahead and download this one.

- ▶ **MadPad** ($0.99)—This app is a breath of fresh air in the App Store. You're encouraged to capture sounds around you—from a trash can lid, a bouncing ball, and so on—and then convert them into listenable tracks. Once you're ready to share your creation with a broader audience, built-in Twitter integration makes doing so a cinch.

- ▶ **PopSugar** (free)—OMG! This is probably *the* perfect app for Twitter integration. Read and tweet about the latest celebrity gossip. It goes hand-in-hand, really.

- ▶ **Showyou** (free)—If you have ever doubted the power and utility of social sharing, this app will win you over. With just a single tap to sign in via Twitter, this app shows you the videos that are being viewed and shared by those you follow. It's like getting the scoop, without ever having to ask, "What are you guys talking about?"

If you're wondering how to keep track of which apps do and don't support native Twitter integration, there's one last app you should download. Once installed, there's an icon to tap that clues you in on a Top 100 list of Twitter-friendly iOS apps. Sifting through here could clue you in on socially-inclined apps that you might otherwise never discover. If you're looking to see if apps you already own have been updated, just ogle the aforementioned Share icon and look for Twitter or Tweet to be an available option.

WHAT ABOUT FACEBOOK?

In iOS 6, Apple decided to give Facebook equal status to Twitter. The recently-IPO'ed social network now has OS-level integration, giving it the same "single sign-in" functionality that Twitter has enjoyed since iOS 5. Everywhere you see a Share button, you'll find both Facebook and Twitter listed. See for yourself in Figure 15-4.

Beyond the built-in iOS integration, there's also a bona fide iPhone application (shown in Figure 15-5), and it's definitely one of the more elaborate, useful, and polished free apps in the App Store. Being that it's gratis, I heartily recommend that you download it, and while you won't be sharing much with it without a copy and a paste, at least iOS makes even that process fairly painless.

FIGURE 15-4: The new Share screen in iOS 6

FIGURE 15-5: Facebook's iPhone app—as useful as it is beautiful

Moreover, the Facebook iPhone app *does* integrate with iOS's Notification Center, so you can customize alerts, see how many unread messages you have by just looking at the app icon, and get alerts of incoming wall posts and the like right on your lock screen.

THOSE OTHER SOCIAL NETWORKING APPS...

Facebook and Twitter are mainstays, for sure, but you're selling yourself short if you stop there. The App Store is home to dozens upon dozens of other social networking and sharing applications, some of which far outclass the official Twitter app that iOS relies on for integration. A few of the following apps also weave in some of the more esoteric chat protocols—fading perhaps, but not forgotten.

▸ **IM+** (free)—You can opt for the $9.99 "Pro" version to add Skype chat, but there's really no need. Download Skype for free if you're interested in doing that. The gratis version has a few advertisements, but they're easy to swallow given the immense amount of functionality that's here. Rather than being a standalone app for one chat or social networking platform, IM+ allows you to punch in your credentials for Windows Live/MSN, Facebook, Yahoo!, Google Talk, AOL, ICQ, MySpace, Twitter, and Jabber, among others.

▶ **GetGlue** (free)—This isn't your everyday social networking tool. So long as you have a Facebook account, you can log in to the app and then check in with whatever you're doing. Unlike Foursquare, which focuses on location, this app focuses on activities—listening to a certain song, watching a certain show, and so on. Your actions are immediately pushed out to your Facebook account, where your friends can Like your statuses and comment on them. Of course, Facebook holdouts (all six of you) can sign up for a dedicated GetGlue account.

▶ **Twitter** (free)—The reason for this inclusion? Even if you have no interest in iOS integration, Twitter is the most polished Twitter app for iPhone. If Twitter wouldn't have purchased TweetDeck, I suspect TweetDeck's iPhone app would have continued being awesome. As it stands though, one of the best social networking apps on the iPhone has been—shall we say, dumbed down—following the company's acquisition by Twitter. If you're a diehard TweetDeck user on the desktop, www.tweetdeck.com still renders beautifully on Safari or Opera Mini.

▶ **Yelp** (free)—Looking for a place to eat? Something to do? Real reviews from real humans? This app has it all; by the truckload I might add. Furthermore, you can converse about your decisions through the Facebook and Twitter integration, and the iPhone-specific layout makes finding things through the embedded Maps a cinch. Of course, the Maps app in iOS 6 isn't necessarily better for those needing mass transit directions, but it's certainly a boon for avid Yelpers.

▶ **Taptu** (free)—It's almost as sexy as Pulse News, but there's a social networking flair here that shouldn't be overlooked. Similar to how Showyou displays videos that your friends and colleagues are viewing, this app shows you news based on what's being shared by both your Facebook *and* Twitter friends. It's a great way to engage and keep track of what your inner circle is (and isn't) paying attention to.

LOCATION-BASED NETWORKING

Location-based networking has boomed in the past few years, likely due to the growing ubiquity of mobile broadband and the rapid emergence of group-based couponing sites such as Groupon and LivingSocial. But even if you aren't interested in saving money (or *spending* money), you have plenty of options to keep yourself on the map while traveling with your iPhone.

iPhone Check-Ins

When you hear "check-in," one entity primarily comes to mind. Foursquare (see Figure 15-6) arguably pioneered the art of making public your location through social networks, and it has grown into a segment all its own. Now users can get deals and other rewards for checking in at a place; for the merchant, each check-in that a user makes public acts as free advertising.

FIGURE 15-6: Foursquare keeps your pals in the loop when it comes to your whereabouts.

Foursquare supports its own proprietary login or Facebook logins. Whenever I check in using the Foursquare app, those alerts are immediately published to both my Facebook and Twitter profiles, allowing me to take the conversation to two places where a great majority of my friends are.

Checking in serves a couple of purposes. For one, it enables your friends and family to know where you are. If you have a few coworkers in a certain area, you might end up getting a call from one if you end up in their neck of the woods. It's also becoming a more realistic way to network. Prior to the check-in movement, Facebook status updates consisted of your location details. With the advent of GPS and mapping IP addresses, you can add credence to those claims. Foursquare and its contemporaries make no bones about it—the digital badge of honor received when checking into a wild or exotic place is very real.

NOTE It's not quite the same, but Apple's gratis Find My Friends app is a must-download for any iPhone owner. It uses your contact list to sift through people you actually want to keep in touch with via location, and if your requests are granted, you'll soon see fellow iOS owners (and Find My Friends users) popping up on a map within the program. The major downside is that it's iOS-only, so it won't track check-ins from Foursquare, Twitter, Facebook, or elsewhere. Plus, it requires an Apple ID to sign in, so families using the same ID can't easily track one another unless they each sign up for a separate account.

Facebook's Move into Location

The Facebook iPhone app allows users to check into nearby locales from within the app, and of course, those check-ins can also be forced to Twitter if you like.

Facebook's iPhone app has quickly become my go-to app when looking for friends in my area, and for check-ins in general. I suggest loading up the Facebook app, tapping that three-lined icon in the top-left corner, and surfing to the Nearby section. If you're connected to the Internet, a map will load showing your current location, as well as the location of friends who are near. It's a frighteningly painless way to see if any of your colleagues or childhood pals are near. If someone is near, sending him or her a Facebook message is only a tap away.

If you prefer to check yourself in while you're at it—and put yourself on the visible map for those looking around for friends to ping—you can tap the Check In icon in the top-right corner.

▶ You can also check in while in the standard News Feed; the Check In icon is just right of center along the top bar in the app.

TIP If you pinch-to-zoom out on the map, you can see where all of your Facebook friends are checked into at the moment. For travel junkies, it's a pretty amazing view, and it's exceptionally easy to access.

Checking In for Deals

Over the past couple of years, a handful of "deals" sites have cropped up with location as the focal point, and "group buying" has been fleshed out in a major way. A decade ago, the only way you could get a bulk discount was to be a major corporation with a direct line to a major supplier, or on a smaller scale, shop at Sam's Club. The trouble there—in addition to needing a significant amount of money to take home individual discounts—was the sheer quantity of product that you ended up with.

Thanks to Groupon and LivingSocial (among many, many others), the cost savings of group buying have been delivered to the everyman. If you've been tuning out the noise, it works as such: every day, Groupon and LivingSocial work with companies small and large in major (and increasingly, minor) areas in order to promote deals to their users. In short, they convince companies to offer a certain service or product at a ridiculous discount, with the understanding that hundreds—if not thousands—of people will flock in and take advantage. Some might say it's making money on quantity instead of margin; others say it's underselling in order to build a larger, more loyal customer base.

Either way, both outfits have beautifully designed iPhone apps that are most effective when you're looking for deals near you. If you show up in a new place with a bit of time to kill, firing up either of these apps can enable you to find local activities, services, and food on the cheap. It immediately takes the legwork out of finding coupons in a new locale, and even when you're home, the coupons come to you.

SUMMARY

Fact is, you'll find entirely too many amazing things on your iPhone not to share them. Apple knows it, and deep in the back of your mind, so do you. With the introduction of iOS 5, Apple unveiled a deep level of Twitter integration, enabling a swath of its core apps to share activities on Twitter. Now that iOS 6 has been released to the public, Facebook is on a level playing field with OS-level integration of its own.

On the topic of location, Foursquare addicts have access to a beautifully designed iOS app, whereas deal hounds will surely spend (and save) a small fortune with Groupon and LivingSocial apps.

Keeping tabs on Facebook and Twitter is a great way to stay in the loop with your friends and colleagues, but it's also an easy place to become overwhelmed. Staying connected to the social network is a 24/7 job, and if you don't forcibly remove yourself from it every so often, you'll quickly become burned out from a never-ending torrent of updates. As they say, network responsibly.

iCloud, the Cloud, and iTunes Match

I've tiptoed around the cloud issue throughout this book, mentioning it here and there as a means to an end. This chapter dives headfirst into the relatively new, unexplored, and unpublicized world of consumer cloud use. In years prior, cloud services were mostly reserved for enterprise users—companies where VPN (virtual private network) access was a requirement due to remote or traveling employees. But as the world becomes more mobile, there's an obvious need to bring consumers into the fold. Without all the headaches involved, of course. Apple's iCloud not only takes the place of MobileMe, but it adds an entirely new layer of sync capabilities. Beyond that, iTunes Match might just be the most galvanizing creation from Apple since the iPhone itself. It, along with Google Music across the way, has turned the music world on its ear, and aside from keeping your music safe from deletion and accessible wherever an Internet connection is available, it has also pushed the industry as a whole closer to the "rent, not own" model. Turns out, Apple isn't the only one piping consumers into the cloud, so I also discuss the best cloud storage iPhone apps and how to best manage your iPhone files across hard drives you'll never actually touch.

WRAPPING YOUR HEAD AROUND THE CLOUD

▶ Lots of clouds are accessed via VPN or FTP. iOS disguises the tunneling and makes it an extension of what you see locally.

What is the cloud, exactly? It's ambiguous. It's everything and nothing all at the same time. It's always online, and it's useful only when you are online. I've probably driven you even further from what the definition of the cloud really is, but as far as the iPhone is concerned, here's what you need to know. The *cloud*, as it's loosely explained, is an offsite storage location for any type of file; the trick is that the off-site locale is constantly connected to the Internet, able and willing to accept new files or upload existing ones on command.

FIGURE 16-1: iCloud selection screen; seen during the initial iPhone setup

In a sense, having access to a cloud storage device expands the amount of content to which a product has access, often exponentially. As I discussed in the opening chapter, you can't buy an iPhone without more than 64GB of local capacity on board. Because there are no expansion slots, the only way to add more material to an iPhone is either to delete what you have to make room, or reach out to the cloud. Obviously, the latter is preferred, and Apple has spent years perfecting what is now known as *iCloud*. In fact, the company spent over *half a billion dollars* building a monolithic data center in the mountains of North Carolina simply to make possible what it has enabled with iCloud (setup screen seen in Figure 16-1) and iTunes Match.

> ▶ This state is amazing. You and your iPhone should go. Maybe we'll bump into each other!

NOTE The cloud is actually breathing new life into the iPhone. As it stands, iOS isn't a "true" desktop operating system. There's no file system, so storing and retrieving files is a challenge. The solution, it seems, is to use an Internet-accessible hard drive whenever an iPhone user needs to access, edit, save, or send a file. Years back, the original iPhone OS skyrocketed to a new level of fame with the launch of the App Store; now, people can't imagine using an iOS product without having immediate access to apps. I suspect that iCloud and iTunes Match are the two new facets to Apple's mobile strategy that'll catapult iOS to the *next* level of stardom. Other platforms will "do cloud," no doubt, but the seamlessness that comes with using it within this ecosystem will be tough to match.

Outside of extending the amount of accessible content to your iPhone, the cloud also serves another monumentally important purpose. It keeps your digital life in sync, across a litany of devices, without you ever having to intervene. Imagine this: you have contacts, e-mail accounts, photos, music, and videos that all matter to you. Some of it is created and uploaded from your iPhone; some of it is created on your work PC; and more is on your Mac at home. Just last year, it was an absolute nightmare attempting to keep content in sync across devices, let alone information. "Did I add this contact in my phone, but not my tablet? Does my PC need its address book updated, too?"

TIP Thankfully, Apple enables users to use different Apple IDs for different services; this is hugely beneficial if you prefer to sync music and app purchases from one "family-owned" Apple ID, but still have separate Apple IDs for programs like FaceTime, Contacts, iMessage, iTunes Home Sharing, and Game Center. There's (almost) nothing more frustrating than your son getting your FaceTime call due to a bungled Apple ID setup. Where it's *vital* to use your own Apple ID is iCloud. If not, you'll have family member appointments, contacts, and all manners of content overlapping your own.

If you ensure that each computer or mobile device is linked into the cloud via the same username (or Apple ID, for the purposes of this book), the cloud can ensure that information uploaded from Device A gets shot down to Devices B, C, D, and E without ever needing your input. Suddenly, completely disconnected devices are at once connected, and information that was once siloed is now readily and immediately available across an entire portfolio of products. If you need another example still, envision an e-mail being sent from your iMac, and then needing to reference that material on your iPhone moments later. Simply visit the Sent folder in the Mail app, and it's there. Now, to set things up so you're maximizing the impact of the cloud on your digital life....

> **WARNING**   Although you can input a separate Apple ID in iCloud and in the Store (where family-owned content can be shared), you *can't* place separate Apple IDs in individual iCloud services. In other words, your entire iCloud portfolio must be connected to a single Apple ID.

Setting Things Up

So, you're sold on using iCloud to make your life easier. Congratulations. And if I didn't already mention that it's 100 percent free, now is probably the time to do it. I'll start with explaining the process on the iPhone, which is where you're apt to set up your contacts list, calendar, e-mail, and so on. Once you've completed that setup (described in detail in the first two chapters), you need only head to Settings → iCloud. From here, you'll be able to flip toggles to On for the items you want to keep synced across devices (shown in Figure 16-2). I'm having a tough time thinking of a reason why you'd prefer not to make any of these available elsewhere, aside from perhaps Notes, which forces you to create a separate @me.com e-mail address to enable it.

iCloud is free for anyone who registers for an Apple ID, which you did when setting up your iPhone or punching in payment information within iTunes to download apps. You get 5GB at no cost, and Apple even excludes your purchased music, apps, books, and TV shows, as well as your Photo Stream, from counting against your free storage. If you have a bulging e-mail account or gobs of music that you *didn't* purchase through iTunes, however, 5GB will almost certainly not be enough for you (bonus storage sizes are shown in Figure 16-3). In my example, I've disabled the syncing of Mail simply because my inbox alone tips the scales at 19GB, and I haven't

> ▶ If you attempt to toggle on a section to sync with iCloud and it detects that it's too large, you'll get a notification right away.

> ▶ If you don't want to pay extra for more storage, make sure you only buy media from Apple. Simple solution! (Wink, wink.)

ponied up the extra dough to send it all to Apple yet. (For what it's worth, it's synced with Google's servers.)

FIGURE 16-2: Don't flip that Mail switch unless you're ponying up for extra storage, or unless you rarely send messages.

NOTE As for those extra pricing options, you can buy an *extra* 10GB of iCloud storage for $20 per year, whereas another 20GB will cost you $40 and an extra 50GB will set you back $100 per year. For clarity, you get to keep your initial 5GB with each of these plans.

You'll need to be in range of a Wi-Fi signal in order to initiate an iCloud sync. Why? You probably don't want up to 5GB of your data flying over the Internet on a 3G connection. Even on so-called "unlimited" data plans grandfathered in from the earliest of iPhone sales, you'll probably get a stern phone call if you push 5GB to the cloud over a cellular data network.

FIGURE 16-3: Extra storage, anyone? Pony up!

▶ Nothing kills the cloud buzz like a spotty connection or sluggish download rates. Time to upgrade your Internet service!

By default, your iPhone will back up to iCloud whenever it's plugged in, locked, and connected to Wi-Fi. If you want to override that list of requirements, just surf to Settings ➔ iCloud ➔ Storage & Backup, and tap the Back Up Now icon at the bottom. I recommend that you have a strong, non-flaky connection when doing so, and if you're on a relatively slow/limited connection, I suggest backing things up overnight so as not to consume the lion's share of the upload capacity. There's nothing worse than killing a friend's upload rate when you're crashing on his couch.

If you're wondering why Music, Apps, and Books aren't listed in the iCloud section of the Settings app, there's a perfectly good explanation for those omissions. There's a seldom-visited section of Settings called Store. Within it, you'll find the missing toggle switches for the aforementioned trio. From here, you can enable any tracks, books, or apps purchased (or just downloaded, in the case of freebies) on your computer's iTunes library to be automatically pushed to your iPhone.

Why separate 'em out from the rest of the group? If you toggle these three as On, you'll lock your Apple ID to this iPhone for 90 days, thwarting future efforts of pals to log in—even briefly—to your iPhone. In other words, think long and hard before automating those three. As beautiful as iCloud syncing is, it might be worth it to manually sync those three services in order to keep your iPhone available to any and all Apple ID logins.

If you *do* decide to enable them, I also recommend leaving the Use Cellular Data option flipped to Off. Data is expensive, and it's a rare occasion when you'd absolutely need to suck down a song or book over the cloud and can't wait for either Wi-Fi or a traditional system-to-iPhone sync. Of course, the best course of action is to leave it Off by default, and then trigger it On for occasions where you specifically want content purchased on another device with your Apple ID to appear instantly on your iPhone.

▶ In many cases, a single iCloud backup can generate overages on AT&T's entry-level iPhone data package. Ouch.

CONTROLLING THE ICLOUD

The control freaks in attendance (it's okay, I'm in that crowd) may be wondering if there's any detailed mechanisms for backing up only certain aspects on your iPhone to the cloud, even beyond the traditional options. Turns out, there is, but it's not particularly simple to find the options. First, head to Settings ➜ iCloud ➜ Storage & Backup. Once there, the journey continues. Exciting! Tap Manage Storage and then your iPhone, and the third bar from the top will inform you of the backup size for your next backup.

Beneath, you can press a Show All Apps button that'll give you a highly detailed look at which apps will be pushing data into your iCloud, and exactly how much each app is responsible for. It's arranged to show the heaviest hitters at the top. If you're looking to lighten the load of a particular backup, you can toggle individual apps off, while still backing up the data associated with the others; sure beats the all-or-nothing approach.

Workarounds Galore

As I alluded to earlier, Apple IDs can be tricky to manage. The most vital thing to keep constant when you're looking to share music, app, and book downloads with family members is the Apple ID entered in the Store section of your Settings app. I recommend creating a universal family e-mail address that's used for all of your purchases, and then sharing those login credentials with your kinfolk. Remember, however, that sharing is—in theory, at least—restricted to five iOS devices per Apple ID.

▶ If you start crafting multiple Apple IDs, make sure you keep a running list of usernames and passwords in a safe place.

▶ Keep in mind that only your main iCloud account can use Photo Stream, Documents & Data, and Backup.

This might mean that you'll be setting up a new Apple ID to share among family, but here's what I recommend. If your personal ID is tied to years of purchases, make that the family ID. Then, use an alternate e-mail address of your own (a work one, perhaps) to use with your new personal services—things like FaceTime, Contacts, Calendar, and iMessage. This way, you aren't splintering iTunes purchases between an old and new ID. That kind of fragmentation will undoubtedly introduce needless headaches into your sharing setup.

If you need even more control over what's connected to which ID, you can do a number of things. For starters, you can head to the Mail ➔ Contacts ➔ Calendars pane within Settings and add iCloud accounts, toggling differing inclusions for each account. The rationale here is that one iCloud account—which syncs only Contacts and Calendars—could be shared with your children, whereas another iCloud account would be used strictly to sync your e-mail, which you don't want anyone else reading.

An important point to mention here is one that often helps basic users get around the pesky 5GB iCloud limit when involving e-mail. It's not uncommon for inboxes to exceed 20GB these days, but if you're a Gmail user, you can use that service for e-mail and iCloud to back up everything else. Google keeps all of your e-mail messages in its cloud, enabling you to access them from practically any device or browser, so there's no need for iCloud to waste space duplicating the effort.

Team Players

▶ If you're using OS X 10.6.8 or earlier, you can't utilize iCloud. You need to upgrade to Lion or Mountain Lion.

Any iOS device can run iCloud, so newer iPhones, iPads, and iPod touch units should be fine. But what about the computers that run alongside them? Apple had to make a few tough choices with iCloud—namely, that it wouldn't support any OS X operating system besides of the latest. For those with OS X 10.7 (Lion) and OS X 10.8 (Mountain Lion), iCloud is neatly tucked with the System Preferences, under Internet & Wireless. If you peek your mouse in there, you'll be able to toggle the same expected list of programs to be synced to the cloud—Mail & Notes, Contacts, Calendars, Bookmarks (applies to Safari only), Photo Stream, Documents & Data, Back to my Mac, and Find my Mac. If enabled—for example—any contacts you add to your Mac's Contacts app will automatically appear on any other iOS product (like your iPhone) and any Windows-based PC that's also tied into the ecosystem.

▶ If you update to Lion for iCloud, you'll lose Rosetta support for legacy apps. Rock, meet hard place.

Yes, I said Windows. Apple threw the millions upon millions of Windows users a bone years back with the unveiling of iTunes for Windows, and it's extending the olive branch once more with iCloud. If you're using Windows 7 or Vista with Service Pack 2, a 40MB download (entitled iCloud Control Panel for Windows) will bring iCloud support to your machine.

Once the add-in is installed, Windows users can cruise to the Windows Start menu and choose Control Panel → Network and Internet → iCloud. Similar to Lion, you'll then be able to toggle the services you want synced with iCloud. For Mail, Contacts, and Calendars & Tasks, you need Outlook 2007 or 2010 installed; Safari 5.1.1 or Internet Explorer 8 or later is required for accessing bookmarks. To enable automatic downloads for your music, apps, and books, open iTunes and click Edit → Preferences → Store. Further details can be found at www.apple.com/icloud/setup/pc.html.

> **WARNING** Careful with setting up multiple devices to use the same Apple ID associated with Photo Stream. Those raunchy shots you took last night at the bar might just end up on mum's iPhone. Can you say "embarrassing?"

CLOUD SYNCHRONIZATION

Think the cloud is just for keeping your contacts in order? Think again. An entire subsection of apps is emerging in order to take advantage of the iPhone's iCloud and iTunes Match functionality, and none is more astounding than djay. It's a paid app that enables your iPhone to be the life of the party. It's iCloud-enabled, so that tracks you build on your Mac, iPhone, and iPad are all in sync, with a tweak on the iPhone shown immediately—in real-time—on your iPod touch. Once you've spun up the tracks over the week and downloaded them from the cloud onto your iPhone, you can hook them up to any number of DJ controllers in order to get the crowd moving. Learn more here: www.digitaldjtips.com/2011/10/cloud-djing-is-here/.

iCloud Web Apps

I'm pretty sure you'll never leave home without your iPhone, Mac, or PC, but in the unlikely event of a catastrophic brain fart, there's actually *another* way to access the information you've gathered in iCloud. Believe it or not, it's... *the Internet*. Apple realized that not everyone would have access to their iOS device or a compatible machine at all times, and in turn, launched icloud.com. Surfing here in any modern web browser will prompt you to log in with your Apple ID and password, and from there, you can easily look at your e-mail, contacts, calendar, iWork (Pages, Numbers, and Keynote), and Find My iPhone, all shown in Figure 16-4.

▶ Anything you add or change on the icloud.com portal will be synced to your other iCloud devices. It's not just a read-only service.

▶ You can add Reminders from icloud.com; it's on the right rail within Calendar.

FIGURE 16-4: The iCloud.com interface; clean, simple, useful.

Although it's certainly convenient be able to access iCloud portals through the web, it's the Find My iPhone functionality that's truly mind-blowing. If you've enabled Find My iPhone on your iPhone (*do it!*), and you've logged into icloud.com with the same Apple ID as the one used on the iPhone, you'll soon see its location emerge on a Google Map. Sure, it's an excellent way to find a phone that accidentally slid between your couch cushions, but it's an even better way to find a highly coveted product that "mysteriously vanished" on the streets of Dodgyville. Once it's located, you can send a message to it (I recommend a plea to call your home phone number) or make it play a sound (great for those who've simply misplaced it in the house). A look at the interface is in Figure 16-5.

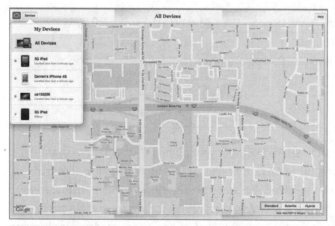

FIGURE 16-5: Hope you never have to use this, but if you do, be thankful it exists.

If things get a bit more serious, you can remotely lock or remotely wipe your iPhone right from the web browser. Of course, you'll need your iPhone to be connected to some form of the Internet in order to get the signal across, but it's fairly unlikely that an iPhone thief would yank it and never once hop online to boast about their misdeeds on Facebook. (Or just hop online, period.) If any of your requests are successful, you'll immediately receive an e-mail from Apple saying as much.

▶ If your iPhone has been stolen and turned off, Find My iPhone will display its last known location.

Google Drive

For a long while, Dropbox was the king of third-party cloud hosting and device syncing. Now, however, there's a formidable opponent: Google. Google Drive has finally come to iOS in the form of an iPhone app that's free on the App Store, and for avid Google Suite and Gmail users, there's nothing better. This app taps into the Google Docs universe that you're probably already familiar with, but also acts as a Dropbox-style "toss anything in it" cloud-hosting service. Thanks to Mac and Windows clients on the desktop side, you're able to upload documents and files from your computer and then have them sync to the Drive app. You can also make entire files or folders available offline from within the app—this is highly useful for making confirmation documents available when you know you'll be traveling overseas without a data connection.

I recommend Drive over Dropbox for a number of reasons. First, Drive gives you 5GB for free, and the expansion options are far cheaper than on Dropbox. Second, anything you create in Google Docs automatically syncs to Drive.

IMPLEMENTING ITUNES MATCH

Now that iCloud is squared away, it's time to make a choice. For the music you've purchased in iTunes over the years, iCloud will automatically back it all up and enable it to be streamed on other iCloud-enabled products, all for free. But the compact disc has existed far longer than the iTunes ecosystem, and if you have many, many gigabytes of digitized music that you didn't procure from iTunes, you'll need iTunes Match to bring those into the fold. Apple describes the cloud-based service as one that brings "the benefits of iTunes in the Cloud" to music that you didn't buy from iTunes.

Indeed, it's built right into the iTunes app on your Mac and PC, and it will let you store your *entire* iTunes library in the cloud for $24.99 per year. I'll break that down a bit further. If you enable iTunes Match, your computer will scan your iTunes library

▶ Apple's matching library currently has 20+ million songs it in. In other words, "a few."

and "match" tracks that it understands with tracks already hosted on Apple's servers. This serves a couple of purposes. For one, the version on Apple's side is a high-quality 256Kbps AAC DRM-free music file; even if your version was ripped a decade ago at a pitiful bit rate, you'll be able to stream a version with higher fidelity.

Secondly, this *dramatically* decreases the time it takes to upload your music gallery into the cloud. I think most folks—save those who relish the opportunity to listen only to the most obscure of tracks—will see well over 75 percent of their music library automatically matched. The remaining tracks will be uploaded to Apple, with your upload rates being the limiting factor. For vast, unsung libraries, it can take a week or more to get your entire library uploaded, but that's probably at the extreme end of things. Thankfully, you don't have to upload all of your tracks at once, and the upload manager will intelligently resume if the connection breaks.

> **TIP** Curious to know which tracks are matched and which are to be uploaded? Eager to know how your uploads are progressing? Within iTunes itself, visit the View option pane within Music, and select View Options. Tick the iCloud Download and iCloud Status selections. Once you press OK, you'll see a status beside every song, and if you want a higher-resolution version of any track on your local hard drive, just click the cloud icon beside it.

OTHER MUSIC ALTERNATIVES

If you're okay sliding away from the iTunes ecosystem, it's worth looking into Pandora, MOG, and Amazon MP3. Pandora is the ideal app for streaming radio, whereas MOG is ideal for creating playlists based on artists you already know and love. Amazon MP3 is a cloud storage locker for music, but it's far more flexible and able to stream and sync to set-top boxes, PCs, and all manners of mobile devices. Because Amazon doesn't have its own OS, it plays nice on pretty much everything.

SUMMARY

Syncing is a necessary evil, even when it's wireless, but Apple's taking a huge step in the direction of effortlessness with the introduction of iCloud. Setting it up is crucial for those with multiple iOS devices, and even those with Macs and PCs can take advantage of keeping their e-mail, contacts, calendars, and documents in sync. Gone are the days of manually moving files, forgetting what is stored where, and never truly knowing which copy is the most recent. When you can't access an iOS device, the icloud.com web interface suffices; plus, it offers an easy way to find your iPhone should it become lost.

Tackling Apple IDs can be daunting for families, but it's worth putting in the effort to segment appropriately. Be careful about enabling iCloud downloads for apps, books, and music, though—enabling those will lock your Apple ID to your iPhone, preventing friends from logging in to your device, even if only temporarily. Backups apply only to your main Apple ID, so if you use the cloud across multiple devices, only those services that are using that ID will be backed up. Apple's take on cloud services might be seamless to the end user, but it's not without its fair share of setup complexities.

iTunes Match takes your music library and a whole slew of devices to an entirely new level. There's no web interface (yet), but if you pay $24.99 per year, all of your tracks will be available to stream instantly from any iOS device or iTunes-equipped computer. Apple will even grant you access to high-resolution files, and because you can download DRM-free copies of them, this will allow you to replace poor-quality rips with superior alternatives.

Ace Accessories

Companies not named Apple have to love Apple. Companies like Kensington, Belkin, Case-Mate, OtterBox, Twelve South, and countless others. The chunk of market share owned by the iPhone range has enabled an entire industry of accessories to sprout up around it. Make no mistake—no iPhone owner will be hurting for options when it comes to peripherals, and in fact, you'll probably have to put the credit card away long before you run out of items to buy. The iPhone is quite the extensible platform. With Wi-Fi and Bluetooth, you can connect a plethora of devices; everything from input products (mice and keyboards, namely) to guitar adapters are all discussed here. This chapter also brushes up on the best protective apparatuses. I discuss tools that are aimed at bolstering productivity, doodads that simply serve to make owners smile, and widgets that no self-proclaimed iPhone addict should travel without. It's a wide, wild world out there in the land of Made-for-iPhone products. I spot the standouts for you in the pages to come.

DECIDING ON A KEYBOARD

The iPhone's virtual keyboard is undoubtedly one of the best in the mobile realm. But sometimes, that's just not enough. Certain keyboard commands and button combinations are nigh impossible to hit on a software keyboard, and for those actively seeking to use the iPhone as a productivity tool, having a physical keyboard around certainly makes things easier. iPhone-compatible keyboards come in all shapes and sizes, aimed at all sorts of different solutions.

Copy and pasting, for example, requires a number of long-presses and icon taps under normal circumstances. But with a keyboard around, it's as easy as pressing Cmd+C to copy, and Cmd+V to paste. Keyboard shortcuts are a huge time saver, and those who invest the time to learn about them can enhance their efficiency greatly. For a wildly comprehensive list, bookmark this link: www.danrodney.com/mac.

Desktop Options

Using your iPhone in an office or another stationary setting? If so, it's probably not a bad idea to invest in a solid, more full-featured keyboard. The iPhone will never truly be a replacement for a bona fide laptop, although it might work as a suitable substitute for more casual users. If you find yourself replying to e-mails or drafting basic documents more and more on your iPhone while at home, here are a few options that will positively improve your input efficiency.

Apple's Wireless Keyboard ($69) is the home crowd favorite, and there's a reason. Apple's own Bluetooth-enabled keyboard is sturdy, rigid, compact, and spun to function beautifully with OS X and iOS. The keyboard commands that make sense in a Mac world are all here, so there's no befuddling key remapping to worry over. Keyboard shortcuts that you've grown familiar with in OS X almost universally translate here, and it's certainly one of the most roomy and most comfortable options out there. To boot, those with Mac machines can easily pair this up with a desktop or notebook using OS X 10.6.8 or higher. Of course, not all of the functions translate to the iPhone—there's no Spaces or Expose function, for example—but at least Apple throws in a couple of AA batteries. Sweet, right?

> **TIP** Pretty much any Bluetooth keyboard will suffice here; if you already own one at home, pair it up and see how it works. You might miss out on having no iPhone-specific hotkeys, but it's always better to make the most of what you have before buying something new.

It's important to note that I expect a number of keyboard + dock combination units to crop up in the coming months to support the iPhone 5's frame and new Lightning port. Keep a close eye on products from Kensington, Belkin, and Case-Mate; historically, those folks have made really solid iOS keyboard accessories.

The Unorthodox Alternatives

Tired of the traditional? Looking for a keyboard with a pinch of creativity? No sweat. From bendable options to those that fold in half, I outline a few of my favorites in the keyboard realm that generally don't get the attention they deserve. (Wondering what a keyboard looks like rolled up? Have a look at Figure 17-1.)

FIGURE 17-1: Scosche freeKEY, all curled up and ready to roll.

▶ **Acase Flexible Portable Wireless Bluetooth Keyboard** ($30)—Be warned, this one's tiny and cramped, but it's also *flexible*. In other words, you can actually roll this keyboard up in the same way you roll a shirt for packing.

▶ **Menotek Flexible Bluetooth Waterproof Mini Keyboard** ($30)—I'll see your flexible keyboard and raise you a *waterproof* flexible keyboard. It's compact, it's thin, and it bends. In fact, you can roll it up tight until you need it. But understand that the lack of rigidity means that the typing experience is far different, and in most ways, subpar compared to a proper keyboard.

▶ **Scosche freeKEY Flexible, Water Resistant Keyboard** ($60)—It's twice as expensive as the others, but it's a name I trust (see Figure 17-1). The quality of the materials is also higher, and while it'll roll up tight, the keys themselves have an above-average amount of travel. It also supports a USB connection; useful for recharging its batteries while still using it on other USB-equipped products.

- **Matias Bluetooth Folding Keyboard** ($85)—The primary benefit of choosing this over one of the more compact keyboards is simple. Folded in half, this keyboard is hardly larger than some of the most diminutive Bluetooth iPhone keyboards, but unfurl it, and you're presented with a full-size keyboard that's ideal for long typing sessions.

- **HiPPiH iEagle Foldable Wireless Keyboard** ($100)—This one is an Apple Store exclusive, and while pricey, it provides a bundled carrying case as well as an iPod touch/iPhone stand.

IPHONE CASES FOR EVERY OCCASION

Protecting your phone is only half of the solution; wrapping it in something that represents you as a person is the other. The iPhone exudes style. If you're going to cover any of it up in the effort of protection, you need a case that gives off its own aura of cool. I should also mention that most of these cases are available for the iPhone 4, 4S, and 5—just be careful to select the right one when you order!

▶ It's worth picking up a screen protector from ZAGG or Griffin, regardless of which case you choose.

- **BookBook for iPhone** ($60)—It's simple, yet beautiful. It's also a great way to conceal the fact that you're walking around with an iPhone. Twelve South's book-themed case tightly holds your iPhone, with the exterior appearing as a well-worn novel. It also folds back on itself to double as a kickstand.

- **Pop! ID Case by Case-Mate** ($40)—It's not as classy as the BookBook, but it's far thinner, and it still contains a slot for your most important credit cards and IDs.

- **Kensington Gel Case** ($20)—This one provides a decent amount of protection from scuffs, but it's clear. And that means you can see the beauty of your phone's backside at any time.

- **OtterBox Defender** ($50+)—If you couldn't care less about keeping your iPhone sleek, this is the case to get. It'll take a severe beating while keeping your precious phone safe, and you'll be glad you chose function over form the first time it takes a major spill.

- **ColcaSac** ($15+)—Here's an environmentally friendly option, and a beautiful one to boot. These are colorful, patterned, soft, and handmade in Salt Lake City, Utah. They don't get much more unique than this, as you can see in Figure 17-2.

FIGURE 17-2: ColcaSac's iPhone case is downright heartwarming.

BLUETOOTH HEADSETS AND HEADPHONES

Corded options get the job done, but there's a very real market for wireless headsets and headphones. Yes, you'll look pretty weird jawing away with a Bluetooth headset in your ear, but hey—you do what you have to.

Trouble is, there are literally hundreds of headset options—all sorts of shapes and sizes, and all sorts of confusion surrounding them. I recommend that you stop fretting and pick the Samsung HM7000 ($40) or the BlueAnt Q2 ($50). Both of these have exceptional audio quality; I suggest picking whichever design floats your boat and calling it a day.

From a listening standpoint, there's AirPlay. But if you're aiming for something a little more personal (yet equally wireless in nature), a set of Bluetooth headphones is your best bet. Jaybird's JF3 Freedom Bluetooth stereo headset ($90) is a lovely option, with outstanding audio quality and a remarkably unobtrusive design. Veho's Bluetooth cans ($110) offer a differently styled solution, and the fold-up design makes them perfect for travel.

HACKS AND WORKAROUNDS

Although Bluetooth keyboards, headsets, and headphones work without any trickery, you're probably wondering if the keyboard's best mate—the mouse—has a place in iOS' heart. Unfortunately, it doesn't. Not according to Apple, anyway. iOS was designed to be controlled completely and entirely by touch, and in a touchable world, a mouse cursor just doesn't have a home.

Just because Apple doesn't support Bluetooth mouse input by default doesn't mean that all hope is lost. If you're willing to jailbreak your device, search for and

▶ With every successive iOS update, Apple usually thwarts the latest jailbreak; it takes a month or so for the jailbreak community to override it. Remember that jailbreaking voids your warranty, though.

install the BTstack Mouse app. Once installed, your iPhone should automatically recognize Apple's Magic Mouse, Magic Trackpad, and pretty much any other Bluetooth mouse you have hanging around.

> **NOTE** If you prefer to use your iPhone to control accessories on the other side—yes, even on the *PC*—I have a handful of app downloads that even a non-jailbroken iPhone can use. I-Clickr PowerPoint Remote for iPhone ($10) is a stellar app for converting your iPhone into a presentation remote, whereas TouchOSC ($5) is useful for controlling audio programs.

NEXT-LEVEL ACCESSORIES

Enough with this whole "productivity" thing. At its core, the iPhone's all about fun, and there are *plenty* of completely unbelievable, thoroughly amazing accessories to bring out the kid in any owner. If you can dream it up, it probably exists, and I've listed a number of my favorites here. It's important to note that all of these work with the Dock Connector found on the iPhone 4 and 4S, and most companies will be updating their lines soon to offer Lightning versions for the iPhone 5.

- ▶ **Sonoma GuitarJack** ($149)—Plug it into your Dock Connector (hopefully a Lightning model will surface soon!), and you'll get an audio interface that plays nice with a wide range of instruments, microphones, and other audio via 1/4-inch instrument and 1/8-inch stereo mic/line inputs. It's hailed as the first device-powered iOS accessory that offers stereo recording, simultaneous voice and instrument recording, 60dB of continuous level control, configurable Pad, Lo-Z and Hi-Z modes, and increased drive for headphones.

- ▶ **ThinkFlood RedEye mini** ($49)—Plug this bantam dongle into your headphone jack, open the RedEye application (free), and you're on your way to controlling every A/V component in your living room via infrared. The app is powerful enough to control your TV, A/V receiver, Blu-ray player, and nearly anything else that supports IR, and the app allows for full customization in order to establish macros and multicomponent commands.

- ▶ **Seagate GoFlex Satellite** ($170)—It's a 500GB, USB-powered, battery-equipped hard drive, but the internal file system and built-in Wi-Fi module allows the unit to stream videos, music, and photos to your iPhone. . . *sans cabling*. It can stream for up to five hours before needing a recharge, and yes, it works perfectly fine as a traditional hard drive all the while.

SUMMARY

You can outfit Apple's iPhone line to the hilt. Although many accessory makers are still in the process of updating their products to work with the new form factor and new Lightning connector on the iPhone 5, you can safely assume that they'll be rolling out updated gear post-haste.

I strongly recommend investing in a case and a screen protector. The display is the most expensive part on an iPhone to replace, and it's also the easiest to mar. No, your iPhone won't look as elegant with something wrapped around it, but it's better to be proactive when it comes to protection. It's really not a question of "if" you'll drop your phone, but when.

The accessory market in general is booming, and whether it's a music controller or a third-party remote attachment, you can find it for sale online.

Jailbreaking and Troubleshooting

Ask twenty people, and you're bound to find one who swears up and down that Apple products simply never have issues. "That's a Windows thing," they'll say. Candidly, Windows has garnered that reputation for a reason, but Apple has most certainly not earned a gold star in Never Failing 101. In my experience, Apple products have failed (and even faltered) less frequently than their Windows-based counterparts, although I suspect much of that is due to the overwhelming amount of malware that targets the operating system with the lion's share of users. It's rare for serious problems to arise on the iPhone, but to say problems are nonexistent would be fibbing. In this chapter, I walk through some of the most common issues, as well as how to get around them, through them, or over them. I also discuss recovery and DFU (Device Firmware Upgrade) modes (useful for getting yourself out of binds). But first, I look at the murky, innovative world of jailbreaking—an action not smiled upon by Apple, but one that can be remarkably enlightening if done with precaution and care.

JAILBREAKING YOUR IPHONE

The mere mention of the word sends shudders down the spines of those who've been burnt by hacks gone wrong before, and to many others, it just *sounds* illegal. Perhaps it's the unadulterated use of the word "jail," or maybe it's the allusion to something going wrong—"breaking." Either way, it's a choice word used to describe an admittedly dangerous technique that gives the end user an unprecedented amount of access to an operating system that ships with extremely rigid rules from the factory.

As it stands, an iPhone can only run programs that are deemed fit and not harmful by Apple. There's precisely one place to download an app, and that's Apple's own App Store. On one hand, it oozes simplicity. On the other, it makes the pondering users wonder what all they are missing. Turns out, there are a smattering of other app stores in existence—none of which are approved (or even publicly recognized) by the folks in Cupertino. You may feel dirty even reading into this as far as you have, but fret not; under the Digital Millennium Copyright Act, jailbreaking Apple devices is legal in the United States, but Apple makes it crystal clear that doing so will void your iPhone's warranty.

▶ If you're familiar with "rooting" on the Android side, jailbreaking is the iOS equivalent.

▶ Apple has actually battled this DMCA ruling. Meanwhile, rival Microsoft is openly allowing people to hack the Kinect. Clearly, different mindsets.

Why Even Bother Jailbreaking?

It's a question I get often: "What do I gain from jailbreaking? Is it worth it? Why should I risk it? What's the first thing I should do if I end up going through with it?" The amount of mystery and intrigue surrounding the art of jailbreaking is actually quite impressive. Almost everyone who owns an iOS device has at least heard casual mention of it, but only the brave dare open up the browser and Google for more information on it.

> **NOTE** Apple's systems have been historically closed, even when they're "open." Take FaceTime, for example. Apple claims that it's an open standard, but to date, no other company has actually integrated it into a shipping product. iTunes might sell DRM-free music, but unless you procure your tunes directly from Apple's music shop, iTunes in the Cloud won't do you any good. (Without paying $24.99 per year for iTunes Match, anyway.) iOS is pretty well sealed, but a rabid community of jailbreakers somehow manages to tear through its seams like clockwork, opening access to uncertified stores and wild applications that most common consumers don't even know exist. It's an underground world, but one worth exploring given the right preparations.

The reality is quite different from the common line that you'll hear. Much like the term "hacking" gets a sour reputation, there are a great number of positive, helpful things that iPhone owners can do by jailbreaking. Beyond the whole "additional access to apps" thing—which I dive into shortly—one of the primary reasons for jailbreaking is to unlock iPhone handsets for use on any carrier worldwide. In fact, that tidbit alone was monumental in keeping jailbreaking legal. U.S. carriers in particular have a knack for selling iPhone handsets that are locked to their network; in other words, if you insert a SIM for any other carrier, it simply won't work. Amazingly, Verizon's iPhone 5 is being sold unlocked, even with new on-contract customers, so those who purchase that model can pop a different SIM in (if you're traveling overseas, for example) and cruise along on the local network.

> **TIP** More useful, however, is the fact that you can take your iPhone to any civilized nation, pick up a rental SIM, and surf away on a local cellular data network—all without roaming or hacking. It's important to note that the iPhone 4 and 4S use Micro SIM cards rather than full-sized SIM cards, whereas the iPhone 5 uses a new Nano SIM.

Beyond all the wireless network talk, there's a very real (and growing) desire to access more applications than the ones Apple lets through its doors. Programmers are capable of producing applications that do more complex tasks than Apple allows. But if an app submitted to the App Store violates any of the company's polices—however questionable those policies may be—that app is rejected by the company. The bubbling desire to truly unlock the potential of Apple's iOS devices (the iPhone included) has helped spur a litany of applications that aren't welcome in the App Store. But they're *more* than welcome in a place called Cydia.

> ▶ Some jailbroken apps, like Wi-Fi Sync, eventually become adopted by Apple for use in its App Store or the core of iOS.

Cydia acts as a tool to search for and install applications that are stored in a great many repositories. All of these, of course, require a jailbroken device to access. Apps within jailbreaking stores can be free or costly; it's just another market entirely outside of Apple's purview. To give you an idea of what you'll find in Cydia that you won't find in the *actual* App Store, consider the MyWi application. It enables jailbroken devices with a 3G/4G radio to share their data signal over Wi-Fi, with no monthly fees raining down from associated carriers. That's usually all I have to mention before people become emphatically interested in the jailbreaking scene.

To recap, the two *primary* reasons people take interest in jailbreaking are to free their iPhones from carrier locks—so that they can pop in any SIM card from any carrier and have their phone work—and to have access to a nearly limitless amount of apps without having to wait for Apple's golden gates to open and allow them onto the official App Store.

What's the Downside to Jailbreaking?

With every successive release of iOS, Apple seems to make it more and more difficult for jailbreakers to gain access. It's a cold war, of sorts. Apple knows it can't stop jailbreaking from a legal standpoint, but it certainly does everything it can to wrap its code in a shatterproof layer. The jailbreaking scene is one that changes and evolves rapidly, with compatibilities changing by the hour some weeks.

The other important tidbit here is the recognition of two major kinds of jailbreaks. There's tethered, and then there's untethered. Both give hints at what they are, but neither just come right out and say it. History has shown that the former nearly always comes before the latter, and I've also found that patience is not only a virtue at the DMV, but in the world of jailbreaking, too. Tethered jailbreaks are easiest for hackers to accomplish, but you're forced to have your iPhone plugged into your computer's USB port for the jailbreak to complete. The first time around, it's not so bad; the problem arises when your iPhone decides to lock up, freeze, or otherwise go on the fritz while you're away from your machine.

A tethered jailbreak requires the assistance of a computer to boot up every single time; in other words, if you power down your iPhone and attempt to turn it back on, you'll be greeted with an unusable product until you can re-tether it to your host computer and try again. If you're constantly carrying around a notebook computer that you can use to revitalize your jailbroken iPhone should it require a reboot, tethered jailbreaks are worth installing. Otherwise, you are well advised to hold off until the untethered counterpart arises.

That variant, predictably, doesn't require the assistance of a connected computer in order to start up or reboot. You can simply use your iPhone as you normally do, without fear of rebooting into a "bricked" state.

▶ To keep up with the changes, follow @MuscleNerd and @chpwn on Twitter. They're tightly involved with the evolution of jailbreaks.

Okay, So How Do You Do It?

One of the reasons that jailbreaking remains a relatively underground activity is the natural fear that a voided warranty could lead to an unwanted repair bill. But perhaps even more significant is just how difficult it is to understand the process, implement the changes, and track the updates. Although the jailbreaking community is as fervent as ever, the lack of standards has led to a fragmented release schedule, non-uniform labeling, and a situation where there are a couple of leaders instead of one common company overseeing things. The "do as you will" mentality that makes the jailbreaking scene so vibrant and innovative is also a pitfall when it comes to actually understanding it.

WHAT'S A BRICK?

"Bricked" is a term thrown around quite often, and it usually refers to an iOS device being unusable for one reason or another. If you attempt to reboot an iPhone using a tethered jailbreak, but there's no computer nearby to tether it to, you'll boot into a black screen that's completely impassable without a partner machine. Some jailbreaks and hacks have been known to "brick" iPhones, rendering them useless when attempting to make phone calls. And I've personally seen my own iPhone bricked when the installation of an iOS 5 beta went awry due to the use of an outdated iTunes build. If you monkey around with your iPhone and eventually reboot into a black screen of hopelessness, you can consider yourself bricked.

The good news, however, is that not all "bricks" remain as such. *True* bricking requires that your iOS device never actually returns to life. In effect, it becomes only marginally more useful than an item used by a common mason. Whenever you jailbreak, bricking is a real possibility. It doesn't happen frequently, but it does happen, and you should be well aware of those consequences before you take a single peek down the rabbit hole.

There's an unhealthy amount of jargon surrounding the entire scene, so I do my best to break it down for you.

▸ **Jailbreaking**—The art of running a software package to unlock your iPhone for use with unauthorized applications.

▸ **Tethered jailbreak**—A jailbreak that requires a host computer to facilitate the iPhone boot process.

▸ **Untethered jailbreak**—A jailbreak that *doesn't* require a host computer to facilitate the iPhone boot process.

▸ **Cydia** (http://cydia.saurik.com)—An app that runs on jailbroken devices; used to find and install unauthorized software packages, including apps, system extensions, and interface tweaks.

▸ **Dev-Team** (http://blog.iphone-dev.org)—A few dedicated hackers who you should follow for the latest in jailbreaking news.

▶ **Ultrasn0w**—An unlocking program designed by the Dev-Team to break carrier-locked iPhones from their shackles, and enable them to function with international SIM cards.

▶ **Redsn0w**—This unlocking program enables jailbreaking in the greater sense, enabling you to install unauthorized apps on your iPhone, iPad, or iPod touch.

When Apple releases a new iOS build, it's an approved copy that's been internally tested for quality. However, jailbreak tools are typically released in beta (or alpha) form, and then new builds are released in quick succession after early adopters report back with bugs and issues.

> **WARNING** As with any alpha or beta software, you should take *great* caution in installing it. Untested and unproven jailbreaks, particularly those in beta form, can potentially damage your iPhone beyond repair. Furthermore, Apple will simply turn the other cheek if you show up for tech support with a jailbroken device. Your only chance for consultation is from others in the jailbreaking community, and while it's an admittedly tight-knit crew that has shown to be exceptionally helpful, this is far from a guaranteed fix.

These days, jailbreaks are mostly software-based. That's to say, users simply download the most recent Redsn0w software package (naming conventions can, and usually do, change over time), plug in their iPhone, and let the software run. Instructions on usage typically arrive either within the software package or on the forum post announcing the new version. You'll be quickly overwhelmed if you rely on Google to find jailbreaks. There *are* a few legitimate alternative sites out there that offer jailbreaks for a fee, but I recommend steering clear. Authentic jailbreaks from the Dev-Team are always made available for free and can be found at http://blog.iphone-dev.org. A screenshot of its site can be seen in Figure 18-1.

The exception to this rule is JailbreakMe (www.jailbreakme.com), which is shown in Figure 18-2. Designed by @comex, this is a simplistic website that enables iOS devices to surf to it, press a button, and have their product jailbroken. It's far and away the easiest method, but it also tends to lag behind software jailbreaks in terms of release. If you're looking for simplicity, though, it's probably worth waiting for JailbreakMe to be compatible with your product and iOS build.

It should be obvious, but I can't stress this enough: back up your iPhone to iTunes before applying a jailbreak. If anything goes awry, you can plug your iPhone back into your computer, select the Restore option, allow iTunes to reformat your tablet, reinstall the latest legitimate iOS build, and then restore your backed-up music, apps,

▶ On a jailbroken iPhone, Cydia is your go-to app store. It's hardly elegant, but it serves the purpose.

documents, and photos. If you forget to back things up (or just opt out), you'll be stuck starting over if your jailbreak renders your iPhone useless.

FIGURE 18-1: The Dev-Team's site isn't flashy, but it's chock-full of information.

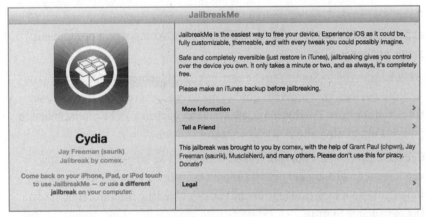

FIGURE 18-2: If you have a compatible device, surfing to this site will initiate the jailbreak process.

▶ Believe it or not, the standard App Store still functions on jailbroken devices.

Furthermore, there may end up being a need for you to lose your jailbreak. It's not unfathomable to run into sluggish performance (or worse) when heedlessly installing uncertified apps, and while the aforementioned method will "unjailbreak" your iPhone and restore it as it came from the factory, you'll need that backup if you're looking to avoid duplicate transfers.

▶ No need to seek Cydia separately; it's included with every jailbreak.

Rather than being a store in and of itself, Cydia is simply a universally accepted tool that provides access to apps and extensions that are hosted elsewhere. You *can* install new "sources" in Cydia that will search repositories of existing apps, but I confess that most of those are designed to encourage and facilitate piracy. In my mind, jailbreaking should be approached by those who simply want access to creatively and passionately designed apps that—for whatever reason—can't find a home in the App Store. Given that Apple's own App Store still functions on jailbroken devices, users should still head there in order to purchase apps that made it in.

The Best Apps for Jailbroken iPhones

If you go through the trouble of jailbreaking your iPhone, be it tethered or untethered, you'll be selling yourself short if you don't dive into a bucket of apps that is unavailable to those who are living on the tame side. The options here are even more unlimited than the conventional App Store, but I break down a few of my suggestions here:

- **Activator** (free)—If you've grown frustrated by the limited multitouch gesture support on the iPhone, here's your extension. It's a beautifully designed, highly practical tool that enables users to customize what gestures do what, and considering that many jailbreak apps require this to be installed, it's a good foundation to have around.

- **OpenSSH** (free)—Tired of moving things around the Apple-approved way? This app enables users to SSH into their iPhone from a computer in order to edit, move, or change files.

- **SBSettings** (free)—Similar to the settings drop-down menu found on many Android devices, this provides quick-and-easy access to toggling many settings and services. Furthermore, an Activator gesture can be programmed to pull this up, tossing one shortcut on top of another.

- **CyDelete** (free)—On a non-jailbroken iPhone, if you long-press on an app you'll see a small X appear over it (Apple's built-in core apps notwithstanding). Cydia apps lack this feature, but by downloading this app, they'll gain the easy delete feature.

- **Action Menu** (free)—It took Apple the better part of eternity to add basic copy and paste functionality to iOS, but the jailbreak community still thinks they can do the company one better. This adds more customizations to handling and moving text, and the (worthwhile) $2.99 Action Menu Plus Pack adds six more actions, including History, Lookup, and the option to instantly tweet text you've selected.

- **QuickGoogle** (free)—If you have Activator installed, just assign a single gesture to bring up a box, which allows you to type in any search term and have it immediately sent to Google.

- **Infiniapps** ($0.99 each)—This suite of apps allows mega multitaskers to shove as many apps as they want into a folder, as many apps as they want into the Dock, and for icons to be placed vertically as well as horizontally.

To say that this is just the tip of the iceberg would be understating things tremendously. The amount of customizations available in the Cydia app store is staggering, and the only way to truly stay on top of what's out there is to follow the beat in related forums and message boards. I recommend heading to iMore.com, ModMyi.com, iPhoneForums.net, MacRumors.com, iPhoneHelp.com, and iFans.com. These sites provide active, informative user forums, and most of them also provide frequently updated tips, tricks, and hacks related to the iPhone and iOS as a whole.

A LOOK AT RECOVERY MODE

Recovery mode is a completely natural mode of operation for the iPhone. Although the title could lead you to believe that it's reserved for situations where your iPhone is in a real pickle, it's actually the state the iPhone slips into whenever a user initiates a standard iOS upgrade or restore.

Every so often, however, Recovery mode decides to take on a life of its own. While uncommon, I've seen iPhones continually restart but never display the Home screen. In the case of an update or restoration being cut short by a yanked cable, a power outage, or a computer freeze, your iPhone may sink into a deep sleep that it simply can't exit. If you're looking to force your seemingly bricked iPhone into a *workable* Recovery mode, you can follow these steps:

1. Disconnect the USB cable from the iPhone, but leave the other end of the cable connected to your computer's USB port.

2. Press and hold the Sleep/Wake button for a few seconds until the red slider appears, slide the slider, and wait for your iPhone to turn off.

3. If you're having trouble turning the device off using this method, press and hold the Sleep/Wake and Home buttons at the same time; once it turns off, release them both immediately.

4. Now that it's off, press *only* the Home button and reconnect the USB cable to the iPhone. If you're on the right track, your device will start to turn on. (Keep holding the Home button!)

5. If your iPhone is extremely low on battery life, you may see a red charging screen; let it proceed to charge and check back in around five minutes.

6. Continue holding the Home button until you see the Connect to iTunes screen; once you spot that, you should release the Home button.

7. Open up iTunes, tap OK on any recovery mode alerts, and use iTunes to restore the iPhone.

Remember, when using recovery mode, you can only *restore* the iPhone. All user content will be erased, but if you had previously synced with iTunes on your computer, you can restore from a previous backup—that'll bring your multimedia, contacts, documents, and so on, back to where they belong. If you still need assistance, give this article a peek: `http://support.apple.com/kb/TS1538`.

> **TIP** If you get stuck in Recovery mode and *really* don't want to complete a restore or firmware update, you can look to TinyUmbrella (`http://thefirmwareumbrella.blogspot.com`) or RecBoot as an alternate way to escape.

A LOOK AT DFU (DEVICE FIRMWARE UPDATE) MODE

To put it bluntly, DFU is Recovery mode on steroids. It's the next level of recovery, with the primary difference being the ability to interface with iTunes *without* loading the iPhone operating system or boot loader. Technobabble got you down? Look at it this way—entering DFU mode enables you to override Apple's mandate that the latest official iOS build be the one applied within iTunes. Recovery mode will allow an iPhone to have the same iOS build reinstalled, or it will allow a newer *official* build to be applied (such as going from iOS 5.0 to iOS 5.0.1). With DFU mode, users can change the firmware in either direction, enabling an iPhone running iOS 5.0.1 to be downgraded to iOS 5.0.

Rather than just using the most recent build at iTunes, you can manually choose an .ipsw file saved to your computer by pressing the Alt/Option key while clicking the Restore button in iTunes. There are myriad reasons why you might want to manually choose an iOS version to install on your iPhone. In some cases, new iOS builds kill compatibility with iOS-friendly car audio interfaces. Perhaps you want to manually install an iOS beta before you're actually supposed to. On occasion, new iOS builds will break compatibility with select apps. And of course, if you accidentally let your jailbroken iPhone update to the newest official iOS build, your jailbreak—and all its associated apps—will be obliterated.

▶ Wondering how to gain access to older versions of iOS? A monstrous library is can be found at www.felixbruns.de/iPod/firmware.

> **WARNING** Remember, new Apple-approved iOS builds kill preexisting jailbreaks.

If you place your iPhone into DFU mode, you can install any firmware you want, provided that you have two things. First, you need the desired .ipsw file, which can be downloaded at www.felixbruns.de/iPod/firmware. Second, you need the version of iTunes that was released when the matching iOS build was released. A fantastic archive of old iTunes versions can be found here: www.oldapps.com/itunes.php.

But here's the thing—you can't easily put two iTunes versions on a single machine. The libraries will conflict, your playlists could be overwritten, and in general, I just don't recommend trying it. Whenever I need to downgrade with an older version of iTunes, I use an older PC that I keep around for hacking tasks such as these. If you have a spare machine, I highly recommend using it.

> **WARNING** Trying to run two copies of iTunes on a single machine is a recipe for disaster (and tears).

Furthermore, you need saved SHSH blobs from an old iOS version in order to install that old version on an iPhone. With that, you also need to bypass Apple's firmware signing security model, which is the final hurdle to getting an iOS build to function with iTunes. An entire how-to guide that explains the ins and outs of SHSH blobs can be found here: www.ijailbreak.com/how-to-save-shsh-blobs.

If you're looking to install a very specific firmware/iOS build on your iPhone, or otherwise gain access to portions of the iPhone that are generally locked down, DFU mode is your access point. Be warned, however, that modifying files on your iPhone could indeed result in a bricked device. And if it's bricked, no Apple warranty will apply.

GETTING YOUR IPHONE INTO DFU MODE

1. Connect your iPhone to your iTunes-equipped machine.

2. Turn your iPhone completely off (hold down the top Sleep/Wake button, and then slide to shut down).

3. Hold down the Sleep/Wake button *and* the Home button for 10 seconds, and then release only the top Sleep/Wake button.

4. Continue to hold down the Home button until you see an iTunes dialog box informing you that an iPhone in Recovery mode has been detected.

5. If you've done this correctly, your iPhone's display will remain solid black. If you see any graphic at all, you're actually in Recovery mode.

TIP DFU mode can be a last-rescue resort for iPhones that are corrupt or stuck for any number of reasons. In theory, the existence of DFU mode should make it impossible to brick your iPhone beyond repair via software. Hardware hacks are another matter, though.

TAKING YOUR IPHONE IN FOR SERVICE

▶ You can find your nearest Apple Store here: www.apple.com/buy/locator. Your nearest Apple Specialist— authorized by Apple to deem themselves "independent dealers and service providers"—can be located here: channelprograms.www.apple.com/Specialist.

If you steer clear of jailbreaking, iPhones are generally reliable. Of course, as with any monolithic consumer electronics company, problems can and do arise. Dealing with Apple's phone support (www.apple.com/contact) is like dealing with anyone's phone support; it's not exactly something anyone wakes up looking forward to. But unlike most rival companies, Apple has a massive advantage when it comes to customer support: Apple Stores and Apple Specialist resellers.

If you're within driving distance of an Apple Store, your best bet is to set up a Genius Bar appointment. Each Apple Store has a Genius Bar stocked with trained employees who do nothing but service Macs, iPhones, and other Apple products. They aren't there to sell you product protection plans you'll never need or a set of orange headphones that your son "would just love"—they're there to fix your gear, period.

Best of all, *it's absolutely free to make a Genius Bar appointment*. Yes, free. Even if your product is out of warranty. Most people find this arrangement truly unfathomable, but by placing trained professionals in front of Apple customers at no charge, the company has created a significant competitive advantage that I've yet to see a rival match.

There's no need to pick up the phone to make an appointment. Just point your web browser to www.apple.com/retail/geniusbar, select the locale nearest you, and choose an available date and time for your appointment. A few clicks later, you'll have an e-mail confirmation and the ability to change or modify it at any time prior. I advise arriving around 10 minutes early on your appointment day, but be prepared to wait another half hour beyond your scheduled time. They aren't late often, but I've seen it happen.

> ▶ Try not to book the final Genius Bar appointment for the day. (Unless you know you'll be brief!)

You should also make every effort to bring *everything* remotely related to your issue. Bring your iPhone, your charger, a USB cable, any accessories that were giving you issues, and even your computer that you use to sync it with (assuming it's portable enough to make the trip). The more devices you bring, the more likely the experts will be to solve what's ailing your poor iPhone. If the problem isn't abuse, and your iPhone's under warranty, you can have it fixed either on the spot or in-store, depending on how serious the issue is. Even when it costs, the Genius will walk you through everything before providing you with an estimate—all for free.

> ▶ When you arrive for your appointment, just notify any employee that you're "here for your Genius Bar appointment." They'll sign you in.

> **NOTE** If you live in a rural or remote area, visiting an Apple Store might not be feasible. Apple Specialist resellers act as extensions to those core stores, and in all of my experiences, they have been more than willing to help. The people who run these shops are your neighbors—locals who have a passion for Apple products and technology in general. In fact, those preferring a personal touch might want to start with an Apple Specialist.
>
> They're authorized to perform the same repairs that bona fide Apple Stores perform, and they generally do it with a bigger smile. As an anecdote, an Apple Specialist in Maine let me borrow a FireWire cable to rescue data from an older MacBook Pro while I was on vacation. *At no charge.* That's the kind of attitudes these resellers have.

SUMMARY

Apple deliberately kept a lot of doors closed in iOS and iTunes, perhaps trying to improve the overall experience for the masses and prevent too much tinkering.

That tinkering, however, can lead to all sorts of beautifully innovative apps and extensions, all of which can be found and utilized on a jailbroken iPhone. Tapping into Cydia will allow new potential to be unlocked on your device, but it also opens it for malware and unoptimized applications to mar the experience.

Dipping your toes into the jailbreaking world while being prudent of what you consume is something that I highly recommend, but only for users who are well-versed in backups and not averse to having to restore their iPhone in case things go awry. There's a certain level of risk associated with deviating from Apple's predefined iOS path, but as with most risk, it brings great reward.

In case something goes south, you have options for getting back on track. Understanding Apple's Recovery and DFU modes is vital to keeping your nerves calm and your iPhone in service. For times when you just need to see the expert, Apple's envious Genius Bar and network of authorized Apple Specialists are there to investigate and solve your issues.

Index